"BUT FIRST A SCHOOL"

"BUT FIRST

THE FIRST FIFTY YEARS OF

A SCHOOL"

THE SCHOOL OF AMERICAN BALLET

JENNIFER DUNNING

ELISABETH SIFTON BOOKS

VIKING

ELISABETH SIFTON BOOKS · VIKING
Viking Penguin Inc., 40 West 23rd Street, New York, New York 10010, U.S.A.
Penguin Books Ltd, Harmondsworth, Middlesex, England
Penguin Books Australia Ltd, Ringwood, Victoria, Australia
Penguin Books Canada Limited, 2801 John Street, Markham, Ontario, Canada L3R 1B4
Penguin Books (N.Z.) Ltd, 182–190 Wairau Road, Auckland 10, New Zealand

First published in 1985 by Viking Penguin Inc.
Published simultaneously in Canada

LIBRARY OF CONGRESS CATALOGING IN PUBLICATION DATA
Dunning, Jennifer.
  "But first a school."
  "Elisabeth Sifton books."
  Bibliography: p.
  Includes index.
  1. School of American Ballet—History. 2. Balanchine, George.
  3. Kirstein, Lincoln, 1907– . I. Title.
GV1788.6.S36D86 1985 792.8'07'107471 85-7625
ISBN 0-670-80407-X

Printed in the United States of America by
R. R. Donnelly & Sons Company, Harrisonburg, Virginia
Set in Sabon
Designed by Beth Tondreau
Page 242 constitutes an extension of this copyright page.

TO ROBERT, WITH ADMIRATION

PREFACE

"Would you come to America to start a ballet company?" The question was simple and direct, posed by Lincoln Kirstein to Georges Balanchine in London in 1933. "But first," Balanchine is said to have answered, "a school."

That response is almost as firm a part of the Balanchine legend as his much-quoted notion that "ballet is woman." Their origins may be lost in time and embellished in myth. But those first talks—held at a party and in a hotel parlor in London in July 1933—led to a collaboration that was to change the look of ballet in America and, indeed, in the world. Kirstein was then a recent Harvard graduate on his annual summer visit to Europe, a brilliant, idealistic young antihero of an American filled with soundly irrational plans for the arts in his country. Balanchine was an equally brilliant young Russian choreographer, stateless and living by his wits. Both wanted to found a ballet company. A permanent group of dancers would give Balanchine the kind of dependable material for ballets that he had had as choreographer for Serge Diaghilev's Ballets Russes. Loving the classical ballet, Kirstein hungered for the development of the classical tradition in his own land. Their plan was that a ballet company must grow out of a ballet school that would prepare young American dancers to work with Balanchine and instill in them a classical technique more solid than that available through the catch-as-catch-can studio lessons then being offered in the United States.

Balanchine had trained as a child in the ballet section of the Imperial Theater School of the Maryinsky Theater, one of the world's great academies. He knew the importance of such schooling, both to give the dancer a sound technical foundation and as a springboard to experimentation. Kirstein, dismayed at the kind of ballet Americans had been exposed to in the twentieth century, knew that his countrymen could have little sense of what the classical tradition was at its best, and of how many years of disciplined training were necessary to reach the right level of achievement. If there was to be an American tradition of ballet, American dancers must establish it. And they would do that at a new American academy to be called the School of American Ballet. But there was much work to be done, in what was largely barren ground.

CONTENTS

Illustrations follow pages 84, 116, *and* 180.

"BUT FIRST A SCHOOL"

INTRODUCTION

"In America we have had no dancers because we have had no schools, and no public that knew good dancing from bad. America has long been the paradise of poor teachers. A man who can do nothing else in the world can teach pretty much anything—and make a living by it—in America. But in nothing has the instruction been poorer than in dancing."[1]

So wrote the American novelist Willa Cather in "Training for the Ballet," a piece written for *McClure's* during her time there as a reporter. The year was 1913. Luigi Albertieri, the foster son and pupil of the great Italian pedagogue Enrico Cecchetti, figures in Cather's article as "a remarkable teacher." And she mentions the Metropolitan Opera Ballet School, founded in 1909 at New York's Metropolitan Opera House in order to provide the opera with suitable corps dancers. But American dancers had few choices as to training, and few of the gifted, developed dance teachers of the time were themselves American.

Yet America had had a struggling but persistent acquaintance with dance, and it had begun early in the eighteenth century. Dancing had been taught at a theater built in 1718 in Williamsburg, Virginia, for theatrical events in the Colonies, like those to be found in London at the time—combined drama, music, and dance. The dance historian Marian Hannah Winter describes the popular dance entertainment of that time as including a variety of styles: there was the harlequinade, a mixed theater piece featuring the mercurial commedia dell'arte character Harlequin, the playing of which had great influence on English stage dancing; popular art forms such as ballads, novels, and opera, and ballet-inspired narrative and pantomime works; rural ballets derived from Scottish and Irish national dances; patriotic pantomimes; and theatrical productions that included country dancing and ballet and national dances. *The Burgo'master Trick'd* and *The Adventures of Harlequin and Scaramouche* are considered the first professional ballets seen in America, danced in 1735 by an Englishman named Henry Holt in Charleston, South Carolina. Two enterprising English choreographers put together a company that toured across the country, but most traveling was done between Baltimore and Charleston (the earliest theatrical centers), New Orleans, and New York and Philadelphia. And it is in New York that historians place the first actual season of ballet in America, in 1792, when Alexandre Placide, a celebrated Parisian performer, and his partner, Suzanne Vaillande, who became America's first woman choreographer, presented a "Dancing Ballot" called *The Bird Catcher*.

The Bird Catcher's cast included John Durang, the first American professional dancer and a noted practitioner of the hornpipe, which he learned by imitation. "I practised at home and I could soon do all his steps beside many more better hornpipe steps," Durang wrote, referring to the itinerant French dancer Roussel, whom he had seen in his home state of Pennsylvania in the 1780s. "The pidgeon-wing I never saw done by any other person and I could not make that out from the front of the house. I contrived to get Mr. Roussel to board at my father's house that I might have the opportunity to dance more correct that I had been used to."[2]

There were no teachers or schools that taught theatrical dancing other than the social and country forms—with a little deportment added—offered by French dancing masters who opened studios or taught at their pupils' homes. "Ballroom dancing was their chief subject and since then ballroom dancing has been considered the chief function of a dancing school," Ann Barzel wrote in 1944. "Ninety percent of the dancing schools in America, outside the professional schools in a few metropolitan centers, teach ballroom dancing as well as theatrical dancing. The tie-up between these two entirely different forms of dance remains a fixed idea in the mind of the public. It is not merely because the same word covers both fields. Their histories really overlap at most points in the United States."[3] A century after those classes in the minuet and rigadoon, dances could be ordered by mail. During the nineteenth century, "drill" books were available for the teaching of such numbers as the "Parasol," "Bubble," and "Cymbal" dances. And by the 1920s acrobatic dancing had become the rage.

Following the revolution in France and the Revolutionary War and repeal of the Puritan antitheater law in the United States, America received an influx of French dancers that continued throughout the nineteenth century. There were more ballet performances for would-be dancers to study, and the climate was favorable for an interest in ballet to grow. France had already had over a century's tradition in the teaching and codification of dance, and some of the dancers traveling about America had been trained at the professional ballet school opened at the Paris Opéra in 1713. A blow to the prevailing "English style" of social and country dancing came in 1821, when a New York theater engaged Claude Labasse, a French ballet master, who in turn brought over a troupe of virtuoso French dancers in 1827: Francisque Hutin, company ballerina, performed such feats as pirouettes and the then new art of dancing on the toes, leaving audiences clamoring for the "new French style of dancing."

With the glittering accomplishments of the visitors from France, the traces of Puritan prudery that had thwarted the development of dance in America were vanquished. But there was still little native interest in training corps dancers to perform with the visiting artists. "Give me de pretty Vimmens: I don't care, den, for de talent," Placide is reported to have said.[4]

That lack of interest was evident on American stages into the first years of the twentieth century. An observer of the phenomenon, writing of a performance in New York in 1826, characterized the corps as "poor half-dressed supernumerary women, now made for the first time in their lives to stand upon one leg, who tottered bashfully and looked as foolish and about as graceful as a plucked goose in the same position."[5] Some of the women were bolder. Paul Taglioni, touring the United States in 1839, was shocked when the corps women recruited in Baltimore sat and smoked on stage as he danced a solo.

Still, the touring French left behind them, as did the Italians who followed later in the century, a number of dancers turned teacher, among them Madame LeComte, who taught Julia Turnbull, one of the earliest American ballerinas and a dancer known for her interpretation of Giselle and other tests of classical technique. But the European performer who had the greatest impact on the fledgling American dancers was Fanny Elssler, the earthy and vivacious Viennese ballerina who crossed the Atlantic in 1840 for a three-month tour and stayed two years in America. Elssler's gifts summoned up the Romantic Era in ballet for American audiences, and she created a furor wherever she danced. Admirers pulled her carriages through the streets and thronged stage doors. Tickets to her performance were auctioned off in one city, and Congress was adjourned when she danced in Washington. Her performances of such popular European ballets as *La Sylphide* and *Le Dieu et la Bayadère* drew the attention of everyone from notables of the time like Ralph Waldo Emerson and Margaret Fuller to those who bought the whiskey bottles marked with her likeness or who assiduously learned the mazurka or cracovienne "as danced by Fanny Elssler."

Philadelphia had become a center for ballet by the time of her arrival, due in large part to the energetic activities of two theater managers in the city and to the teaching of Paul H. Hazard, a member of the Paris Opéra Ballet, who made his American debut as a dancer in 1830 and opened a school in Philadelphia during that decade. (Among his pupils were Augusta Maywood, the first—and for well over a century, the only—American ballerina to achieve fame in Europe, and Mary Ann Lee, the first American Giselle.) Hazard's was just one of several studios in Philadelphia, where LeComte and Charles Durang, the son of John, were also to establish schools.

Teachers like Hazard, LeComte, and Durang taught a "French style" that called for crisp footwork, pliant feet, and soft, gracious arms and upper bodies in classes that, at Durang's school at least, included "bending of knees in all positions," "grands and petits battements," "rond de jambes on the ground and in the air," "tems de courante," "coupés à la premiere, seconde et compsée," "attitudes," "grands rond-de-jambes," "tems de chaconne," "grands fouettés facing," "pas de bourrée," "pirouettes," and "tems de vigueur."[6] Barzel suggests, however, that few schools offered such thorough technical training, stressing instead set dance routines, marching on point, and curtsying.

Elssler's artistic influence was not deep. But she did make a point of recruiting American dancers to perform with her, and a good many youngsters learned by her example. Working with or studying Elssler and taking class from James Sylvain, her partner and ballet master, had as great an effect on Lee, Turnbull, and George Washington Smith, the first American Albrecht in *Giselle*, as any academic training in ballet or performing. Sylvain was, in fact, Smith's principal teacher. Lee went on to Paris to study with Jean Coralli, a choreographer of *Giselle*, and learned authentic versions of the ballet and several other popular works. She later organized a small troupe, with which she and Smith toured the United States for two years. And both returned to Philadelphia to open ballet schools late in their careers. Smith also danced with distinction in the Ronzani Ballet Troupe, which arrived in the United States in 1856, one of the first Italian ballet companies to tour the country.

The level of American ballet teaching and ballet in general in America and Europe sank during the second half of the nineteenth century. But the influence of the Italians and the dancer-teachers they left behind persisted into the 1930s, when American training and performing began to establish themselves.

For one thing, the peripatetic Italians needed corps dancers for their touring productions, and as the quality of teaching dropped the need for at least minimally trained dancers grew, creating a generation of pathetic farm and factory girls across the country of the sort depicted in Theodore Dreiser's *Sister Carrie,* women drawn by the glamorous-seeming world of the stage into a life that would leave them without work skills or the hope of leading any respectable life. Theatrical dancing was marginally acceptable as a profession for men, but the "ballet girls" were considered too immoral even to work as maids or behind shop counters.

With *The Black Crook,* the need for ballet girls reached its peak. This extravagant American theatrical production opened in 1866 in New York and was seldom out of performance there or on the road for the next forty years, establishing a taste for spectacle in the American public and influencing the development of the American music hall, vaudeville, and musical theater. Many of the European dancers imported for its cast of 150 dancers stayed in America to teach, most notably Maria Bonfanti, a prima ballerina at La Scala in Milan who served as one of the first production's stars and who set up a studio first near Union Square, then on Broadway, next to the old Palace Theater.

Bonfanti taught both professionals and amateurs, and among her students was Ruth St. Denis, at an institution that ended its days on East Fifty-ninth Street, just a few blocks from where the first School of American Ballet was established fifteen years later. Another noted New York teacher was Elizabetta Menzeli, who had picked up training in cities throughout Europe and who arrived in America in 1876 as a performer in *Ali Baba,* one of the many successors to *The Black Crook.* She later established the

Knickerbocker Conservatory on East Sixteenth Street, also near Union Square and the theaters, an "ecole chorographie classic et pantomime" that offered lessons in "Artistic DANCING and Pantomime in all its Branches, Elocution for Pulpit, Stage, Platform and Parlor, Dramatic Art, in its full meaning and purpose, and Music, through its every form."

Her first classes, conducted in the 1880s in her mirrorless back parlor, cost twelve dollars for a month of daily lessons, and Menzeli assured a reporter that it would take three months to train a starting soloist but a year to prepare a lead dancer. She "insisted on good positions, extreme turnout, articulate feet, well-placed arms," Barzel noted in 1944. "She was a perfectionist in the vocabulary of steps she did teach. Petite batterie was especially stressed and small brilliant beats were worked on indefatigably. Pirouettes were incidental (although circles of piqué turns were taught). The neglect of pirouettes was partly due to the soft type of toe shoe worn until the last few decades. Even when the box toe slipper was invented, Madame, like all the classic artists of her day, frowned on it as a cheap device to aid the music hall dancer. Menzeli insisted that her pupils learn to dance on their toes in soft slippers that had been slightly stiffened by darning. The slippers had to be worn very tight to give the foot any support at all. Menzeli was not conservative in every way. While most of the 'artistes' of the day frowned on 'French dancing,' i.e. can can, high kicks and splits, she allowed her pupils to stretch and acquire high extensions and even to do the splits."[7]

The aim of many teachers of the time was just to strengthen their students' feet enough to enable them to pose, though not dance, on their toes.

In the same era the Christensens, a Danish family with training at the Royal Opera in Copenhagen, migrated to the American West. There three generations of the family spread the art of ballet to Salt Lake City and Ogden, Portland, Seattle, and San Francisco, where Willam, a third-generation Christensen, founded the San Francisco Ballet. (His brothers Harold and Lew went east, after a stint in vaudeville, and studied at the School of American Ballet in its first year. Lew Christensen continued his association with the School and the early companies of Lincoln Kirstein and George Balanchine, and was Balanchine's first American Apollo in the ballet of the same name.)

The last noted representative of the Italian school in America was Malvina Cavallazzi, who had trained at La Scala, danced in London, and served as prima ballerina of the Metropolitan Opera when it opened in 1883. A formidable personage, she was invited to return to establish the Opera's ballet school, created to train American dancers to perform with the opera company. There, she became responsible for an atmosphere of strict standards in discipline and dress for an institution that was a landmark in the history of ballet training in America. Though founded to produce opera dancers, the Metropolitan approached its task on a scale and with a seriousness of purpose that were unusual for the time. Students were taken on for free professional training on the condition that they would be under contract to dance with the Metropolitan during the last three years of their four-year training period. It must have been a tempting proposition. Cather notes that the young working women of the day served in sweatshops and department stores for six dollars a week, while the ballet paid fifteen to twenty dollars, though the student body did include young women from the upper-middle class. With fifty women enrolled in the school by its fourth year and twenty-four American women in the Metropolitan ballet in 1913, she predicted that by the following year there would be a fully American ballet for the first time in the history of opera in the United States.

"From my first experience in teaching them, I saw that American girls had a peculiar aptitude for dancing," Pauline Verhoeven, successor to Cavallazzi, told Cather, in comments echoed by other foreign teachers of the time. "In the first place they are strong, and that is a great point. After the first year the work is hard, and the girl must be strong. She must be on the floor for at least two hours every day, and she is working all of that time, using not only her muscles but her mind and her will. After the easy exercises of the first year, there is no mere going through the drill; it is a continual struggle to improve, to get the mastery of one's body little by little. The American girls have, on the whole, better figures than the girls I have seen and worked with in classes abroad. But their chief advantage is that they are not afraid. They have more confidence than French or Italian girls. They suffer no chagrin from making mistakes; they are always ready to try."[8] They were better nourished, too, and so better able to be strong, as Anna Pavlova noted on a visit to the Metropolitan school. "There is material to reflect upon in that sentence," Cather observes, "as well as suggestions of personal history."[9]

She mentions such classroom exercises as "various battements," the "rond de jambe on the floor," and the entrechat quatre as being undertaken at the Metropolitan, and notes that the best dancers seem to have the brightest eyes. The school had re-established the use of the barre, out of fashion for a time in American studios and thought to be too advanced for most students. There was one area, however, in which American women continued to be faulted in their dancing. Luigi Albertieri objected to American dancers' seeming inability to use their arms, which he described as "something terrible. I don't know why it is they can not learn to be alive and graceful with the arms," he groaned to Cather. "Their arms mean nothing to them; they are like the arms of a dead woman. Maybe it is that people use their arms more in other countries, and here they are taught to keep them still."[10]

Albertieri was a leading teacher in the years just before the advent of the Russian dancer-teacher in America, which began in the second decade of the century. He came to the United States in 1895 and promptly dazzled Americans with his pirouettes. Albertieri was known as an exacting traditionalist in his years as ballet master at the Chicago and Metropolitan operas, after which, in 1915, he founded a school in New York.

Stefano Mascagno was another noted Italian teacher of the time, a product of the San Carlo Theater in Naples who had his greatest effect on the training of American ballet teachers, giving them classes that were, in many cases, the first real instruction they had received in even simplified ballet technique. Mascagno opened a school in the United States in 1915 and taught for the next twenty years, numbering Willam Christensen among his pupils.

Louis H. Chalif occupies a more ambiguous position in the history of ballet in America. Trained at the Odessa Municipal Theater in Russia, where he became ballet master, Chalif came to the United States in 1904, danced with the Metropolitan Opera, and opened the Chalif Russian Normal School in 1907 in New York. The classes offered were in classical ballet, toe, and national, folk, ballroom, and interpretive dancing. His school was the largest in the country for many years, and a theatrical shoemaker reported that the sale of toe shoes in the United States began with the Chalif school.[11] His textbooks on ballet technique were popular with teachers, and by 1934, when the School of American Ballet was founded, an advertisement in the January issue of *Dance Magazine* recommended home study of five textbooks with 850 clearly described dances and ballets. It was Chalif who renamed the grand jeté en tournant the "tour jeté," as the step is now called in America.[12]

The triumphant appearance of Pavlova and her partner, Mikhail Mordkin, at the Metropolitan Opera in 1910 marked the start of the Russian era in performing and teaching ballet in the United States. The low esteem in which ballet was then held in America is suggested by the fact that Pavlova, in what was her American debut, came on stage at about eleven o'clock in the evening, after four acts of *Werther*, to dance a forty-minute version of *Coppélia*. She was to serve as a one-woman propagator of the art for the next fifteen years, however, in tours that took her to nearly every corner of the United States. And Pavlova's was the only ballet troupe to tour so widely and so regularly. The Russian influence was consolidated by a visit to America in 1916 by Diaghilev's Ballets Russes, complete with Vaslav Nijinsky, greeted as "well-nigh perfect," though it was noted he had grown heavier and sadder, and Adolph Bolm, a leading member of the Ballets Russes, who was to remain in the United States and become an important figure in American ballet. But there was little professional ballet in America between Pavlova's last tour and the first visit of the Ballets Russes de Monte Carlo in 1933. Like Elssler before them, Pavlova and Nijinsky left only a legacy of dreams and the pale imitations of the Russian ballerina's dances that sprang up in her wake on stages and in parlors around the country. Solid home-grown performing, which would help to establish an atmosphere for ballet in the country, came with the early companies created by Kirstein and Balanchine and with the Philadelphia-based Littlefield Ballet of the 1930s, which toured Europe successfully in 1937.

What the Russian influence did establish, however, was a teaching tradition. With whom had the first students in the School of American Ballet studied previously? The roster included Bolm, Mordkin, and Michel Fokine. Bolm made his name in Chicago, where he served as ballet master and premier danseur with the Chicago Civic Opera in the early 1920s, passing along his Maryinsky heritage and the neo-Italian style of Cecchetti that he had later absorbed. Bolm was greatly interested in producing modern American ballet, choreographing in 1928 the first production of Igor Stravinsky's *Apollon Musagète*. By the early 1930s he was creating dances for film musicals. He joined the San Francisco Opera, whose dance component was the forerunner of the San Francisco Ballet, serving as the opera's choreographer and ballet master and establishing a ballet school there. Bolm also performed, choreographed for, and served as ballet master at Ballet Theatre early in the 1940s. He was a pioneering figure in American ballet, but his gift for vivid portraiture on stage was not matched by an equally vivid way with academic ballet technique in the classroom. Ruth Page, who studied with Bolm in his studio on East Fifty-ninth Street, remembers him as a "lazy" teacher who was more involved in producing for his little Ballet Intime company.[13]

Chicago was a center of activity for many of the Russians, among them Laurent Novikoff, a former partner of Pavlova who was known for his inspired teaching of boys, and Serge Oukrainsky, who with Andreas Pavley founded the official ballet of the Chicago Opera. A host of "foremost American ballerinas, formerly with Pavlova" sprang up as teachers in studios across the country, and a move was begun to Russianize or change American names. Perhaps the best known of Pavlova's actual partners was Mordkin, who had thrilled American audiences with his virile dancing. His studio in Carnegie Hall, opened in 1927, was a popular place to study, though he, too, taught in a rather haphazard fashion, intent more on getting his pupils onto the stage than on instilling in them a strong technique. After ten years' work with his American pupils, he was able to create the Mordkin Ballet from a student company, and that provided the base for the establishment, in 1939, of Ballet Theatre.

But Fokine was probably the most popular Russian teacher in New York. His studio at 4 Riverside Drive offered, in 1934, "modern Russian ballet, the necessary foundation for all forms of dance, character dance—rhythmic exercises," and "plastic and expressive movement" for beginning through advanced students, with "ladies' physical culture" and special classes for children and "business girls." The outstanding Russian rebel against the strictures of the academic ballet as practiced in the reign of Marius Petipa at the Maryinsky Theater, Fokine did not stress perfect technique or established ballet conventions, but sought to draw the quality of movement from his students, teaching them excerpts from his ballets to get them dancing.

One of his students was John Taras, later a member of Kir-

stein's Ballet Caravan company and a teacher and long-time ballet master at the New York City Ballet. Taras took his first ballet
class with the Russian iconoclast. "I decided to go and learn how
to be a choreographer," he recalls. "The Romola Nijinsky book
about Nijinsky was just out in New York. I read about Fokine in
it and then I saw an advertisement in *The New York Times* for
classes in a house on Riverside Drive. Classes cost five dollars each,
which was a lot. And Fokine wasn't a teacher for beginners. The
first class I took there we did his *Schéhérazade.*" Professionals
danced alongside the teen-aged beginner. "I learned every step in
Les Sylphides, but I never learned about turnout." Fokine, too,
was bent upon production, and his small company performed in-
frequently but with popular success from the early 1920s to his
death in 1942.

The level and variety of training had improved greatly in the
years since Durang studied Roussel from the audience, though in
a random, changeable way that never built on any solid tradition.
American studios had now begun to teach ballet dancing instead
of dances. The Metropolitan offered increasingly thorough training. With the School of American Ballet, it approached the ideal
of a professional training school for dancers in the 1930s, though
both were far from the ideal of the European and Soviet state-
supported dance academy. But from its inception the Metropolitan offered little opportunity for performing and even less for
performing anything very meaningful to a trained young American ballet dancer with a growing ambition and sense of standards, and so it lost many of its apprentice dancers to musical
theater long before they completed their obligations to the
opera.

Dance performances were being given more often and taken
more seriously by the 1930s, due in part to the glitter of the visiting Russian companies. But in one sense little had changed. A
problem remained that John Martin, dance critic of *The New York
Times,* addressed passionately in that newspaper in 1933. "Miss

Bowman has gone as far as it is possible for a ballet dancer to go under the present system in this country," Martin wrote of Patricia Bowman, later the popular ballerina of Radio City Music Hall.

> Yet even those of her less successful fellows who look most longingly at her financial security would by an overwhelming majority vote rather to change places, if they might, with some European ballerina whose income and security are vastly inferior but whose artistic reputation is higher. Miss Bowman herself, because she is known to take her work seriously and to be ambitious about it, must frequently find herself beating fruitlessly against the stone wall which imprisons the American ballerina.
>
> The matter of merit does not enter into the question, for Miss Bowman can dance circles around at least a dozen English, French and Russian ballerinas whose names have more international glamor than her own. . . . The system under which she is working allows her to be nothing more than a pretty machine, no matter how extensive her talents may be.[14]

There was no place for the American dancer to perform ballet—except in a half-formed vision entertained by Kirstein and Balanchine.

I. 1933

Lincoln Kirstein and Georges Balanchine had their first real conversation at a fashionable London cocktail party on July 11, 1933, following a performance by Balanchine's Les Ballets 1933. The company was then having a reasonable artistic success at London's Savoy Theatre. But it offered no competition at the box office to the Ballets Russes de Monte Carlo, which had just opened triumphantly at the Alhambra. Formed by René Blum as a continuation of Serge Diaghilev's company, the Ballets Russes had recruited Balanchine as its choreographer in 1931 but, fired the following year, Balanchine had gone on to found Les Ballets 1933. To the artists and socialites in attendance at the Savoy, among whom Kirstein had friends, Balanchine's progressive new company was the true successor to the Diaghilev tradition. Like the Diaghilev company, Les Ballets 1933 was as much a departure from the canons of tsarist ballet as it was from the sterile European ballet of the day. And its very existence asserted that ballet was an art form as important—and provocative—as any of the arts.

Kirstein had encountered Balanchine briefly backstage at the Savoy, looking tired and sick when he came out to greet Romola Nijinsky, with whom Kirstein was writing a book on Vaslav Nijinsky, her husband. He met Balanchine again at a rehearsal in Paris, which he attended with the artist Pavel Tchelitchew, who had designed the sets for Balanchine's *Errante*. But at the home of Kirk Askew, an art dealer and Harvard friend of Kirstein's, the two men began, at last, to talk.

"I made a headlong onslaught; what Balanchine thought of an anonymous youth who in exaggerated desperation proposed an entire future career in half an hour, he did not say, except that he must think it over," Kirstein has recalled. "I consoled myself that, at the least or most, it was not absolutely impossible. He was not in the best of health and had no personal security whatever. But since we had met, he now knew of another possibility."[1]

Kirstein found Balanchine charming but worn, and full of talk about French dancers and the ballet conventions handed down by Petipa. He spoke of his current problems working within the reduced means of Les Ballets 1933. What he could do in America, Balanchine said, with twenty women, five men, and the promise of American feet and spirit!

Five days later, Balanchine visited Kirstein for lunch and more talk of America. Kirstein suggested their American ballet company be formed under the auspices of an American institution, the Wadsworth Atheneum of Hartford. There was talk of bringing the dancers Tamara Toumanova and Roman Jasinski, both members of Les Ballets 1933, to America with him. And where the young Toumanova went, her mother followed: her mother would cook for the Russians. Kirstein's excitement became contagious. For Balanchine, America was now the dream of a lifetime—not just the home of women as wonderful as Ginger Rogers, but the place where the theater could be, for him, a sacred temple.

Kirstein had envisioned the new American company as small but developing slowly while Balanchine worked on new ballets and saw something of the United States. Details began to form and cohere. Romola Nijinsky and Kirstein would give public lectures, with the American dancers demonstrating. She would give them the rights to her husband's four ballets, as well as four more that had never been produced. Balanchine owned half the ballets in the repertory of Les Ballets 1933. It might be, as Romola Nijinsky prophesied, that the tubercular Balanchine would last only two years. But a good start could be made in those two years toward establishing an American ballet. And it must be made immediately. That night Kirstein wrote a sixteen-page letter in a neat but rapid hand to his friend A. Everett Austin, Jr., a leading museum director of his era who was then the head of the Wadsworth Atheneum.

"This will be the most important letter I will ever write you as you will see," Kirstein said in a letter he later described as more enthusiastic than honest.

> My pen burns my hand as I write: words will not flow into the ink fast enough. We have a real chance to have an American ballet within 3 yrs. time. When I say ballet—I mean a trained company of young dancers—not Russians—but Americans with Russian stars to start with—a company superior to the dregs of the old Diaghilev Company which will come to N.Y. this winter and create an enormous success purely because though they aren't much they are better than anything New York will have seen since Nijinsky.
>
> Do you know Georges Balanchine? If not he is a Georgian called Georgei Balanchavidze [sic]. He is, personally, enchanting—dark, very slight—a superb dancer and the most ingenious technician in ballet I have ever seen. . . . He is 28 yrs. old—a product of the Imperial schools. He has split from the Prince de Monaco as he wants to proceed, with new ideas and young dancers instead of going on with the decadence of the Diaghilev troupe. . . .

Kirstein proposed, he wrote, that a free ballet school be established in Hartford, at a safe distance from the distraction of New York society and the lure of the Broadway theater. The adolescent students—four white girls, four white boys, and eight black youngsters—would learn by doing, getting their technique from the classroom and from working on Balanchine's new ballets. The chosen dancers would sign contracts to remain with the company for five years, and within three months Balanchine could start producing. Initially, the company would perform not in commercial theaters but on the museum and university circuit. As the school became established, children from eight years old and up would be accepted for a complete training program. No tuition would be charged at the school, which would be supported by the performances and by ground-breaking lecture-demonstrations by Kirstein, Romola Nijinsky, Toumanova, and Jasinski. Kirstein himself would speak for a hundred dollars a lecture in thirteen cities along the East Coast. But an immediate six thousand dollars was needed to guarantee a year's expenses and passage to and from the United States for Balanchine, Toumanova and her mother, and Jasinski. And the institutional backing of the Atheneum, with its new theater, would be a necessity.

Kirstein suggested five names of friends who, like himself, would be willing to become patrons. By February 1934, Hartford would have four performances of new ballets. Kirstein had already begun to discuss with Balanchine ideas for seven ballets with scenarios based on American folk legends. And Balanchine was willing to commit himself to spending five years creating an American school and company.

"This school can be the basis of a national culture as intense as the great Russian Renaissance of Diaghilev," Kirstein continued in his letter to Austin. "We must start small. But imagine it— we are exactly as if we were in 1910—offered a dancer only less good than an unformed Nijinsky, an incipient Karsavina—a maître de ballet as good as Fokine—who would also be delighted to cooperate. It will not be easy. It will be hard to get good young dancers willing to stand or fall by the *company*." For, Kirstein wrote, there would be no stars in this company. But they must grab Balanchine. "He is an honest man, a serious artist, and I'd stake my life on his talent." Balanchine was easy to work with,

Kirstein added, and could come to the United States in October or earlier.

"Please, Please, Chick if you have any love for anything we both do adore—rack your brains and try to make this all come true. If not as I outline, then some other way must be feasible. We have both done harder things than to raise $6,000. . . . We have the future in our hands. For Christ's sweet sake let us honor it."[2]

Balanchine and Kirstein met several days later at the Batts Hotel in Mayfair, where Kirstein was staying. Balanchine arrived several hours late, having learned, as he told the apprehensive Kirstein, that he must replace an injured lead dancer that night. Out of practice and tired from rehearsals, Balanchine was frank but remote. There was little to keep him in Europe, he acknowledged. He was leaving for Paris on July 21, but would talk further with Kirstein. And then he left the hotel.

Kirstein sat for a time in the hotel parlor, which, he recalled, was "dusty with propriety and full of provincial beauties who had come up to London to be presented at court."[3] Three girls in white court dresses, plumes nodding in their hair, sat having tea at the next table, just back, Kirstein imagined, from an appointment with the court photographer and reminding him of the poignant young beauties of Balanchine's *Cotillon*. "I could not discover whether they were the three Muses of Apollo or the three Fates," Kirstein would remember. "My mind jumped forward in time and I saw the completed school achieved and functioning, and even more, a great stage swarming with dancers the school had trained, situated somewhere in America. It was exasperating to think concretely of ways and means to make the mirage a miraculous reality."[4]

The tall, gawky, twenty-six-year-old who dreamed on in that London hotel parlor could have been a character drawn by Henry

James: a monied, well-connected young American whose abundance of gifts and keen intelligence and wit had left him shy, arrogant, and filled with a rueful, self-flagellating sensitivity. Exuberantly optimistic, yet possessed of an ingrained pessimism, Lincoln Edward Kirstein was ill-prepared for life in an everyday world. He was, however, eminently equipped to determine the course of the history of dance in America.

Born in 1907 in Rochester, New York, Kirstein was the son of fond but firm parents. Louis Kirstein, who had named his first son after his favorite president, was an executive and a partner in William Filene Sons, the Boston department store, a philanthropist and businessman who was to exert some influence in the administration of Franklin Delano Roosevelt. The family moved to Boston in 1912, and schooling followed for Kirstein at Phillips Exeter Academy, where his first publication occurred with the printing in the school journal of a play set in Tibet.

After graduation from the Berkshire School, a move on to Harvard University seemed inevitable in the course of this proper American education. But Louis Kirstein insisted that his son work for a year in a stained-glass factory in Boston in order, he said, to learn something concrete before college. And Kirstein looks back on the experience as having taught him something about the technique and execution of a craft.

He entered Harvard in 1926, and in his years there gave evidence of the range of interests and skills that would contribute to his haunting, lifelong sense of himself as an informed dilettante. He had bought his first picture at ten. Gifted in drawing and a more than competent pianist, Kirstein began to collect art in earnest at Harvard and wrote about painting and the then uncredited art form of photography. The first issue of *Hound & Horn*, an influential quarterly on the arts that Kirstein helped to found and edit at Harvard, was published in 1927. The following year he and two classmates, one of them Edward M. M. Warburg, who was to figure prominently in the founding of the School of American Ballet, created the Harvard Society for Contemporary Art, a precursor to New York's Museum of Modern Art. While at Harvard, Kirstein came to know leading writers of the day, connections that, with his family's social ties, were to serve him well in the difficult business of founding and sustaining an American ballet academy and company.

In the years to come, Kirstein would gain the solid but unpublished reputation of a formidable man of the arts. Nothing, it seemed, escaped his interest and ambition, particularly among the American art forms that had begun to draw the support of young American intellectuals during the nationalistic 1920s. He wrote frequently for *Hound & Horn,* whose end was hastened after seven years of existence by Kirstein's consuming interest in the establishment of the School of American Ballet. *Hound & Horn* brought him into contact with many writers—T. S. Eliot, Ezra Pound, Edmund Wilson, e. e. cummings, and Katherine Anne Porter. And it was Eliot's essay, "Tradition and the Individual Talent," that influenced his belief that new art, like that of George Balanchine, must come out of the solid traditions of the past. "The first principle is that Creation is a unique act," Kirstein later said. "It happened once and everything else is invention and discovery."[5]

When he was twenty-five, Kirstein published a memorable first novel, *Flesh Is Heir.* (His *Rhymes of a PFC,* a book of poetry published in 1964, became, like the novel, a lost American classic.) "Murals by American Painters and Photographers," an exhibition he put together for the Museum of Modern Art in 1932, was one of his earliest monumental attempts to bring the work of American artists to the public eye. It was also one of his most controversial, erupting as it did into a clamor over the leftist sentiments expressed in one of the murals. Kirstein was instrumental in establishing the career of the photographer Walker Evans and was responsible for the revival of interest in the work of the sculptor Elie Nadelman. He helped to found the short-lived journal *Films* in 1939. During his war years with the U.S. Army, from 1943 to 1945, Kirstein assisted in the finding of art looted by the Nazis, and supervised its recovery. In 1955, he produced *A Mid-*

summer Night's Dream for the first season of the American Shakespeare Festival Theatre Academy at Stratford, Connecticut, of which he was a founder. He produced a medieval mystery play and Japanese theater and ritual sports, and wrote a play on Lincoln's assassination. An art critic for *The New Republic,* a participant in the civil-rights marches of 1965, and active even in the promotion of dressage, Kirstein became a true—and intensely involved—Renaissance man, honored by foreign governments and called upon to serve as artistic adviser to his own.

But it is as an authority on and advocate of dance that Kirstein is best known. A chief benefactor of what is now the Dance Collection of the New York Public Library at Lincoln Center, Kirstein established and edited *Dance Index,* an influential journal published between 1942 and 1948, and has written a series of formidably opinionated, brilliant polemical and scholarly books on the history, politics, and techniques of dancing. Dance was an interest Kirstein traces with characteristic irony back to a childhood rebellion at the age of nine, with a vengeful instinct to run away from home and become a dancer when his parents forbade him to see Diaghilev's Ballets Russes in Boston.

His early aesthetic training had come, informally, with visits to the ballet with a cousin only a few years older than he but full of eye-opening opinions on quality in theater and dance. Together, they attended performances by Anna Pavlova in the spring of 1920 for five nights' running at Boston's Symphony Hall, and Kirstein understood that dance was a learned and disciplined craft rather than the apparently spontaneous outcropping of the soul. Two years later, he visited London and the Continent for the first of many summers. There the economist Maynard Keynes, married to the Diaghilev ballerina Lydia Lopokova, continued Kirstein's education in ballet.

A diary he kept at Exeter reveals that by his mid-teens Kirstein wanted to become a dancer—as well as a portraitist, diplomat, and novelist. "Dancing is not hard; you have to feel free and keep time,"[6] he wrote, looking back on childhood memories of a

22

fleeting encounter with dancing lessons, disguised as rhythmic exercises and taught by a disciple of Isadora Duncan at Kirstein's summer camp in 1919. Thirteen years later, he planted himself at the barre of Michel Fokine's Riverside Drive studio in New York and began the work of learning ballet technique first-hand from a "living monument."[7]

The legend of the Russian émigré's important role as choreographer to the Maryinsky and Serge Diaghilev had gained Fokine a reputation as New York's leading practitioner of ballet, though his classes were, in truth, idiosyncratic. "I know Fokine thinks it's ridiculous," Kirstein later wrote, "I only want to learn the structure of his teaching, but he thinks I'm some sort of mad millionaire (like Ida Rubinstein) who dreams of dancing. Do I want to start an 'American ballet'? I do, but of course this sounds crazy. I am incapable of lifting a leg."[8]

Kirstein persisted in this "exercise in free will."[9] He listened to Fokine's instructions and drew him out in conversation, writing down what he said. One day it could, Kirstein thought, become a book. "By birth, training or merit I could never belong, but by association with Fokine, something might rub off on me. . . . I absorbed from his *barre* exercises a modicum of what is necessary in the schooling of professionals. I learned the consummate logic in the progression of academic exercises from first steps to ultimate virtuosity."[10]

When the teenaged Kirstein finally encountered the Diaghilev company in London, he became a recognizable approximation of what he later called a "balleptomaine." "The first blaze of its great adventure was over," Kirstein recalled. "A small theatre housed the company, and it was by no means a good season. But I never knew that. It was exactly as if I had come home to that splendid country for which I knew I had been destined, but which up to that time I could not seem to find."[11]

Kirstein had seen two cabaret numbers Balanchine choreographed for Chauve Souris, but his first Balanchine ballet was *Le Fils Prodigue*, which he saw at Covent Garden in 1929. His earliest exposure to the young Russian dancer and choreographer had come three years before. "Diaghilev is bankrupt," Kirstein wrote of a remembered visit to the Ballets Russes in London in June 1926. "Anyway, the present theater is dreary and smaller than the Lyceum in Rochester. I expected more. Not much dancing; not enough dancers. But one exciting moment. In *Firebird* the magician Kastchei was made up as Genghis Khan; Mongolian, with long fingernails like gilded claws, a frightful vulture. In a fantastically evil way he manipulated the others. Afterward, to a restaurant; there he was, among the other dancers. I wanted to ask him for a drink, but didn't dare." [12] The Kastchei was Balanchine, he discovered, a good dancer who had impressed Diaghilev with his choreography but was not himself a member of the impresario's inner circle.

"The ballet disintegrated after Diaghilev's death, and perhaps circumstances will not allow the full development of this brilliant choreographer," Kirstein wrote of Balanchine in the July–September 1930 issue of *Hound & Horn*. Otherwise, Kirstein foresaw, the Russian choreographer "must certainly have developed into one of the ablest of Diaghilev's designers, for not only was his energy and invention prodigious, but he well understood the dangers attendant on the unintelligent if entertaining implications of the 'clever' acrobatic Massine dance."

Balanchine's ballets, he suggested with startling prescience, "had the spareness, the lack of decoration which is by no means a lack of refinement, the splendid capacity to display individual gestures against a background of unrhythmical massed gesture. . . . The ballet of Balanchine was more difficult to follow, perhaps, required more of an effort, in so much as the human eye accepts more readily easy variations, just as the human ear accustoms itself more readily to tones in transitions bounded by the more obvious tonal intervals. . . . The last period of the [Diaghilev] ballet was and must be considered a period of transition, not of decadence. Balanchine in the *Cat* and in *Apollo* was leading out of mere ingenuity into a revivified, purer, cleaner classicism."

Kirstein's ballet experiences came together like elements in a collage: summer performances in Europe and fringe participation in the glamorous gossip surrounding them, chance attendance in 1929 in Venice at a funeral he later heard was Diaghilev's, Kirstein's lessons with Fokine and his lecturing on dance for his friend Warburg, then teaching at Bryn Mawr, and the beginning of a collaboration with Romola Nijinsky, during which Kirstein became fascinated by the history and structure of the ballet academy of the Imperial School at St. Petersburg, which had trained Nijinsky and Balanchine and could trace its heritage to the Royal Academy of Dancing founded in Paris during the reign of Louis XIV.

Kirstein's ambitious progress toward the establishment of an American ballet school and company began to quicken. In New York, several months before his meeting with Balanchine in 1933, he worried at a rumor that the impresario Sol Hurok had bought Diaghilev's repertory and might tour it under the Ballets Russes de Monte Carlo, which became Ballet Russe de Monte Carlo by 1938. If that were true, any money available for an American ballet would be quickly drained off. Living on an allowance too modest to support his plans for an American ballet, Kirstein sailed for Europe that summer with the knowledge that he could call on his skeptical but generous friend Warburg for financial help should a plan present itself for the formation of an American company. And Austin, he knew, was building a new wing on the Wadsworth Atheneum in Hartford, which might be the perfect place to install a company and a school.

"The closer I found myself to the furnace of activity," Kirstein has written, "the more intoxicated I became. Using the flimsiest support as my strongest arm, I involved or precipitated Warburg, Austin, and myself with a blind conviction and impersonation of authority which should have surprised us all had I retained any objective insight."[13] With his two friends at a safe distance across an ocean, Kirstein felt headily free to act. What did he want? the painter Tchelitchew asked the gangling young

25

American shortly before carrying him off to the rehearsal of Les Ballets 1933. To create an American ballet, Kirstein told him. An idiotic idea, he knew, but it was supported by the interest of the American expatriate composer Virgil Thomson, who listened receptively to Kirstein's sketchy plans, informed, as Kirstein has put it, by big hopes and small experiences, then disabused him of his wilder notions.

Kirstein made his choice. Balanchine and Les Ballets 1933 had introduced him to the fabled Russian ballet at its best, he felt, and that would be the model for the new American ballet. "Everything [Balanchine] did spoke for the present, of immediacy, by surprise, with brilliance: for 1933," Kirstein wrote. He had seen Balanchine's "concrete examples of fantasy and ceaseless invention" night after night that season. "There was a magical transference of private caprice onto a public platform. Studio talk and studio planning were projected in a heroic dimension, far larger than life. Everything was intensified through the physicality of the dancing itself, through the power, athletics, and lyricism of ballet's language. This was where I wanted to live. This was what I wanted to do; here I was learning how it should be done."[14]

But how was Kirstein to get to Balanchine? At last, the meeting came, in the Askew kitchen, a meeting carefully engineered but apparently perfectly spontaneous. "I was at a party in London," Balanchine recalled forty-nine years later at a press conference in New York announcing the start of the School of American Ballet's fiftieth anniversary fund-raising campaign. "Suddenly an enormous man, who was Lincoln, asked, 'You'd like to come to America?' I thought. I said, 'All right, I'll do it.' "

As he had told Kirstein, Balanchine had nothing to lose at that point in his life. While still a student, he had shocked balletomanes and teachers with his ballet experiments. Just four years after graduation, he joined and then became a choreographer to the most famous ballet company in the world. But he now had little work and no sign of a meaningful future in Europe, with its stultified ballet traditions and postwar turbulence.

Beneath the calm authority with which Balanchine worked with dancers often older than he, beneath the sure touch of his burgeoning creativity, beneath the inherent gaiety of his manner, there lay a practicality rooted in a nearly lifelong rootlessness. The ordered environment of the Imperial School had replaced the less stable one he had known at home, but was itself ruptured when the Bolshevik Revolution turned Russian society upside down in 1917, midway through his training years. Serge Diaghilev had signed him on in 1924, then died suddenly five years later. The company as suddenly dispersed, leaving the dancers, most of them Russian émigrés, without the institution that had given them a sense of community. Balanchine found employment in one European capital or another, but it was scattered, piecemeal, and often unappreciated. Les Ballets 1933, with which he had hoped to forge an instrument of his choreography, went under after two brief seasons, the victim in part of fashion and commercial rivalry. Why not try America, the land of the sporty young, the skyscraper, and the cowboy? It had beckoned before and had the merit, at least, of novelty.

Born in 1904 in St. Petersburg to a musically inclined young mother and older father, a composer known as "the Georgian Glinka," Georgi Melitonovich Balanchivadze was, like Kirstein, the first son and second of three children. His earliest years were happy, if not luxurious, but disaster struck when his convivial father won a large lottery prize and splurged the family into bankruptcy and himself into imprisonment. What was to seem, at first, another disaster overtook Balanchine at ten. The year before, he had accompanied his mother and sister to an audition at the Imperial School. At the suggestion of a family friend, Balanchine took the audition, too, and was one of eight or nine boys to be accepted. His sister was not. And a year later, as a boarding pupil, he would find himself left behind by his family at the school, alone in an uncongenial atmosphere where pointless-seeming steps and gestures were drilled into him day after day.

There was no respite in academic classes, in which he tended to do poorly. And none of the other children cared, it seemed, to make the effort to breach his aloofness and ignore the nervous twitch of the upper lip that earned him the nickname of "rat." Felia Doubrovska, who graduated from the Imperial School the year he entered and was to become one of the School of American Ballet's leading teachers, remembered a very young Balanchine watching rehearsals with a polite but probing gaze, absorbing everything he saw, often scrutinizing the dancers' feet.

Life was regimented, though not unduly so, as Balanchine recalled. The pupils—about sixty girls and forty boys—wore uniforms and were for the most part boarders. The School was housed on two floors of a spaciously proportioned Baroque building in a cul-de-sac leading to the Alexandrinsky Theater. The students' lives were lived out in separate dormitories, two big studios and a small one, a small theater and church, and classrooms for academic study. Balanchine, considered an exceptionally expressive young dancer, occasionally acted at the Alexandrinsky in plays requiring young boys. But Maryinsky students seldom ventured outside the School for anything but performing. "We were sort of like pages," Balanchine recalled. "We were trained to music and drama."[15]

It was a life in some ways comparable to that of the students in the school Balanchine was to found in the United States. Though the children of the School of American Ballet do not wear uniforms and there are no dormitories, their lives are equivalently formal, spent in four big, light-filled studios tucked into a third-floor wing of the Juilliard School, just two blocks from the New York State Theater, where the New York City Ballet performs. Like the Imperial School, Juilliard has its own theater, where the School of American Ballet's annual Spring Workshop Performances take place, an important and demanding event around which much of the life and energy of the School and its students center. The children scurrying or trudging to Workshop rehearsals through the months are, as Balanchine was, being trained for a vocation.

Balanchine ran away to the suburban home of an aunt, who returned him immediately to the School. And gradually there began to be compensations. Pianos were scattered through the ornate old building and, already trained in music, Balanchine played them in free moments. One day he peered through a keyhole into a studio where Samuel Andreyanov, a leading Maryinsky dancer and Balanchine's favorite teacher, was coaching three young Maryinsky ballerinas. One of them was Elizaveta Gerdt, whose long, slender body and cool purity of style attracted the young Balanchine to her dancing and possibly imprinted in him his notion of an ideal. "I saw this working and it was very interesting," he later recalled. "It was like a little game. So since then I decided that it would be very interesting to look at something like that."[16]

A taste of performing further palliated the bitterness of school life when Balanchine danced children's roles in the Maryinsky production of *The Sleeping Beauty*. Around him on the stage of the beautiful Maryinsky Theater moved dancers who had gone through the same training as he, in the same building, taught by many of the same teachers. And they moved in a world of color, light, and lavish spectacle produced for the pleasure of the Tsar— "Little Father" to the ballet students and the authority that had traditionally supported the theaters, their free schools, and the performing companies in St. Petersburg and Moscow.

The stage of the Maryinsky, noted for its purist approach to ballet and its technical perfection, was an exciting place for the children of the Imperial School to be, and they were exposed early and routinely to performing with the parent company. Balanchine's favorite role was that of the monkey in Marius Petipa's *La Fille du Pharaon,* in which he got to race through treetops as Mathilda Kchessinska, the prima ballerina assoluta, tried to shoot him down with a bow and arrow. Some four decades later, sequestered in an upstairs wardrobe room at New York's City Center, Balanchine coached a small student from Brooklyn named Eliot Feld in the intricacies of miming the Little Prince in the New York City Ballet's production of *The Nutcracker*, a part Balanchine had played as a child at the Maryinsky, where he had learned the art of mime from the great Pavel Gerdt.

Classes with Andreyanov, an elegant, manly dancer and a sensitive teacher, were another bright spot. There, the young Balanchine learned a highly developed, fluent style of classical ballet: a carefully preserved blend of several important traditions embodied in the work of such nineteenth-century visitors to Russia as Marius Petipa, the French dancer and choreographer; Enrico Cecchetti, the Italian dancer and teacher; and Christian Johansson, a Swedish dancer and teacher acquainted with the work of August Bournonville, the Danish choreographer. Though Russian ballet was then synonymous with Petipa and his expansive, technically refined, and classically articulated ballet spectacles, it also displayed the precision and clarity of the French school and the virtuosic technique of the Italians. Heightened by a vivid resonance many defined as Russian "soul," it was dance that traced its lineage to the earliest sources of the classical ballet.

The blindered life of the Maryinsky School came to an end in October 1917. Bolshevik sailors raced through the dormitories looking for counterrevolutionaries. Soon, the School was closed and the ballet company, now seen as a decadent plaything of the Tsar, disbanded. Lenin addressed the public from the balcony of a palace that had belonged to Kchessinska and was now the headquarters of the Bolshevik party. Many of the Maryinsky children, once fed chocolates by the Tsar, were forced to forage for food in the chaotic, barricaded streets of the once-serene city and along the banks of the Neva River, where army barges were now moored. His family moved out of the city, but Balanchine, just thirteen, was left behind with his aunt on the chance that the School might reopen. It was the last he saw of his mother and sister. Odd jobs as a messenger and a pianist in a shabby little neighborhood movie theater enabled Balanchine to eat. Food was a more valuable currency than paper money. For a performance organized by metalworkers a leading Russian ballerina of the time, Ekaterina Geltzer, accepted five casseroles, a saw, and an ax as her fee.[17]

The children returned to the School, reopened in 1918 as the Petrograd Theater School, with a new independence that led them to demand such reforms as classes in aesthetics, staging, and set design, and the provision of boxes from which older students could watch performances at the imperial theaters. They returned, too, to a new life. Classes in Marxist doctrine had been added to the curriculum. Divertissement programs became the vogue, often danced at Communist Party meetings. The young dancers' diet was spartan. They pulled down the school draperies and cut and sewed them into clothes. The studios were so cold that the children took to burning the wood from the parquet floors in order to keep warm.

Even the performers were not exempt from the difficult new conditions. The dancers' bare shoulders steamed and their breaths clouded on a stage on which the temperature could fall as low as six degrees below zero.[18] Soldiers and workmen filled the theaters now, dressed in sheepskin coats and felt boots and stamping their feet to keep warm as they watched ballets by Petipa, Lev Ivanov, and Fokine. But Balanchine worked steadily and sociably at the School, also serving as a favorite piano accompanist for dancers earning a little money at club and factory engagements.

"In the old days, you first were a choreographer and then you became one," Balanchine told his biographer Bernard Taper.[19] As a very young child he had staged family performances inspired by theater his parents had taken him to. Responding, perhaps, to increasing production activity within the School itself, he created *La Nuit (Night)*, a romantic duet whose untraditional structure and simple costuming created something of a scandal among the more conservative members of the faculty, but a ballet that was well received by the students and performed long after through-out the city.

"We were accustomed to seeing in the former Maryinsky Theater and in the school the usual adagio développés, tradi-tional turns from fourth position which the ballerina performed with support from her partner," wrote Vera Kostrovitskaya, a fellow student who later danced with the experimentalist Young Ballet. "Before the turns, there would be fear on her face, and a relieved smile at the conclusion. There was none of that here. Rubinstein's 'Night,' in Balanchine's dance, was a lyrical duet of restrained passion—half poses, half arabesques . . . tender pas-sages of adagio without the conventional movements of legs raised on the principle 'the higher, the better.' Of course, later on in various concert pieces, artists performed love duets, called ada-gios, with disregard for the traditions of Petipa. But then, and es-pecially in the school, this was completely new. And in 1921, there were still few who appeared on stage in tunics. Dancing on pointe was done only in tutus."[20]

Poème, a piece in which Balanchine and Alexandra Danilova danced together, drew charges of obscenity from some teachers and a clamor from students who wanted to dance in Balanchine's ballets. "The irreproachably formed Danilova with her finely moulded, severe features framed in golden hair, wearing a trans-parent bright blue tunic, was the embodiment of pure, cold beauty," Kostrovitskaya wrote, in words that could be used of Balanchine's ballets today.

> Balanchine, also very handsome, lifted Danilova in the classic ara-besque and lowered her softly on pointe. The adagio began, but again without the usual turns and technical tricks (although Danilova had many opportunities to do them). Sometimes these performances were accompanied without violin, only by a piano, but the lines of the dance were so melodious that one could always imagine the violin's presence anyway. At the end of "Poème," Balanchine carried Da-nilova off, lifting her high in an arabesque with his arms extended. One had the impression that she herself, without a partner's sup-

port, was gliding through the air away from the audience to finish "singing" her dance somewhere far, far away. The "Poème" gave rise to many imitations.[21]

There was evidence here, already, of the extreme musicality and the preference for a simple, active body line that would alter the look of a ballet a half century later and demand a new kind of dancer. Balanchine's easy practicality, rare among choreographers then and now, would come into play shortly after, when he designed *Marche Funèbre* so that the ballet could be performed not only on the circular stage for which it was created, but also on a traditional proscenium stage if necessary. His fourth dance for the Young Ballet, *Marche Funèbre* would serve, restaged, as an audition project for Diaghilev the following year, in 1924.

Balanchine had graduated with honors in 1921 and moved into the corps de ballet at the State Academic Theater of Opera and Ballet (formerly the Maryinsky), where he was to receive favorable public notice for his vivid dancing and wickedly funny pantomime. Already enrolled in the Petrograd Conservatory of Music, where he studied musical theory, technique, and composition and learned the art of rapid, easy musical improvisation, Balanchine also gave in agreeably to the many requests from young fellow dancers for quick creations for concert programs, and busied himself preparing dances for the women he admired, who were often transformed on stage by his choreography.

But the culminating experience of Balanchine's last years in Russia was his work with the Young Ballet, an informally constituted group of dancers, artists, and writers whose first program, presented in June 1923, was called *The Evolution of Ballet: From Petipa Through Fokine to Balanchivadze*. A grandish sort of title, it nonetheless perfectly expressed the quality of those restless, excited years of the 1920s in Russia. The world had split open. Old and restrictive rules and customs no longer obtained. And the Russian arts lived through a burst of unparalleled innovative glory before settling into fitful life as vehicles for propaganda, their expressive function determined by the imagined limitations and appetite for realism of the common man, after Stalin succeeded Lenin as leader of the Soviet Union in 1924.

The idealized relationships of ballet could not be sustained unchanged in a revolutionary society. The old and traditional were largely suspect. The new, in those few, brief years, was the exciting topic of late-night and even public disputation among the friends who gathered around the dancer Pyotr Gusev, Yuri Slonimsky (later a leading Soviet writer on dance), the ballet designer Vladimir Dimitriev, and Balanchine, at seventeen the youngest in the group but clearly the leader. Vladimir Tatlin had founded Constructivism. Kasimir Malevich, the first Suprematist, created one of the earliest abstract paintings, a white square on a white ground. Vsevolod Meyerhold developed "Biomechanics," a training system and acting style that broke down gesture and movement into physical components. "All is new! Stop and marvel!" Vladimir Mayakovsky wrote in his *Mystery Bouffe*, the first Soviet play. It became a rallying cry for the young. And Balanchine luxuriated in the sensuous new rhythms of Scriabin and Prokofiev, though sensing near "cacophony"[22] in an initial hearing of Stravinsky's *Le Rossignol*, to which, ironically enough, he was later to set his first ballet for Diaghilev. Yet Balanchine also came to acknowledge his debt to Petipa, whose ballets provided a foundation and the material for his eventual extension of the range of classical methodology. And even in those iconoclastic years he referred to Fokine's *Chopiniana* as his favorite ballet—the work of an earlier iconoclast that taught him dances need not have plots.[23]

Music and its relation to dance were being re-examined. The Moscow ballet master Nikolai Foregger had created *Dance of the Machines*: with dancers impersonating machine components, it called for "dances of the pavement, of rushing motor-cars, the accuracy of machine work, the speed of the present-day crowd, the grandeur of skyscrapers."[24] The Russians were also exposed to the exploration and development of training for rhythmic sensitivity of the Swiss educator Emile Jaques-Dalcroze. "Music is energy," wrote Boris Asafiev, a musical theorist who supported Balanchine's early experiments. "More than that, it is energetic; there are wonderful possibilities for making visible that which is heard."[25] Already musical, Balanchine got first-hand exposure to a new view of music and dance when he performed in *Dance Symphony*, a 1923 ballet by Fyodor Lopukhov, the young dancer, choreographer, and teacher who had become director of the State Theater the year before. Danced to Beethoven's Fourth Symphony and performed only once, the ballet was plotless and argued for dance that was "free and self-contained,"[26] deriving only from its music. Gusev, Balanchine's classmate and fellow performer, saw Lopukhov's indirect influence in *Symphony in C*, choreographed by Balanchine in 1947.[27] And Kirstein suggested the Lopukhov work served as a prototype for *Serenade*, Balanchine's first American ballet.[28] But the most forceful and direct influence on Balanchine in those years was the adventurous Kasyan Goleizovsky, a dancer and then influential experimentalist choreographer, whose intricately posed and acrobatic dance spectacles he observed for the first time in 1921. "Seeing Goleizovsky was what first gave me the courage to try something on my own," Balanchine has said.[29] A long-haired "hippie," as Balanchine described his young self,[30] he thought immediately of opening a studio with Goleizovsky.

Ballet flourished in unprecedented popularity among the bourgeoisie and proletariat in the 1920s. New studios sprang up. All the young women took ballet class, it seemed, and dreamed of becoming the ballerinas that had been the aristocracy of Russia's aristocrats. The democratization of ballet was reflected in a new interest in Russian folk dance, acrobatics, and clowning, and their relationship to the traditions of the classical ballet. Like Balanchine, Goleizovsky loved the music hall; he helped to produce mass theatrical spectacles and was deeply interested in the aesthetics of sports. Goleizovsky's innovations—impressionistic studies performed barefooted, scantily costumed, and set to the music of such composers as Scriabin, Richard Strauss, and Debussy—may also have been influenced, as had been the early work of Fokine, by Isadora Duncan's dances. They made bold, if rather narrow, new use of par-terre acrobatics and unusual lifts that also surfaced in Balanchine's early ballets and soon became part of the Soviet ballet vocabulary.

In five years, Balanchine created thirty ballets, designed movement for three plays and an opera, and put together numerous cabaret pieces for his friends, while performing at the State Theater and studying at the Conservatory. Much was crammed into those years of experimentation in the worlds of ballet, theater, music, and visual arts, and Balanchine witnessed and sought much of it out. "Some of what was tried then in Petrograd and Moscow would seem much later in the West almost like the discovery of the twentieth century; decades of bitter practical experience would be necessary before coming to the conclusions that we reached at the end of the 1920s," Slonimsky has written.[31] For some, the conclusion was to abandon experiment and move on to the preservation or contemporary re-analysis of the classical ballets of old. Other experimenters were suppressed by the state and still others, like Goleizovsky, continued doggedly to choreograph in obscurity.

Balanchine learned to work with dancers in the single year of the Young Ballet's existence. The company sewed its own costumes and rehearsed on its own time. For its first formal program, Balanchine asked the dancers to choose favorite repertory pieces and choreograph others. The first earnings were handed out by Balanchine to the company members on the basis of the greatest need. Working with his peers, he formulated what was to be his lifelong vision of the dancer as interpreter of the ballet, both servant to and ruler of the choreographer. He accepted an invitation to become ballet master at the Maly Opera Theater, and continued to forge a style—and gain notoriety—with the Young Ballet.

"From the old classic adagio to modernism (a foxtrot), his style

36

for the moment involves a skillful combination of extremes," a Petrograd newspaper critic wrote revealingly in a 1924 appraisal of Balanchine's work with the Young Ballet. "It is difficult to say at which stage of his creative work he established himself definitively, but through his efforts a fresh stream has flowed into choreography which no one can now stop. Balanchine is bold and insolent, but in his insolence one can see genuine creativity and beauty. Balanchine's character dances are much less successful than the classical and abstract ones. They lack vividness and color, strong temperamental movements. Although in the classical work he does misuse poses, he combines them in such an interesting way and creates such beautiful if unexpected transitions that one can grudgingly excuse this defect." For "everything hackneyed and conventional," the critic continued, "Balanchine managed to find new, liberating forms."[32]

The Young Ballet disbanded that summer, the victim in large part of the increasing popularity of its individual collaborators, as well as of threats from the State Theater, and mixed reviews and public response to such oddities as ballets danced to chanted poetry. Balanchine sought permission to stage Stravinsky's *Le Sacre du Printemps* at the State Theater but received no answer. The Young Ballet presented its final performance on June 15, 1924. Later that summer, Balanchine hurriedly left Russia on a German steamer bound for Szczecin, in the company of three dancers, three singers, a conductor, and a second acquaintance named Vladimir Dimitriew. A former singer at the Maryinsky Opera and an admirer of Balanchine's work, Dimitriew had managed to coax permission from the Soviet authorities for the group to embark on a summer holiday tour of Germany, to be financed by his earnings as a croupier in a gambling casino.

Despite threats from the authorities that brought the musicians home, Dimitriew and the dancers continued on the tour. And Balanchine did not return to Russia until 1962, when the New York City Ballet danced at the Kirov Theater, once the Maryinsky, where Balanchine had performed as a child. "Welcome to

Moscow, home of the classic ballet!" a local reporter said at Balanchine's return, greeting him as the company arrived in that city at the start of its Soviet tour. "I beg your pardon," Balanchine responded. "Russia is the home of the romantic ballet. The home of classic ballet is now America."[33]

The Soviet State Dancers, as Dimitriew had rather grandly named the bedraggled group, arrived in Berlin in 1924 nearly penniless and without any dependable means of support, though well fed for the first time in seven years. Russian émigrés rallied around them and there was a tour of summer resorts on the Rhine. The group made its way to London for an unsuccessful booking in a variety show at the Empire Theatre, where it appeared as the Principal Dancers of the Russian State Ballet. When their work permits expired, the dancers were providentially summoned to Paris to audition for the great Diaghilev, whose keen nose for the new had sniffed them out in London.

Looking, as always, for good performers, Diaghilev accepted all four dancers, and Balanchine, his young wife, Tamara Gevergeyeva (later Geva), Danilova, and Nicholas Efimov joined Diaghilev's Ballets Russes. The following year Balanchine officially became the company choreographer. The second great episode in his education and preparation for America had begun. "It is because of Diaghilev that I am whatever I am today," Balanchine once said.

At twenty-one, Balanchine was already formed as a choreographer and coolly professional about his work. But Diaghilev, who once said he could mold a choreographer from an inkwell, embarked on a refining process with the raw young Russian, whom he renamed a more pronounceable Georges Balanchine. Go to galleries and churches, Diaghilev told Balanchine in Florence, and look at the paintings. And Balanchine eventually learned to see and cherish them for himself. Throw away the Scriabin, a somewhat sullen Balanchine was instructed, and Diaghilev handed him Stravinsky's *Le Rossignol* to set a new ballet to. A fairy tale, it starred a fourteen-year-old English dancer named Alicia Markova, found by Balanchine in one of the London studios run by the Russian émigré ballet teachers drawn to the city in the wake of the Diaghilev seasons. His next ballet for Diaghilev was an earthy farce, and three comic pieces followed.

Balanchine was disturbed by the inferior quality of many of Diaghilev's forty dancers, and later called the company a "disaster." But there was a lesson in that. Without a school or a dependable source of good dancers, Diaghilev had been used to acquiring performers from the Russian academies in St. Petersburg and Moscow, at which dancers received more thorough and sophisticated training than they were wont to at the studios and schools that had opened in London and Paris. But the Revolution had left Diaghilev without new dancers, as the Soviet state closed it on itself, forcing him to depend increasingly on chic visual effects and what were to Balanchine irritating libretti. Balanchine's *La Chatte* was danced in a transparent Constructivist set with costumes covered in mica, designed by Naum Gabo and Antoine Pevsner, and told of a love affair between a man and a cat.

The ballets Balanchine created for Diaghilev over the next two years did include *Apollon Musagète* and *Le Fils Prodigue*, both signature masterworks. In *Le Fils Prodigue*, a last work for Diaghilev's Ballets Russes that was presented in 1929, Balanchine used stylized acrobatic dance that reminded some of the cabaret to retell vividly the Biblical story. And Diaghilev observed that *Apollon Musagète*, a plotless, crystalline evocation of its Stravinsky score that Balanchine finished in 1928, was "pure classicism, such as we have not seen since Petipa's."[34] For Balanchine, the ballet was a turning point that taught him to look to and extend the traditions of the past. The score reminded him of something "white on white"—the effect, curiously enough, of the Malevich canvas—and he worked in close cooperation with the composer, in whom he sensed a kindred spirit.

Apollon Musagète taught Balanchine to refine to the clearest, most inevitable essentials and to work within a single tone or quality, an ability that served him well in *Le Fils Prodigue*. But

Diaghilev died three months after the premiere of that ballet, effectively ending the young choreographer's European career. Balanchine, Geva said, hated to dance, and a severe knee injury had curtailed his performing career in 1927. He was now a choreographer looking for work—at the Paris Opéra (with a project that ended in a bout with tuberculosis), in fashionable London revues, and at the Royal Danish Ballet, where he staged Diaghilev works.

His year with the Ballets Russes de Monte Carlo left Balanchine with a profound and lifelong distaste for the double-dealing Colonel de Basil, who had joined Blum in running the company. But out of that year came his touching and beautiful *Cotillon*, inspired by the innocent sophistication of three ballerinas in their early teens whom Balanchine had recruited for the company. And he created dance after dance for Les Ballets 1933, an endeavor undertaken with Edward James, a rich young socialite intent on mending relations with his estranged wife, Tilly Losch, around whom the new company was to be built.

Six new ballets formed the company's repertory, among them *Les Songes, Errante,* and *Mozartiana*, which New York would see just two years later, danced by the Kirstein-Balanchine American Ballet, and *Les Sept Péchés Capitaux*, recreated in *The Seven Deadly Sins* for the New York City Ballet in 1958.

For Balanchine, Les Ballets 1933 must have seemed a life-or-death proposition artistically. But the ballets were not the stuff of blockbuster seasons. "I was born into a world of cause and effect and grew up in a world of chance," Stravinsky once said.[35] Molded with extraordinary completeness in Russia and refined in Europe by the aesthete Diaghilev, Balanchine was once more thrown out into an anomic world, where even the comfort of working within the ephemeral but sustaining community of a ballet company seemed denied him. He had thought before of going to America. Now a strange young American had made him an improbable offer.

Balanchine left London with Dimitriew for Paris and a rest in the south of France. Would Kirstein ever see them again? The address they gave him was vague and faintly mysterious, and despite his mystical turn of mind, Kirstein was a practiced fatalist. But the machinery for the new plan had been put into operation. In the United States, Austin received pledges of three thousand dollars from such donors as Warburg and the future architect Philip Johnson. The Atheneum was willing to receive the dancers, given a solid contract. Austin telegraphed to Kirstein in London. A second wire followed. Austin could now guarantee the entire six thousand dollars.

Could Austin, Kirstein cabled right back, guarantee living expenses for Balanchine, Toumanova, and Jasinski for a year? No salaries would be necessary, but the dancers would need letters of recommendation from the Atheneum in order to secure entry permits to the United States. By mid-August 1933, Kirstein had met with a worried Balanchine and Dimitriew and discovered the beleaguered Russians—or the managerial Dimitriew, at least—had thought beyond the immediate financial provisions to wonder about the Atheneum's eventual relationship with a commercially successful company and school. And would six thousand dollars be enough?

It might be sensible, Kirstein suggested in a letter to Austin, to establish a private corporation to be called the School of American Classical Dancing "or some such Nationalist title"[36] to run the planned company and, even more importantly, the school. Eight to ten advanced students and the same number of children would make a good start. And Balanchine had even talked of creating a course in ballet composition, then a novel idea. Once just a feverish dream, the school and company were becoming a suddenly sobering business proposition.

Details began, inexorably, to fall into place. Austin sent on the necessary letters, Balanchine and Dimitriew left for the south of France, and Kirstein sailed for America. Shortly after his arrival, he received a cable from Balanchine. Had a decision been made yet? Off Kirstein went to the Warburg estate in White Plains, New York, to work a little more propaganda. It was a visit Warburg remembered well. He'd never seen a ballet, but Kirstein's visits were usually exciting. He listened carefully as talk tumbled out about his friend's "latest madness." Could Warburg guarantee his help? "I agreed to, little knowing what I was letting myself in for," Warburg recalled.[37] And Kirstein wired Balanchine that the plan was set.

Three weeks passed, however, with no word from Balanchine or Dimitriew. Had the two absconded with the money, money deposited to Balanchine's account, or just decided not to risk the venture? Warburg had the three thousand dollars traced and found it remained untouched in the Paris bank to which it had been wired—the address in the south of France was wrong. Having decided that Kirstein had changed his mind or been unable to raise the money, Balanchine had accepted another job, though he withdrew from it when contact with the Americans was finally re-established.

Kirstein continued lobbying among family, college friends, and colleagues in the arts. And then another bomb fell. Toumanova and Jasinski would not be necessary for the plan, Balanchine cabled. ("I don't know what happened," Jasinski says. "When we left London after the problems with James, Mr. Balanchine told us he'd take Toumanova and me to the United States to build a school and a company, with us as first dancers. I went on vacation to Monte Carlo with Balanchine, and he told me he'd had a telegram from Toumanova's mother that they'd signed a contract with de Basil. Without Toumanova, they didn't need me any more. Balanchine said he'd go first and see what possibilities there were in the United States, then he'd write and bring me over. But I had no money. I couldn't wait.")

Instead, Balanchine cabled, he would bring a very good teacher named Pierre Vladimiroff, once a leading dancer with the Maryinsky. A few days later, Balanchine cabled again to say that he and Dimitriew would come alone. But the momentum had increased to the point where Kirstein, despite his apprehension, continued to negotiate with immigration officials. He courted journalists, among them John Martin of *The New York Times*, who had seen and liked Balanchine's revue choreography in London in 1930 and had written of Balanchine's desire to come to the United States.

Balanchine and Dimitriew arrived in New York on October 17, 1933, and, after a brief flurry of trouble with immigration officers, were allowed to land. Balanchine practiced his American slang and asked not to be taken to visit any cathedrals. The two men walked the streets with Kirstein, looking at the city sights, and Kirstein and Dimitriew talked of the business of the new school. The Balanchine of those first days, Warburg recalled, was "a remarkable little man. He looked ill, which he was. He was also shy, gentle and very precise, while Dimitriew was a big bear of a Russian businessman with ice water in his veins and a constant smile which revealed voracious clenched teeth." [38]

If Dimitriew and Balanchine wondered at the nest of well-intentioned dilettantes into which they seemed to have fallen, the older Russian's intentions were entertained with suspicion by the genial, ironic Warburg. "Dimitriew had a field day. He had two little rich boys with no or not much knowledge about ballet, even though Lincoln knew more about it than any American. When the school was incorporated, I went through my lawyers to protect myself against the Russians. Lincoln however turned into a fifth column and moved over to the Russians. He spent his time with Balanchine and that left me with Dimitriew, who kept the squeeze on me." [39]

And then it was off to Hartford. "Balanchine arrived from Paris on Tuesday, left for Hartford on Thursday and is presumably busy at this moment on details of the project," Martin wrote in the *Times* on October 22. He was, but those details had taken on an alarming hue. From the beginning, the visit to Hartford was a failure. The three were met by a deputation of local dancing teachers distressed at the founding in their city of a free school run by a Russian. And although Balanchine and Dimitriew liked the museum facilities, they found the stage too small for ballet.

Hartford, they explained to the astonished Kirstein, would be impossible. A school, simply a company, or even just a few performances in New York began to be mentioned. By late October, New York had been settled upon as the site of any American ballet school or company they might found. Of course, there was always Europe to return to. Leaving Austin deeply hurt, and regretting it long after their rapprochement, Kirstein continued to confer with Dimitriew on the school prospectus and to work out immigration problems. It seemed as though the two would leave the country, but Balanchine suddenly fell ill in New York City, suffering, once more, from tuberculosis. The two were forced to stay, giving Kirstein a little extra time in which to work.

Doggedly, half welcoming failure as a relief, he set about finding a home in New York for the School. Vladimiroff had declined to join the faculty, though he later agreed to teach out of friendship for the ailing Balanchine. But Kirstein walked the streets of Manhattan for a week until he found space suitable for a ballet school. Notice in the *Times* had not brought them any students, but at least the School would have a home on the fourth floor of Tuxedo Hall, a small, shabby building at 637 Madison Avenue, at Fifty-ninth Street, which had housed a number of other dance studios including, legendarily, that of Isadora Duncan. It was a single room, but the tenant next door agreed to move out.

The new studio threatened at first to resist the necessary renovations. An iron post stood in the center of a wall cutting across the open space that Balanchine insisted he needed, a space that would have been approximately the size of a large stage and almost as big as the room at the Imperial School where Balanchine had worked on his first dances. Here, Kirstein felt, was a metaphorical summation of all their difficulties. But a week before the School was to open, Dimitriew found that another wall could be removed, creating the necessary amount of space. A movable wall was installed, giving the School the possibility of having two smaller studios and also the facility for a performing area and space for an audience. A bench was installed around the stubborn post, on which students were to lounge and chat over the next twenty-two years, in a foyer later handsomely redesigned by Philip Johnson.

Students had begun to get in touch with the School. Contracts had been negotiated just a month before Balanchine and Dimitriew had arrived in the United States, and talk now thrived on what would be taught and who would teach it. Only American students would be admitted to the School, Martin had announced, where they would learn classical ballet technique, character dance, and adagio or partnering, and attend lectures on art, architecture, period costuming, and music. Pupils would follow a system of instruction based on that of the Imperial School of Russia. It was hoped, he added, that as many as one hundred students would enroll in the new, national academy of dance.

Kirstein envisioned even more. The new School would exist "to further the tradition of classical theatrical dancing in order to provide adequate material for growth of a new art in America."[40] It would develop "a national ballet corresponding to the famous Russian Ballet but created by American artists to express an American tradition," an early announcement read. "The curriculum constitutes a complete education in the art of dance, and has been designed to train the permanent company of an American Ballet whose productions will be presented throughout the country under the direction of M. Balanchine."

Catalogues were printed. What would be danced at a concert planned for March, in which the School's advanced students would appear? Tempers flared at the dawdling of the workmen and the tenant next door. But on December 19 the name plate was designed for the front door. Kirstein mailed out announcements of the School's impending opening.

Prospective students continued to drift in, including Ruthanna Boris, a teen-aged dancer with the Metropolitan Opera Ballet, who later became a ballerina of the Ballet Russe de Monte Carlo as well as a ballet choreographer. Her audition was peculiar. Balanchine was "gorgeous"-looking, the bubbly teen-ager observed, and Vladimiroff austere. Vladimiroff gave her a barre or warmup exercises followed by center combinations from Balanchine that "flew." Then he told Boris to do a double pirouette, which Metropolitan dancers were not allowed to attempt. She couldn't, she said. Do it, he responded. "So I tried and he spanked me and I went around twice and fell down. I looked at him and I knew this guy was making jokes."[41]

Three visiting Russian dancers came for a look and left impressed. Kirstein braved the Christmas crowds at Macy's to buy furniture for the foyer, still wondering if there would ever be a school or a company. But two days after Christmas, he was at work washing and polishing the classroom mirrors.

A few preliminary classes started on December 29, five days ahead of the School's official opening date. Some twenty-two students had enrolled, to attend a morning class for the advanced women and a late-afternoon one for advanced men, all company material, and an evening class for rank beginners. Vladimiroff noted an improvement in the students in just one day. Meanwhile, though Kirstein was able only reluctantly to ask the pupils for their fees, an American Ballet now promised to become a reality. And 1933, so crowded with improbable achievement, closed with a New Year's Eve party in the studio for the founders and friends of the School of American Ballet.

II. 1934

"So in 1934 we opened the School here," Balanchine said at the press conference held in 1982. "From then on I don't count. That's my biography." The School opened its doors on January 1 for auditions. It was, Kirstein recalled ten years later, like "the parties parents make their children give. The small hosts hope that *someone* will show up."[1] When classes began officially the following day, thirty-two students had enrolled at the new School. Two months later, fifty students were attending classes graded on four levels of skill and experience.

The nucleus of professional dancers in the group of intermediate and advanced students chosen by Balanchine came from Catherine Littlefield's school in Philadelphia, accompanied by her sister Dorothie, who was to teach the beginners' class and perform with the planned company. Only a few beginning students turned up, and there were no children. Serious, disciplined ballet classes in New York in the 1930s were not just rare but served mostly adults. In a time when children learned "routines," with their teachers bent on producing legions of tiny, curly-haired Harriet Hoctors, the School's emphasis on solid training principles could not guarantee the kind of quick results then favored in the studios that welcomed children.

Balanchine was beginning to be known in the United States by those who had seen his *Cotillon* and *La Concurrence* performed by the touring Ballets Russes de Monte Carlo. Kirstein was known—among the intelligentsia, at least—for editing *Hound & Horn*, for writing, and for organizing art exhibitions. If these were fairly rarefied credentials, the School's first announcement in *American Dancer* (later *Dance Magazine*), was no less impressive. "A complete education in the art of dance," it promised, "toward the creation of an American Ballet Company."[2] And the promise was soon fulfilled. Within ten weeks of the School's opening, Balanchine began work on *Serenade*, his first American ballet and a dance that celebrated his new students.

"The most that the School has achieved in the first six weeks of its history is the fact of its existence," Kirstein wrote in a report issued in March of that year. "The Russian element in the administration is thoroughly acquainted with the American scene and the organization of the School's mechanics proceeds smoothly."[3] Whether this was wishful thinking or hyperbole, there was seldom an entirely peaceful atmosphere behind the scenes that year.

Having taken charge of Warburg and Kirstein, Dimitriew frequently expressed his scorn for the "dilettantisme" of the two young Americans with whom he had had the misfortune to become involved. Kirstein worried but watched excitedly, even taking parts of classes to acquaint himself with the business of building dancers. At the same time, he endured a coruscating, haphazard education in management from Dimitriew.

For a time, Kirstein gave nervous weekly lectures to the students on the history and aesthetics of dance. His tasks, all unofficial, ran the gamut from squiring representatives of foundations through classes to hammering soundproofing into ceilings and giving an underaged dancer her lessons in hygiene and civics. Some of the students saw him as a friend and an adviser, to Dimitriew's disgust. There were trips to Washington and even Montreal to straighten out the tangled immigration problems of his Russians and to talk, always with dread, to influential family friends about the new School of American Ballet and its needs.

Warburg wound through the studio like a cheerful refrain, stopping to comment on rehearsals and joke with dancers. And Balanchine continued to work, seemingly impervious to such problems as dwindling enrollment, then suddenly too-crowded classes, rumors of new American schools to be established by other Russians, and the loss of some of the more experienced dancers to musical theater or dance groups that could pay them wages and give them a measure of security. Conversation ranged from his ideas for new ballets and thoughts on the nature of music to occasional, exotic stories of the Diaghilev circle as seen, as Kirstein put it, from the slave quarters.

Balanchine grew increasingly tired-looking, and there were recurrent tuberculosis scares. Toward the end of the first month he suffered a day of quiet despondency brought on, it seemed, by his realization that the instruments of his new ballets were essentially untried students and that this spring, for the first time in ten years, he would produce no new dances. The next night, however, Balanchine was at work on a new solo for *Mozartiana*. He was too preoccupied with the business of inventing dancers and designing dances, as Kirstein later described it, to worry about everyday disasters, often engineered by Dimitriew as instruction for two young Americans naïve enough to attempt the establishment of a ballet school.

Dimitriew's fury stamped the School's official first day: the classroom mirrors didn't hang quite straight. Kirstein's anticipation of a small opening celebration was quickly quashed. He must stay, the Russian insisted, in the office and "superintend," rather than watch Balanchine teach class. A bad telephone connection kept Kirstein from informing his father of the opening with a due sense of occasion.

What had been wrought by this strange amalgam of personalities? The facility that greeted the students that opening day in 1934 was a spacious one with high ceilings. Most of the classes were given in a large studio with big windows. One wall was lined with mirrors, the other three with ballet barres. A smaller studio was designated the children's classroom. A waiting room, an administrator's office, and three dressing rooms with showers completed the facility.

The School was on the fourth floor, reached by an old and rickety elevator, with painters' lofts on the fifth, top floor. The offices on the third floor included the premises of the tailor who had moved to make room for the School, only to find himself sewing to the thud of Balanchine and the advanced students as they whirled through mazurkas in character class. The Tuxedo Ballroom took up the second floor, and the ground floor was occupied by Sammy's Delicatessen, a favorite hangout of the dancers, which was soon offering a George Balanchine sandwich.

"I felt it was absolutely the most fabulous place I'd ever been or seen," Elise Reiman says of the School. Reiman, a member of two Balanchine-Kirstein companies and, by its fiftieth anniversary, a children's teacher for twenty-eight years at the School, came to New York in 1934 to study with Balanchine and perform with the projected company, which she'd read about in *Vogue*. Reiman had trained and performed with Adolph Bolm, but the School of American Ballet was a new experience.

"Everything was so different," Reiman recalls. She had started studying ballet as a child in her home town of Terre Haute, Indiana. "It was ludicrous: I loved to dance and my sister had a friend who was a dancing teacher with no students. Then I studied with Bolm in Chicago. Everything was stressed differently at the School. Balanchine always had a thing about starting class with battements tendus. There were fantastic ports de bras then. Once I saw him, I never wanted to leave." It was Vladimiroff who noticed her first. "He was teaching class one day when Balanchine came in. Vladimiroff pointed to me. 'I want you to see this one,' he said. The only thing I had was good feet. A good arch, though the feet were sickled. Balanchine talked with me later, and invited me into the company right away. 'Of course,' he said, 'you'll have to work on your feet.' "

Reiman came into the School during its second term. "It was very exciting to be there at that time. Balanchine was sort of experimenting a little bit, and we had a sense that he and his new ballets would be different. Lots of artists came to watch. There were just a few of us. It was like a family. Ballet wasn't popular then. There was no money, though Warburg was pouring it in, thank goodness."

Many of the young women students had crushes on Balanchine. "He was very kind," Reiman says. "Lots of fun, but very serious at the same time. He'd take anybody—whoever was going out the door with him—to lunch or dinner. He was a very generous man. Warburg was adorable. And Lincoln. There were parties at the studio all the time. Lincoln's mother and father came and I knew them a little bit. They were sweet. One night, I remember, Vladimiroff and Balanchine did some famous pas de deux together just for fun, with Balanchine dancing the woman's role. We were all young, and it was a ball, though we worked very hard and it was strict." ("Lily cups of ginger ale," Warburg grumbles happily about the parties. "After rehearsals we did adjourn to the Russian Tea Room, the four of us and Kopechke— [Nicholas] Kopeikine the pianist. And we'd listen to them talk about how they'd had nothing to eat in Russia but herring heads.")

John Taras, who went on to become a ballet master at the American Ballet Theatre, arrived at the School six years later, but he remembers it with a sense of surprise similar to that of Reiman. "It was a *school*," Taras says. "Everywhere else was a studio where someone taught, with small rooms that made moving difficult. The big studio at the School was an enormous space. You could travel, and that was the way Balanchine wanted it. He wanted the dancers to cover space. To move. You can see that in *Serenade*. We were constantly watched, too. Lincoln would bring in everyone." He mentions Tchelitchew, W. H. Auden, Glenway

Wescott, the novelist, and George Platt Lynes, whose photographs provide a glamorous record of Balanchine, Kirstein, and the dancers. "It was absolutely marvelous. You felt part of an artistic community." It was, as Kirstein put it, a paradoxical education, with the faculty representing both the traditional and the offspring of that tradition in Pierre Vladimiroff and Dorothie Littlefield, in an atmosphere of Prussian grimness shot through with gaiety and affection.

Vladimir Dimitriew, the School's director until 1940, when Kirstein bought out his shares, was almost universally unloved. But he had his uses: he'd managed to get Balanchine out of Russia and into an audition with Diaghilev, and he had helped him to found Les Ballets 1933. And Balanchine had insisted that he be part of the package when Kirstein invited the choreographer to America. Kirstein had some sympathy for Dimitriew, his initial fear of the man being mixed with admiration for his management skills and a certain pity for the lonely life he led until 1964, when he died in New York. The sudden depredations of the Revolution, early statelessness, and shifting artistic bases had left Balanchine with a capable, almost feckless charm. Dimitriew survived to become a jack-of-all-trades, a cynical misanthrope for whom the theater, symbol to him of all disorder in the world, was simply a means of economic survival that, adorned by two rich young Americans, even represented a considerable step toward prosperity.

"Few were ever relaxed around him, except when he judged we had had as much riddling and needling as we could take," Kirstein has written. "He orchestrated or choreographed both explosions and reconciliations; he would take us to excellent Russian restaurants, to get us drunk. Before midnight tolled, Warburg or I would have signed another check, ensuring the school's existence for another few months. My father understood and admired him; since he considered me a financial idiot, there was some security in Dimitriew's unyielding penny-pinching."[4]

Not even Balanchine was spared Dimitriew's acid tongue. All

that Balanchine was interested in, Dimitriew told Kirstein early that first year, was pianos, automobiles, and girls. What did Balanchine see in him? "I think he needed Vladimir," Taras says. "Balanchine was shy. He was all alone. He couldn't do it alone." And it is undeniable that Dimitriew lent exotic color to the School's earliest days. Survivors of his reign remember the man with delighted horror. "I was scared to death of him," Reiman says. "I remember that he put peepholes in the doors to the studios. He'd look through them to see who was working and who was not."

Dimitriew's penury extended to the students. "Balanchine said once that he tried giving the good girls ten dollars to study," remembers Georgia Hiden, a member of three of the Balanchine-Kirstein companies and an early student at the School. "But Dimitriew didn't see the point of dancers getting anything. And he was there all the time. I remember once some of the students were coming back from lunch. One girl had bought a few pairs of stockings. 'You don't need but one pair,' Dimitriew told her. 'Dancers don't need all that.' " Dimitriew had envisioned coming to America to start an academy comparable to the Imperial School, though his experience as an educator was less than Kirstein may have been led to imagine at the start. He kept an iron hand on the teachers, watching to see that Vladimiroff did not rest unduly on his laurels. Vladimiroff, too, knew Dimitriew's wrath. He left the School in 1937 and did not return until Dimitriew departed.

Called "the ideal partner" by a Russian critic, Vladimiroff had danced with the famed Kchessinska, Lubov Egorova, and Olga Spessivtseva, whom he'd partnered in 1921 in *The Sleeping Princess,* Diaghilev's exquisite but doomed revival of the Petipa classic *The Sleeping Beauty.* But Vladimiroff was a star in his own right in Russia, an athletic, musical premier danseur and gifted mime who had specialized in interpreting the Fokine repertory until the choreographer had suggested he had better do more classical ballets so that the public would know that he knew how to dance. So exciting was his performing that balletomanes paid him the legendary homage of pulling his carriage through the streets after the ballet. And Balanchine had admired him greatly while a student at the Maryinsky, where Vladimiroff had graduated ten years ahead of him. "He used to say Vladimiroff could stay up in the air so long he could write his name with both hands—the left one going backward," Suki Schorer, a former member of the New York City Ballet and a teacher at the School of American Ballet, recalls. Jacques d'Amboise, another former member of the company, heard Balanchine describe Vladimiroff as having been a better classical dancer than Nijinsky. "When the Bolshoi came over to the United States in 1959, the dancers all rushed over to see Vladimiroff and take his class," d'Amboise says.

But Vladimiroff somehow never caught on as a dancer in America, where he was known principally as a partner to Anna Pavlova, with whom he danced from 1928 to her death in 1931. He had begun to teach informally at the Maryinsky when noted dancers like Tamara Karsavina and the great academic theorist Agrippina Vaganova, intrigued by the exercises he invented for himself, asked him to give them barre work. In his thirty years at the School of American Ballet, where he taught until 1967, three years before his death, Vladimiroff became an admired ballet teacher and was appreciated as a vital link to the classical tradition of nineteenth-century Russian ballet.

"Vladimiroff was very gentle," Natalie Molostwoff, director of the School in 1984, says. "Very unassuming. Very simple." Not notably strict in class, Vladimiroff taught by example rather than explanation, as have most of the Russian teachers at the School. And to see him teach, students and observers of his classes say, was to witness a textbook embodiment of the essential traditions of classical dancing. "He had a wonderful, elegant style," Taras says of Vladimiroff's partnering and repertory classes. "His steps had flow," Hiden recalls. "They felt right. And he was a perfect gentleman." Vladimiroff, Reiman feels, would not have been a good teacher for beginners. "But his classes were lovely," she says. "He gave wonderful jumping combinations from the Maryinsky."

"After Balanchine, Vladimiroff was *the* great teacher,"

d'Amboise, says, looking back on his days at the School in the 1940s, when he studied with the two, as well as with Anatole Oboukhoff. "With Balanchine and Oboukhoff, he epitomized the Petipa school, the pre-Soviet manners, that are gone now. With the Soviets, everything is big. Up. For Vladimiroff, princes didn't look up. He used to teach pirouettes starting low on the heel to give you control. He hated excess. You never prepared with a run. You never looked where you were going. Everything was on the balls of the feet: you never put your heel down. You always walked a line." His style recalled to d'Amboise the fact that the earliest ballet performers danced in heeled shoes and cumbrous dress.

Littlefield, on the other hand, had a fresh-faced American glamour to her, and the broad shoulders and short, slightly plump body that then characterized many American women ballet dancers. A mere eighteen years old when she arrived at the School, Littlefield had trained with her mother and sister in Philadelphia. She had studied with some of the Italians teaching in New York in the 1920s and finished her training in Paris, where she went with her sister to learn from the Russian expatriate teachers who had settled there. She was a devoted admirer of Balanchine. "A big, bouncing field-hockey girl" is how Warburg remembers Littlefield. "That was what we started with," he says. "Some had had ballet training. But we had to have lessons in how to take a curtain call. Their idea of taking a bow was to wave to their families in the third row."

Littlefield had, Kirstein noted in the School's first year, "an excellent sense of American limitations and possibilities."[5] Working in consultation with Balanchine and Vladimiroff, from whom she took classes, Littlefield shared the teaching load and helped to conduct rehearsals at the School before leaving it to join the American Ballet, the first of the Balanchine-Kirstein companies, in 1935. She went on to perform with the Philadelphia Ballet and Chicago Civic Opera Company, danced for Balanchine in 1946 in the Broadway musical *Song of Norway,* and worked with her sister staging Broadway musicals and ice shows until her death in

1952. Her solid, straightforward teaching style made her particularly good with beginning students.

The fifth member of the staff that first year was Eugenie Ouroussow, a gracious and efficient young Russian gentlewoman whom Dimitriew chose as his assistant just before the School opened. "She was a princess, actually," recalls Muriel Stuart, a teacher at the School since 1935. "And very beautiful, but very simple. Very human." Director of the School at the time of her death in 1975, Ouroussow had, it seemed, all the necessary gifts, balancing a blithe sense of humor with what one friend remembers as an incredible resourcefulness. A born diplomat and full of common sense, Ouroussow was eminently suited to serve, as Kirstein wrote in a memorial tribute, "as a liaison officer between two brash Americans and half-a-dozen Russian theater-people unaccustomed both to their perplexing manners and amateur attitude towards professional business in the instruction of a difficult discipline." Four years after coming to the School, Ouroussow was joined by her friend Molostwoff. "The School was so small then," Molostwoff recalls. "Eugenie and I took attendance, sent out bills, and tried to break even, which we did. We managed to survive and even put a little money aside for emergencies." (By 1984, the School had an administrative staff of twelve.)

Ouroussow had virtually taken over the directorship of the School by 1943, when Kirstein went off to war. Her handsome face stares out from a photograph hung on a wall facing the entrance to the School's Juilliard headquarters, its meditative expression giving little away to the uninitiated about a woman whose favorite hobby was fishing and who worked with Edmund Wilson on Russian translation. The face seems to serve as the icon of a patron whose presence is still felt in the School and whose abiding calm is reflected to a surprising extent within the sanctum of the School in its fiftieth year.

The operating budget for the School in the first year was, Kirstein recalls, approximately $50,000. "All in red ink," Warburg comments. (In 1984, it was $1.4 million.) Dimitriew's accounts for the first three months of 1934 survive, meticulously recording such expenditures as "timbres," "Scott papers," "Petites cashes," and three "avances" to Ouroussow in a total amount of $25. Vladimiroff was paid $100 a week for the first two weeks and $150 thereafter. Balanchine and Dimitriew earned a weekly salary of $100 each, the resident pianist $60, Littlefield $25, and Ouroussow $20 every week. Rent for the floor appears to have been $275 a month.

Among the students Dimitriew logged in those first months were "Mr. Erick Hawkins," today the noted modern-dance choreographer; "Mlle. Leda Anchutina," a brilliant young dancer who would become a leading member of the American Ballet, "Mrrs. Christensen," "Mr. Paul Haakon," then a popular ballet solo performer, and "Miss Patricia Bowman," later to become ballerina of the Roxy Theater as well as of Radio City Music Hall, and a charter member of Ballet Theatre. Fees paid on any particular day ranged from $1.50 to $30, the latter the average fee for a month of "complete instruction" for the 60 percent of the student body not on scholarship.

That first month, Balanchine celebrated his thirtieth birthday, his first in his new home country, by demonstrating the five positions of ballet in a "class of explanation" that opened with a speech by Warburg. The School was open, generally from ten or ten-thirty in the morning to seven or seven-thirty at night, six days a week, with the actual curriculum for the men's and women's classes for advanced and professional students including technique, adagio, character, and even variations or solo repertory classes from time to time, as well as instruction by Dimitriew in stage makeup, and Kirstein's lectures on the arts. Warburg wanted the dancers to study music, but it was felt that the School could not afford to offer such classes. And Balanchine expressed the hope that the following year he might conduct a class for choreographers, although colleagues recall that he later said he did not believe choreography could be taught.

For the time being, Balanchine taught both advanced and beginning students, though the latter only occasionally and with bad grace. Even then, he was given to working on individual steps through exhaustive repetition, and to teasing the students with quietly wry, cryptic anecdotes, explanations, and teaching ploys, a habit for which he was famous in later years. "Hold it, hold it, hold it," he might call to a classful of students surging into a position at the end of a combination; then he would disappear from the room. Some preferred Balanchine's classes for their poetry; others thought them poor pedagogy.

By March, Balanchine was holding afternoon practice or "rehearsal" classes four times a week. He had begun, on January 6, in a class whose significance was felt by all those present, to work for the first time on a scene from one of his own ballets, now called *Errante*, a haunted dance he'd created for Les Ballets 1933. Twelve days later he began to stage *Mozartiana* for his advanced students. The plan had always been to focus on eventual professional appearances with a new American ballet company, and Balanchine was impatient to start to work. Now the dancers became not just potential performers but the raw material of creation. For on March 14, Balanchine began to choreograph *Serenade*.

He had been working on changes in *Errante* that evening in the rehearsal class when he turned to the new ballet. His mind was blank, he said. Would Kirstein pray for him? Then he lined up the seventeen women in class according to height and slowly began to create what he called "a hymn to ward off sin." Pulling out two dancers, he watched them move first in toe shoes, then without, and decided they should not work on toe. Then came a few gestures for the arms and hands, which seemed to Kirstein to have Balanchine's distinctive quality. Dimitriew was quick to dismiss the perception. How did Kirstein know how the ballet would turn out? Balanchine had had, after all, his failures. But *Serenade* was, in its way, as much a turning point in Balanchine's creative life as *Apollon Musagète*. This initial American ballet, created for the student dancers of his new American School, was first of all a further commitment to the "plotless ballet."

There had been the slightest pretext for a plot in *Apollon Musagète*, inherent in the music Stravinsky had composed after a period of contemplation of a ballet to be based on some aspect of Greek mythology and danced, ideally, in the academic classical-ballet idiom as a pure "ballet blanc." Scored for a string orchestra in order to achieve a homogeneous, austere effect, the ballet contained programmatic hints having to do with Apollo and three of the nine Muses, overseers of the arts and sciences in mythology, whose gifts seemed the most appropriate inspirations for choreography. In Balanchine's hands, the god received a serene and almost playful education from his three young companion Muses in dance of a surprisingly unheroic tinge.

For his first American ballet, Balanchine chose Tchaikovsky's Serenade in C Major for String Orchestra, like *Apollon Musagète* scored for strings alone. It was probably familiar music to Balanchine, since it had been used by Fokine for a 1915 ballet called *Eros*, in which Vladimiroff had danced during Balanchine's early years at the Imperial School. It was music that had poured out, Tchaikovsky wrote in a letter to a friend, from "an inward impulse" of an urgency comparable, one imagines, to that of Balanchine's desire to begin, once more, the work of making dances. Though not programmatic in any way, the score unfolds in an undercurrent of suggestive atmosphere, from the first expansive, annunciatory chords, through haunting reversions to the theme to which the ballet's magical opening moments are set, and on through a buoyant melodic waltz to a last movement that hurtles forward, eddying with brisk assertion back to the opening theme.

For Balanchine, making a ballet was the choreographer's way of showing how he understood a piece of music. That the atmosphere of the Tchaikovsky score becomes visible on stage seems as much a function of Balanchine's growing interest in creating ballets in which the dance might be heard and the music seen as of the subject matter of the ballet, with its suggestion of the

American dancer acquiring discipline and technique, or even in the throes of young romance. But Balanchine did incorporate classroom events into the ballet. And its first moment, when ranks of dancers suddenly, in one quick move, open out their feet into the first position of classical ballet, has a tone that is irresistibly symbolic.

"He had to find a way for Americans to look grand and noble, yet not be embarrassed about it," the critic Edwin Denby wrote. "The Russian way is for each dancer to *feel* what he is expressing. The Americans weren't ready to do that. By concentrating on form and the whole ensemble, Balanchine was able to bypass the uncertainties of the individual dancer. The thrill of 'Serenade' depends on the sweetness of the bond between all the young dancers. The dancing and the behavior are as exact as in a strict ballet class. The bond is made by the music, by the hereditary classic steps, and by a collective look the dancers in action have unconsciously—their American young look. That local look had never before been used as a dramatic effect in classic ballet."[6]

Serenade is essentially an exegesis of classical ballet and those who dance it, whether the mostly chubby neophytes of the first cast or the streamlined products of the School of American Ballet fifty years later. At its heart lies the corps of women on whom the curtain rises, a mass of bodies whose free and sweeping flow through the ballet suggests that Balanchine was, indeed, influenced by Fokine's *Chopiniana*. Soloists split from the group from time to time for fleeting variations. "I had never seen anyone run in and out all the time that way," Reiman, one of the ballet's early soloists, says of those dances. "When you did solos, you stayed put."

Of almost the same emotional weight and a similar impact are the classroom "accidents" or exigencies that Balanchine incorporated into the ballet. A woman arrives late and has to find her place within the group, which leaves as a man enters to partner her in the waltz that makes up the ballet's second section. A woman falls. A male partner for her is brought in by another woman, who stays to dance with them, then leads him off again. It is the woman who has fallen who rises again, but rises in lonely, somewhat dangerous splendor in the ballet's stunning close, when she is carried slowly off the stage, standing on the shoulders of three males, her body arching back and her arms opening wide as she is transported into the light.

It is possible to see, in that culminating moment, a statement of the hard principle that today guides the School of American Ballet and troubles some observers. Ballet is an unyielding discipline, a vocation rather than a pastime, which demands serious commitment and, often, physical and emotional sacrifice. Transfigured, those who become the elect, that closing moment in *Serenade* suggests, are poised alone and at risk above the crowd. Even the persistently unrhetorical Balanchine, in an unguarded moment, saw fatefulness in *Serenade*, though of a fate that had to do with man's romantic destiny.

"Too fancy," he remarked when told of Denby's analysis of *Serenade*. "I was just trying to teach my students some little lessons and make a ballet that wouldn't show how badly they danced."[7] By his own account, Balanchine devised the ballet as an exercise in stage technique to give the students, many of whom had never performed, an idea of the relationship between classroom steps and stage dancing by working with them on a completely new ballet that would, eventually, be performed.

From the start, *Serenade* was not just a lesson but a creation of the young dancers' own time, unlike the more familiar nineteenth-century classics. And it signaled the mutual and inextricable interdependence that would characterize the relationship of the first Balanchine-Kirstein companies with the School of American Ballet.

Balanchine continued to refine the ballet, adding a new third section for the Ballet Russe de Monte Carlo in 1940, set to the score's closing movement, which he had not used in the first version. *Serenade* grew with Balanchine and the company, becoming more theatrical and more polished technically as he went on working on it with an unusually sustained interest. The only one of Balanchine's American ballets choreographed in his first six years in the United States to remain in the New York City Ballet's repertory, *Serenade* has been performed continually by the company, and it was danced by the students in the School's fiftieth-anniversary-year Spring Workshop. Balanchine has given *Serenade* to more companies throughout the years, both in America and abroad, than any other ballet. It was in the repertories of forty-four companies by 1984.

And yet its beginnings were so simple and so characteristic of Balanchine's practicality and lack of presumption. There were seventeen women to work with. He would start with them all, ranging them in diagonal rows that did not reveal the unevenness of their number. And what could be more reassuring, at the start of this unusual and clearly important collaboration, than simple movements for the hands? The ballet would, however, use their sometimes painfully acquired classical technique. Bodies rooted firmly in the reassuring springboard of the floor, their feet opened next into first position, that first letter of the ballet's alphabet.

Students tended to come and go in those early months. Occasionally Balanchine would be despondent at the chaos of it all. He had always created his ballets in the studio rather than plotting them to any great extent before rehearsal, seldom turning away observers. Work on *Serenade* began in a closed studio. But Balanchine was able to use the element of ragged chance in this new American ballet. When nine women turned up for the next class, he choreographed a next section that used only nine dancers. Five women turned up for the third class, and *Serenade* continued with a dance for five.

A dancer came late to class one evening and inserted herself into the group's formation at that point in the ballet, automatically achieving the rank of soloist. Rushing off the floor with the group during another rehearsal, a dancer fell and began to cry.

Balanchine told the pianist to keep playing, and that moment and its poignancy are preserved in *Serenade*. And when Warburg objected to the stiff line of the women's raised arms in the opening moment of the ballet, which reminded him of the Nazi salute, Balanchine softened the arms, keeping the hands in a gesture that struck Kirstein as resembling a shielding of the eyes from "some intolerable lunar light."[8] That opening moment was to draw tears from Martha Graham. "It was simplicity itself," she observed, "but the simplicity of a very great master—one who, we know, will later on be just as intricate as he pleases."[9]

Serenade has moved critics throughout the world to comment in ways that shed light on the entire Balanchine oeuvre. All that that first American ballet called for from its dancers was a clean and unrhetorical technique. And it would come to be a favorite among City Ballet dancers, whom it made feel, simply, beautiful.

Though John Martin regarded the ballet, initially, as merely "serviceable," Denby saw in *Serenade* evidence of Balanchine's status as heir to Petipa in the clarity, grandeur, and humaneness of his classicism. *Serenade* "presents that beauty which is the province of dance alone, the beauty of highly trained bodies moving rhythmically through space, experiencing adventures in design, exploring the air in leaps, exploiting the endless possibilities of movement sequence," the critic Walter Terry wrote. "There is beauty also in the almost intangible theme of 'Serenade,' in the communication of romantic searching, of waiting, of longing, of finding."[10]

In 1954, the Japanese critic Eguchi described the ballet as "a masterpiece of sheer musical movements." "The end result: no dancers remained in our memory; only the structural beauty of extreme refinement."[11] And Yuri Slonimsky wrote, revealingly, in 1972:

In this work, Balanchine declares himself heir to the traditions established by L. Ivanov and M. Fokine in "Swan Lake" and "Chopiniana." From the first measures he introduces the innovative "dance of the arms" to interpret Tchaikovsky's music—a world of contradictory emotional urges, lyric meditations, doubts, limpid sadness, and the trouble-fraught quest for happiness. Balanchine enriches the classic dance of his predecessors with the new body movements . . . "single-voiced" and "multi-voiced" modulations of the corps de ballet, retardations and accelerations of the dance melody, changes in rhythm (not only inward but outward), plastic caesuras, and so on. It is no wonder that Balanchine's staging of this work has remained alive for nearly forty years in many of the world's theaters.[12]

Chameleonlike, *Serenade* adapts to situation. Over the years its solos have been danced by varying numbers of soloists and, as Kirstein noted, the ballet seemed to fill almost every space it was performed in. Its first performance took place on a bare pine platform designed by Dimitriew for a concert presented by the Producing Company of the School of American Ballet early in June 1934, for invited friends, out of doors at the Warburg estate in White Plains.

"And so I was persuaded—and in turn I convinced my long-suffering parents—that what I wanted most for my twenty-sixth birthday on June 1934, was to have these ballets performed in the garden at our family place," Warburg has recalled.

We invited some two hundred guests and erected a platform on a stretch of lawn (which, incidentally, never recovered from the shock). With rather primitive spotlight facilities and a piano hidden in the bushes, we introduced the American Ballet to a rather astonished group of friends. The first scene was "Serenade," one of the perennial standbys of the ballet repertoire now at Lincoln Center. With the music of Tchaikovsky, the lights went up on the assembled group of dancers, each one standing with arm outstretched, looking towards the heavens. It was a moving moment. I can never look at that scene now without remembering the White Plains performance. No sooner had the dancers become visible when, as if in answer to their raised arms, the heavens opened up, and it poured!"[13]

That first performance had been under discussion for a month or two, in a time of increasingly optimistic activity. A manager was sought for the planned company. Though performances seemed much more a matter of hopeful certainty than business, Kirstein envisioned a tour of college towns by the fall, the proceeds of which, after the dancers had been paid, would help to support the School. There was talk, which came to nothing, of expanding the School's facilities. By mid-May, as storms raged around him over the practical and artistic preparations for the White Plains engagement, Balanchine had begun work on another work to be called, variously, *Touchdown* and *Alma Mater*, a project suggested by Warburg and drawn from his scenario on American college life.

With that last-minute disarray before an opening that is as much a part of theater tradition as the promise of disaster held by a good dress rehearsal, the School moved inexorably toward the White Plains performance on June 9, hesitantly announced by its producers as a "demonstration" though planned as a prelude to the formation of a professional company. By mid-afternoon the day before, the young dancers had departed for White Plains in the company of three parents, a wardrobe mistress, and boxes of costumes assembled and delivered just in time.

There were sudden injuries as the dancers rehearsed and posed for publicity photographs. The weather turned cold, and everyone got hungry as the rehearsal went on into the night. The skies grew grayer the following day, though the weather had been promised as "fair and warmer." A light rain interrupted the afternoon rehearsal, and the dancers moved to shelter and sang together until the shower ended. Kirstein stared moodily at a flag fluttering nearby. Tarpaulins covering the stage and piano were removed and put back on again with each change of weather.

Guests began arriving. Dressed for a rehearsal of *Mozartiana*, the dancers performed the ballet as the weather grew better for a time. Then, with the torrent that greeted the start of *Serenade*, Kirstein announced the cancellation of the program and invited the audience to return the following evening, to the dismay of Warburg's mother. Where, on a Sunday, would she find enough additional food for everyone? And how, Dimitriew snarled, could the Warburgs have expected the ballet company to be fed like pigs, as the dancers settled down for a postperformance party in the family garage?

The following day began more calmly, with the company setting out for White Plains once more in the late afternoon, this time with a full complement of family members and friends. There was more food than the day before. The audience was at least as large and notable. And *Serenade* began in only a light rain, to which the dancers and pianists remained impervious. The School had had its first performance, which it celebrated that evening with a party in New York.

The next day, Balanchine returned to work on the Warburg ballet, and the students went back to their classes in a lingering fever of excitement that would dissipate within a week, as the end of the term approached. With the exception of the Metropolitan Opera School, no New York dance studio had ever closed for the summer, as the School would do from July 3 through August 26. Influential visitors continued to drop by, however, and everyone on the staff but Balanchine continued to worry about money for productions by the barely fledgling company.

Would the students return for a second term, Kirstein wondered? They did, although the School was able to offer only ten scholarships, twelve fewer than the term before. The studio was full. The students looked much thinner. Vladimiroff's men's classes were becoming increasingly popular. More and more well-known dancers were taking class at the School. It was possible to pick out, in one advanced women's class in mid-September, Alexandra Danilova, Felia Doubrovska, Nina Verchinina of the various Ballets Russes, and Kyra Blanc, a former Goleizovsky dancer and member of the Bolshoi Ballet and Ballets Russes. Dimitriew's wife and "a sweet little thing," as Warburg remembers her, Blanc was to join the staff in 1939, becoming its first children's teacher two years later. She had, d'Amboise noted, "a perfect fifth" position.

Danilova began work with Balanchine on reconstructing *Apollon Musagète*, which he rehearsed with five School casts. Littlefield returned, but only to perform, and Dimitriew and Kirstein hastily searched for replacement teachers for the poorly attended beginners' class, resisting the urge to dump those students into an intermediate class, as other New York studios did.

Opportunities for film and Broadway musical work had begun to come in for Balanchine, offering also the promise of student employment. But Balanchine continued to dream of a finely produced ballet season. There was talk of a modest bus tour for twenty-eight of the School's best student dancers as a tryout for a New York season. A chance encounter between Kirstein and Austin led to an invitation for the dancers to appear in February at the Avery Memorial Theater at the Wadsworth Atheneum in Hartford. It became increasingly clear, too, that the School must maintain an identity independent of any company, and talks began about drawing up corporate structures for each, a legal arrangement that took effect in 1935. Encouraging requests for company performances began to trickle in. Balanchine finished *Touchdown* and started work on two other new ballets. The dancers' first payday occurred on October 12. Five days later, on the first anniversary of the arrival of Balanchine and Dimitriew in America, three dates were set in early December for the dancers' first public, professional performances.

What should the company be called? Would there be work for the dancers after Hartford? Warburg came through, once more, with money for the productions. The Hartford stage was the size of the School's small studio, but a respectable number of artists and socialites were expected to attend. Tickets, considered expensive at a seven-dollar top, sold slowly for a three-ballet program that included *Touchdown* (now renamed *Alma Mater*), *Transcendence* (Balanchine's new ballet to Liszt), and *Mozartiana*, replaced on closing night by *Serenade*. Two pianos substituted for an orchestra, and the dancers had performed better in rehearsals. But just a year after its inauspicious beginnings in the same city, the School had returned to Hartford and produced its American ballet.

III. THE FIRST
THIRTY YEARS

April, 1938: New York.
. . . Balanchine demoralized . . . Dimitriew prophesying doom; Warburg
fed up. School, O.K.[1]   —Lincoln Kirstein

F ew of the students could have imagined they were attending
the School of American Ballet to learn deportment. For George
Balanchine, creation and public performance were clearly of par-
amount importance. And so the early history of the School and
the Balanchine-Kirstein companies, precursors to the New York
City Ballet, are linked inseparably.

But the School of American Ballet's first thirty years are colored by a curious dichotomy. The School itself seemed to continue imperturbably, as it does today, appearing to run itself. If
the first ten years were a time of daunting crises and disappoint-
ments for the School's founders as they worked to establish their
American ballet company, common sense and high spirits pre-
vailed in the fourth-floor studios at 637 Madison Avenue. Eugenie Ouroussow's tact had a great deal to do with that, as did

intent, daily grappling with the demanding work of learning to dance under the firm hand of teachers who even then approached a common goal in surprisingly individual ways.

The American Ballet, founded in 1935 and the first of five companies formed by Balanchine and Lincoln Kirstein, sank into oblivion. Kirstein's Ballet Caravan exhausted its limited human resources on spartan touring schedules. After a single season nothing came of the American Ballet Caravan, the amalgamation of Ballet Caravan and the American Ballet that toured South America in 1941. But the School continued, becoming a streamlined professional academy as it grew. Its most obvious and attractive goal—the training of young American dancers to perform on stage in American ballet—did seem nebulous to the point of impossibility during most of that difficult first decade. Youngsters who attend the School today may dream of one day dancing with the New York City Ballet, and if they are not accepted they have a wide range of professional companies across the nation and in Europe in which American dancers may perform. But in the mid-1930s, there were few such outlets. For most American dancers, there could be no realistic hope of performing classical ballet with any continuity. The prominent representative of ballet in the United States, the Ballet Russe de Monte Carlo, favored Russian dancers, and the Ballet Russe was in increasing artistic and financial disarray—a process slowed, ironically enough, by Balanchine's work with the company in 1944–46, when he restaged ballets, created new ones, and worked to enliven the dancers.

New York's Metropolitan Opera Ballet, geared as it was to serve up danced interludes in opera productions, offered little chance for ambitious young performers. And employment with smaller troupes like that of Michel Fokine tended to be short-lived or fluctuating. Ballet was for Russians. American ballet looked in those years as if it would never establish a hold.

Kirstein drove back to New York from Hartford, the day after the company's season at the Avery Memorial Theater, full of anticipation at the thought of a New York season to come in just three months. Some of the dancers had proved too inexperienced to perform; they must be let go. Nine ballets had been announced for New York, four of them, possibly, new revivals. There was a chance that Balanchine might create an entirely new ballet based on Harriet Beecher Stowe's *Uncle Tom's Cabin*, with a scenario by e. e. cummings and a score by Virgil Thomson. There was work to be done. But the American Ballet had acquitted itself, without disgrace, at its first public performances.

If the reviews had been mixed, the company had been received well by its audiences. And the influential John Martin had treated the company seriously, if with an ominous note of warning, in a long open letter to the American Ballet published in *The New York Times*. "The bravos of the comparatively small company of the ermine-clad are transitory," Martin wrote. The undeniably gifted Balanchine would need time to acquire a sense of things American and might, in the meantime, "put the stamp of Europe upon his pupils and dancers in these sensitive formative years." Native American choreographers must be encouraged. And as for the company's developing audiences, Martin wrote, "only let them see as soon and as often as possible that the American ballet is classless in its appeal, functional rather than decorative and expressive of a home-grown and not an imported outlook."[2]

The American Ballet made an auspicious debut in New York, however, doing well enough to extend its run through an unscheduled second week at the Adelphi Theater, where it had opened on March 1 in a repertory of six ballets. Twenty-six dancers then studying at the School of American Ballet were joined by Paul Haakon and Tamara Geva, by then a glamorous veteran of the Broadway musical. Some of the student dancers had already had stage experience. Others had had very little or none. Marie-Jeanne, the first American-trained Balanchine ballerina, had begun to study ballet at the age of fourteen, early in 1934, with the opening of the School of American Ballet, and she found herself performing three months later at White Plains.

Given that range of experience, the program that Balanchine,

Kirstein, and Warburg put together was remarkable for its variety and sophistication. Holding up the "American" end were *Serenade* and Warburg's *Alma Mater*, in which a brainless Yale football hero and a raccoon-coated villain, complete with two-seat bicycle, vie for the attentions of a dim-witted flapper. Balanchine had tried, but the ballet was little more than a revue sketch. Warburg conceded that it was a mishandled flop, though the dancers and their audiences loved it. "It would have been fine had Balanchine been willing to go to a football game, but he wanted to do an American *Bourrée Fantasque*," he says of the ballet, which was inspired by the Yale sagas of Ralph Henry Barbour, a popular novelist of the time. Warburg's fur coat was borrowed to complete the costumes designed by John Held, Jr., the cartoonist. "I could never wear it again. I think it's at the Smithsonian."

Dreams, created for Les Ballets 1933, had been a hit in Paris, but its depiction of a lonely ballerina's tortured nightmare failed to engage the New York audiences. *Errante* seemed equally obscure, a hallucinatory dance of great visual beauty derived from mysterious costumes and decor by Tchelitchew. The atmospheric, technically demanding *Transcendence*, created for the Hartford performances, was set to music by Liszt—notably his "Mephisto" Waltz—and based on a mystic scenario by Kirstein that involved a hooded man and a girl whom he mesmerizes. The program was completed by *Reminiscence*, a suite of lightweight classical divertissements. Critics praised the level of performing the company exhibited in it, but only Martin liked the ballet, which was the single work on the program that he praised wholeheartedly. *Alma Mater* was "relatively unimportant," *Dreams* was "scarcely worth the labor that has been spent on it," *Errante* was "cosmic nonsense, and *Transcendence* "largely incomprehensible."[3]

Five months later, writing about the company's performances at New York's Lewisohn Stadium, Martin threw down the gauntlet. He had earlier praised the clean, dignified style of the dancers, but now he urged Kirstein to "charge the whole experience to date to profit and loss . . . and get to work starting an American ballet."[4]

Kirstein responded in kind. "American ballet is not tap-dancing, though it may use it," he wrote in a telling letter to the *Times*.

> It is not the Virginia reel, though country dances can be added to its context. Nor is it the hypnotized idiosyncrasies of a small group of concert-dancers who happen to have been born in America, and who draw their ideas from Central Europe. Ballet in America is a form of dance expression no more indigenous than American violin or piano playing. Mr. Martin feels Russians are unsuitable to transmit this 400-year-old medium of Italian, French, German, Scandinavian and Slav origin and collaboration to fit the capacities of native Americans without corrupting them by foreign tricks.
>
> The American Ballet is interested in the development of ballet on the continent of America. That an enthusiasm for this kind of dance exists can be proved by the existence of the School of American Ballet, which has given instruction to over 300 students in a year and a half, to a successful New York engagement of the ballet company composed entirely of artists trained by its teachers, and by its fourteen weeks of advance booking outside of New York for 1935–36.[5]

But disaster struck the American Ballet a week into the tour Kirstein described, set out upon with much familial fanfare and the whir of newsreel cameras as dancers and musicians boarded two buses at Rockefeller Plaza. All went well until the company reached Scranton, where it was discovered that the booking manager had absconded with the receipts. Not only would proceeds from the tour not help to support the School, as Kirstein had hoped, but there would be no tour. "I found myself the nearest thing to an asset within miles," Warburg recalled years later.[6]

The dancers were sent back to New York and given two weeks of pay and scholarships at the School, though it reportedly took one company member a month to muster the courage to return home to Brooklyn and admit the failure to his family. But the Metropolitan Opera beckoned. And under the circumstances, it was hardly surprising that Kirstein and Warburg turned eagerly to the Metropolitan, which invited the American Ballet to become a resident under the aegis of Edward Johnson, the Metropolitan's new general manager.

Balanchine was delighted at the opportunity to work in a place that reminded him, at first, of the Maryinsky. Kirstein's ingrained pessimism deserted him. He and Warburg were astonished at the company's good luck. Not only would it have an opulent home base, with summers free for touring, but the Metropolitan agreed that the company might present occasional ballet evenings in addition to Balanchine's opera assignments.

It was a surprising achievement for a company barely two years old, but from the start the collaboration was a failure. Rehearsal time was limited, production values were haphazard, and the facilities offered the dancers were cramped and dank. Elise Reiman, who lived through those three years, says, "I still can't go to the opera today." The management showed little interest in the company or the promised ballet evenings. Balanchine's opera ballets unsettled conservative critics and audiences, and his sensual dances for *Aida* were singled out for special alarm.

With the Tchelitchew-Kirstein-Balanchine staging of Gluck's *Orpheus and Eurydice* in May 1936, the American Ballet had one of the most stunning failures in the history of twentieth-century ballet. The singers were hidden in the orchestra pit. The opera was presented without an intermission. And Tchelitchew had fashioned a startling vision of hell and heaven from chicken wire, dead tree branches, and cheesecloth. Metropolitan audiences had never experienced anything like it. ("At those prices, there wasn't a brain in the house," Warburg observed.) Most critics were equally disturbed. Some were flippant. Others, like Olin Downes, music critic of *The New York Times*, spouted indignant pejoratives. *Orpheus and Eurydice* was "ugly," "futile," "impudent," "meddlesome," "far-fetched and ridiculous manoeuvring," "bad," "dull," and "pretentious dilettantism." The production was canceled by the Metropolitan after only two performances.

Ten years later, the artist boasted to Balanchine that his designs for an unproduced version of the Balanchine-Hindemith *The Four Temperaments* would wipe out all choreography and obliterate the music. Tchelitchew had helped the American Ballet to find a following, if an elitist one, and had played an important role in developing the company's artistic credo. But his visionary concept of the Gluck opera virtually obliterated the American Ballet. "Our audience was totally unprepared for an interpretation that transformed vaguely familiar myth and music into a heroicized domestic tragedy of artist, wife and work; hell as a forced-labor camp; eternity as no happy heaven, but a paradisaical planetarium where time and space crossed," Kirstein later wrote.[7]

Warburg remembers the production fondly. "What happens in the second act?" he asked Tchelitchew early on. "It's wonderful," Tchelitchew responded. "Yes, but what's wonderful?" Warburg pushed. "She climbs very slowly up the mountain," Tchelitchew said. "When she reaches the top, she turns her back, facing the precipice." He paused. ". . . and lets her hair down." Warburg was delighted. "A killer," he said. "We can't lose on that." But they did, and his delight turned to misgiving. " 'For this,' I thought, 'I'm spending my patrimony.' "

Balanchine had begun to work on Broadway, and in 1936, with his second musical, *On Your Toes,* he had a hit. It was one of many theater and film musicals and operettas for which he would create dances over the next fifteen years, earning himself extra money to plow back into his company and creating jobs for dancers from the School. "George Balanchine has done an ace job on the terp angle," *Variety* declared.[8]

With his work in musicals, Balanchine won new respect for the "dance arranger," soon to be referred to in program credits, at his request, as the "choreographer." He also raised the level of show dancing, thus opening up more opportunities for work for dancers with serious ballet training. "If the rules of Equity permitted, probably the dancers would be glad to pay Mr. Balanchine something for the privilege of appearing under his direction, for he has released them from the bondage of hack dancing and ugliness," Brooks Atkinson wrote in the *Times*.[9]

Kirstein saw the Balanchine of these years as an "homme perdu," and Balanchine himself felt like a lion tamer with no lions,[10] as he later told Taper. But it is likely that his experiments with show dancing had a broadening effect on his style of "American" ballet.

Kirstein, too, had embarked on an enterprise that would not only bring more employment to dancers from the School and to the American Ballet during summer layoff, but would also serve as an important spur to the development of native ballet in the United States. From the spring of 1936 through the fall season in 1940, the small troupe of dancers and neophyte American choreographers calling themselves the Ballet Caravan (later the American Ballet Caravan) crisscrossed the country, inventing a repertory of their own like the American modern dancers of the day, and presenting ballets on familiar folk themes and situations from everyday life that in effect "eliminated the footlights," as George Amberg put it.

Balanchine had resisted Kirstein's suggestions for ballets like the one on *Uncle Tom's Cabin*. For him, America was simply a land of "lovely bodies," though he would come to celebrate his vision of its spirit and culture in the mid-1950s with ballets like *Western Symphony* and *Stars and Stripes*. For Kirstein, as moved by folk themes as were other American intellectuals of the time, the American ballet was not just a product of collaboration among "the best American painters, musicians, poets and eventually choreographers," as he had declared in an early announcement of the founding of the School of American Ballet. The American ballet had also to do with the kind of outlaw antihero who gave Eugene Loring's *Billy the Kid* its name, as well as the pump jockey, truck drivers, and gangsters who populated Lew Christensen's *Filling Station*, two of Ballet Caravan's most popular works.

Anatole Chujoy, a supporter of regional ballet and an admirer of Kirstein's project, thought Ballet Caravan's programs well danced but atheatrical and dry. Kirstein was to describe the company's nearly four years of arduous existence as "an era of instruction rather than construction" for everyone involved. "And yet there was no other way to do it at the time," he noted, "even if one would never do it again. It was an education of a sort, for all of us, audience, dancers, directors."[11]

It cost Kirstein about a hundred thousand dollars of his own funds to present, and he was unable to realize his plans for a New York season to be shared with leading modern dancers of the day, foreign guest choreographers, and chamber opera ensembles, though that would come about in another ten years. Diaghilev, Chujoy pointed out, had gone through a decade of comparable investigation of Russian folklore. But Ballet Caravan did what Diaghilev ultimately failed to do, which was to find and involve a new audience of tremendous geographic range, planting the seeds for a new kind of dance as it went. Most of the dancers and the choreographers, who included William Dollar and Erick Hawkins, were charter members of the student body at the School of American Ballet. And not until the formation of Ballet Caravan, company member Alicia Alonso recalled, was she able to perform exclusively as a ballet dancer.

Such projects did nothing to enhance the reputations of Balanchine and Kirstein at the Metropolitan Opera. A successful single-program Stravinsky Festival in the spring of 1937, in which the American Ballet presented *Apollon Musagète*, along with *Le Baiser de la Fée* and *The Card Party*, both new ballets by Balanchine, did little to change the Metropolitan's increasing hostility toward the company. In March 1938, Johnson announced that the company's contract would not be renewed for the following season, and later suggested that the American Ballet had been lacking in the chief requirements for an opera ballet: modesty, unobtrusiveness, and a respect for tradition. "He is an artist and could do fine things, but he has no wings," Balanchine said of Johnson. And the tradition of ballet at the Metropolitan, he retorted in an uncharacteristic public display of temper, was "bad ballet."[12]

Kirstein resigned from the American Ballet's board of directors in May 1937 to devote himself to running the School and working with Ballet Caravan, which ended in a burst of giddy glory in the spring of 1940, when the company was commissioned to perform in twelve shows a day for six months at the World's Fair in Flushing Meadow, New York, in *A Thousand Times Neigh!*, Dollar's expert and even witty eighteen-minute promotional venture for the Ford Motor Company. Warburg, who had been subsidizing the American Ballet, had resigned from the company's directorship late in 1937. "I asked myself: Why do I want to continue being involved in this strange form of torture?" Warburg explained years later.[13] Family pressure led him to resign also from the board of the School of American Ballet just as Kirstein was leaving the American Ballet. Balanchine quit the board at the same time to devote himself to creating dances, and he and Dimitriew were left to run the American Ballet. The company ceased performing in 1938. "What the American Ballet . . . did do was to acquaint a number of native-born dancers with a new spirit in stage dancing, a spirit expressing the essence of the nervous contemporary age as apart from the romantic spirit of the rose," Kirstein observed several years after the company's demise.[14]

But the School had never seemed healthier. In 1938, it held its first summer course, conducted that year in Bermuda. "We had the most marvelous time," Muriel Stuart says. "It was not really businesslike. But the School's never been businesslike." Stuart had joined the faculty three years earlier and was to become one of its best-known teachers. She, Balanchine, Vladimiroff, and Anatole Oboukhoff, who was to join the faculty in 1941, formed the core of a staff that included other pedagogues and visiting guest teachers, often noted performers, who gave classes in ballet, modern and character dance, and music theory. "It was quite an assortment," John Taras recalls. And each teacher had a distinctive presence and idea of how a pupil should move, though all proceeded from a technique rooted in the classical tradition of the Imperial School.

Stuart could trace her lineage to the Russian academy as a dancer trained from the start by Anna Pavlova, who had graduated from the Imperial School twenty-two years before Balanchine. Stuart began her training at eight, after two years in a neighborhood "fancy-dancing" school in the town near London where she grew up. Pavlova had advertised that she was beginning a class for very young girls. At the audition, she was fascinated by the way Stuart moved with the music at a sudden change of rhythm. Stuart began to perform with Pavlova at thirteen, and continued to dance with her company for ten years, until 1926, when she left to marry. She performed briefly and choreographed for the Chicago Civic Opera, settling to teach in San Francisco and Los Angeles in the late 1920s and 1930s.

Pavlova had passed on to Stuart a sense of poetic lyricism and spirituality. The Russian dancer was also interested in ethnic dance forms, and Stuart found herself exploring new American dance. During her time in California, she studied modern dance with Harald Kreutzberg and dance composition with Louis Horst, the musician and theorist who served as adviser to Martha Graham and other American modern-dance pioneers. It was to study with Graham that Stuart came east to New York. And shortly after, recommended by Graham and Agnes de Mille, she was invited to teach at the School. Stuart remembers teaching a sample class to the sound of whispered Russian. Soon after, she was at work teaching classical techniques to the women and later a kind of fluid, hybrid style in classes open to all.

"Dimitriew was very nice to me," she says. "And after I'd been there a year or two he called me into the office. 'Isn't there something else that the students can do but bend their knees and stand in fifth position?' he asked. 'I understand you study modern dance. There must be something else you can teach the girls. It would be awfully good for them.'

"They called it 'plastique.' It wasn't modern dance exactly. My dear, if I'd sat them on the floor they'd have died. It was running and jumping and dropping. Balanchine liked that very much. He thought something would happen so the dancers wouldn't look like wooden soldiers." Taras remembers the class as providing the students with a chance to move and use their bodies more. "We worked so much on backs," he says. "There is such an emphasis on technical correctness," Stuart notes wryly. "Getting the students into these terrible positions that are against any sense of movement and don't come naturally."

Still a member of the faculty in 1984, Stuart is known for the beauty of her line and her "gift for movement," as Georgia Hiden puts it. Stuart herself doubts that musicality and artistry can be taught, though she remains on a covert lookout for the kind of poetic lyricism embodied in Allegra Kent, a favorite former pupil. "It's either innate or it ain't," one student remembers her saying of rhythm.

"She made combinations that danced," recalls Jacques d'Amboise, who studied with Stuart in the 1940s. "Her use of the arms and upper carriage was extraordinary. Very similar to Oboukhoff. The grand gesture. Nothing little, nothing small." But Stuart, the co-author with Kirstein of *The Classic Ballet*, a respected manual of ballet technique, is also one of the School's most theoretically oriented teachers, verbally stressing method and precise placement as much as she teaches it by demonstration. That combination can extend the physical imagination, preparing the student, as Kirstein once said, for Balanchine's violations of the classic order.

Classes were small and the students not very advanced when Stuart arrived at the School. There were few male students. By the time Oboukhoff joined the faculty, the quality and level of skill had risen considerably. Oboukhoff, whom students adored, were terrified by, or adored in terror, brought a new atmosphere of edgy alertness to the studio. Kirstein has described him as "a strong, even harsh teacher who frequently behaved as if he were training big cats, horses, or poodles rather than adolescent bipeds. He barked commands and corrections like a drill sergeant; his own gestures seemed violent to the point of physical aggression; yet he was the gentlest of men as well as the strictest and clearest of analysts."[15]

A particularly gifted teacher of the young male, Oboukhoff is remembered by his students as a disciplinarian who was also a colorful character, a teacher who gave exhausting, very structured, technically demanding classes that managed, at the same time, to be highly inventive. Vladimiroff could seem remote. "I don't think he ever adjusted to the United States," d'Amboise says. "I think he lived and belonged in the world of St. Petersburg and the ballet." But Oboukhoff was an admirer of the pretty women students in his classes and a teacher who clearly enjoyed his work. A famous habit was to stand very close, snapping his fingers in the students' faces as they did their barre. "He was like a circus trainer," Taras says. "A lion tamer. You'd be standing there doing pliés and he would be there, close up, looking at you." D'Amboise remembers Oboukhoff's "terrific frown." "But he wasn't mean. He was gentle. I later found out his extraordinary mannerisms were caused by a stutter." D'Amboise imitates Oboukhoff growling "Good morning" into a towel at the start of class. "He carried Life Savers with him all the time. And he'd give you one if you did a combination well." While Vladimiroff usually dressed in neat workpants and a short-sleeved polo shirt, Oboukhoff favored tailored black linen pants and a flowing white shirt.

Like Vladimiroff, Oboukhoff was known for his elegant ports de bras. And Oboukhoff built strength, a particularly useful gift during the New York City Ballet's earliest years, when performers might dance four ballets every night during the season, since the company was then so small. "You thought you were dead after the barre," Taras recalls. "Yet everything after that was easy. It was an extraordinary way of teaching. His enchainements were long. They'd last perhaps ten minutes and include almost everything, from adagio to allegro to some jumps as another combination at the end." Hiden remembers Oboukhoff roaring, "That way! To Moscow!" in Russian as the dancers leaped through the final jump of the class. "There was a schism, though denied," she says. "When you did something bad in class, Oboukhoff would say: 'Where do you think you are? In Moscow?'"

Their classes complemented each other. "Oboukhoff taught by example and repetition," d'Amboise says. "He was relentless. You'd have about a thirty-minute barre, then long, complex, sustained adagios that incorporated the barre work. Vladimiroff taught by variety. He gave the most beautiful, incredible, joyful combinations, with difficult steps. The barre was short. Just a warmup, like Balanchine. And there was a lot of allegro in Vladimiroff's class. You could get thirty-five minutes of jumping."

Oboukhoff had graduated from the Imperial School the year Balanchine entered it, and achieved the rank of premier danseur at the Maryinsky Theater, where he soon established himself as a danseur noble in lead roles in the classics. "Balanchine used to say that Oboukhoff was like a king coming down the hall at the Maryinsky," d'Amboise recalls. He left Russia in 1920 and went on to dance in small ballet troupes in Europe and Latin America as well as the Ballets Russes de Monte Carlo before he joined the School of American Ballet, where he taught until his death in 1962. Watching Oboukhoff teach, Stuart remembers, she contemplated changing her own style. "But Balanchine said, 'No, no, everybody has their way.' Of course, if we didn't get them into fifth position . . ."

Erick Hawkins worked at the School as an assistant instructor, as did other early students, among them William Dollar and Lew Christensen. Taras recalls taking class with Merce Cunningham, who taught at the School in the mid-1940s; John Cage, the avant-garde composer and Cunningham's collaborator, served occasionally as class accompanist. The School continued its flirtation with modern dance until 1969, employing such teachers as Dorothy Bird, Anna Sokolow, and Janet Collins. "I pushed for modern dance when I thought it was an alternative," Kirstein says.

The School has also offered character dancing through the years, ranging from polkas, mazurkas, and Spanish dance to English country dancing, taught, most notably, by José Fernandez, Yurek Lazowski, and Robert Parker and Ronald Smedley of the British Folk Dance Society. If the general repertory no longer demands such training—as did Petipa ballet with its national-dance divertissements—character classes can offer the young ballet dancer a chance at flamboyant, all-out movement as a freeing relaxation from the rigid technical demands of classical ballet.

"George always transfigured character dance into something else," Kirstein says. "The nearest thing we have is jazz, and he invented his own kind in *Who Cares?*. Not Broadway, but certainly musical-comedy dancing." In 1984, the School initiated social-dancing classes for the girls and boys in the advanced and intermediate classes. Lessons in music theory, initiated in 1940, have also been given sporadically through the years, and were part of the School's curriculum during its fiftieth-anniversary year, though only interested students participated.

The other members of the faculty in the School's first decade were Anatole Vilzak and Ludmila Schollar, both graduates of the Imperial School who had danced with the Maryinsky, and various Ballets Russes companies. Vilzak performed with the American Ballet at the Metropolitan, and the two joined the staff in the mid-1930s, with Schollar teaching variations classes and Vilzak giving partnering instruction. They left the School in 1940 at the instigation of Dimitriew and set up their own school in New York, subsequently joining the faculty of the San Francisco Ballet school. ("Dimitriew did do us one favor, though," Molostwoff says. "It was he who called to tell us Oboukhoff was in New York and that we should get him as a teacher.")

"You never knew who'd teach," Hiden says. "You just thought,

'I wonder what's going to happen today.' Balanchine's classes were always changing. You'd have to move. He'd push you into the air. Then after a while he'd give you classes on a dime. I asked him once and he said that people would get well trained, and stay in fifth position when he wanted them to move. Then they'd move, but get sloppy and have to be pulled back. Another time, for a short period, all we worked on were our hands, which he said were dead. That came from something Nijinsky apparently wrote about observing babies' curled hands and wrists. But I don't remember Balanchine talking that much. It was strictly work.

"The big studio was large but it was very crowded. All the girls admired Vilzak. His classes were fun. He loved to mix you up—give you steps that were a puzzle. Each of the men wore a different after-shave cologne, but his was the best. Like hot cinnamon buns. And there were a lot of nuts in the class. There was one girl who would go up on half toe and fall asleep. They sent her to talk with Balanchine, who told her to read *War and Peace*. She did, and then came back to him. 'What should I do now?' she asked. 'Read it again,' he told her."

Gradually it became obvious that the School was less and less interested in anyone but serious students working toward a professional career. In 1942 the School started a short-lived class for laymen, or "monster" classes, as Kirstein called them, to help subsidize the School and its scholarship programs. "We had to stop because they all wanted to be promoted," Molostwoff exclaims.

Children under twelve began to be enrolled in 1936. Five years later Kyra Blanc began a Children's Division in which students from eight to twelve were given their own fundamentals classes after school and on Saturday mornings, classes that were restricted to children only and were separate from the mixed ones the youngest students had previously attended. The School now offered five divisions of study, ranging from children's to professional classes. The second, or Beginners' Division, offered basic

A classroom at the Imperial School, St. Petersburg, circa 1913—George Balanchine's heritage and the tradition the School of American Ballet drew upon. Alexandra Danilova, standing at right; Balanchine, seated at far left. *(Collection Alexandra Danilova)*

A ballet class at the Imperial School, St. Petersburg, circa 1912–13. Note the violinist accompanying the class. *(Collection Alexandra Danilova)*

GEORGE BALANCHINE,
circa 1934, a founder of the School
of American Ballet with Lincoln
Kirstein, Edward M. M. Warburg,
and Vladimir Dimitriew. *Photo:
Paul Hansen (Dance Collection, The
New York Public Library)*

Left: EDWARD
M. M. WARBURG,
1930s. *Photo: George Platt
Lynes (Dance Collection,
The New York Public
Library)*

Below: VLADIMIR
DIMITRIEW,
1930s, first director
of the School. *Photo:
Ralph Oggiano*

LINCOLN KIRSTEIN, president of the School of American Ballet, looks at a portrait of himself by George Platt Lynes, circa 1934, on exhibit in "First, a School . . . The School of American Ballet's First Fifty Years," the first of the School's fiftieth-anniversary celebrations, at The New York Public Library's Library and Museum of the Performing Arts, 1983. *Photo: Carolyn George*

Classroom at Tuxedo Hall, 637 Madison Avenue, at the
northeast corner of Madison and 59th Street, the home of the
School from December 1933 to February 1956. It was said to
have been the studio in which Isadora Duncan once worked.
Note its large dimensions. *(Collection of Ballet Society)*

Above: Rehearsal of *Serenade,* the first ballet George Balanchine created in America, by students from the School of American Ballet, June 1934, at the estate of Felix Warburg, White Plains, New York. Balanchine stands, right, center, working gamely on in the midst of confusion. Warburg's son, Edward, had been coaxed by his colleagues at the School to ask for the performance, presented to invited friends, as a birthday present. The ballet was next performed by the Producing Company of the School of American Ballet, antecedent to the Balanchine–Kirstein American Ballet. It remains in the repertory of the New York City Ballet and many other companies in the United States and around the world. *(Collection of Ballet Society)*

Opposite, above: The first performance of *Serenade,* June 10, 1934, at the Warburg estate. *(Dance Collection, The New York Public Library)*

Opposite, below: Serenade, as performed by the students of the School of American Ballet fifty years later, at the School's Workshop Performances at the Juilliard Theater, May 1984. *Photo: Paul Kolnik*

Above: The American Ballet (1935–1938). Group portrait of the company, in costume for George Balanchine's *Alma Mater,* first performed by the company in 1935. Vladimir Dimitriew, Lincoln Kirstein, Edward M. M. Warburg, and Balanchine may be seen standing, left, center. Among the dancers pictured are Erick Hawkins, Elise Reiman, Annabelle Lyon, Giselle (Gisella) Caccialanza, Ruthanna Boris, William Dollar, and Eugene Loring. *(Dance Collection, The New York Public Library)*

Opposite, above: The American Ballet at the Metropolitan Opera House. Annabelle Lyon and Lew Christensen in George Balanchine's *Orpheus and Eurydice,* 1936. Its unconventional staging, and Pavel Tchelitchew's sets and costumes, caused a scandal that hastened the end of the American Ballet. *Photo: George Platt Lynes (Dance Collection, The New York Public Library)*

Opposite, below: Ballet Caravan (1936–1940). Left to right: Eugene Loring, Lew Christensen, and Fred Danieli in Loring's *Billy the Kid,* an American folkloric ballet created for the company in 1938. *Photo: George Platt Lynes (Dance Collection, The New York Public Library)*

American Ballet Caravan (1941). Left to right: Marie-Jeanne, William Dollar, and Mary Jane Shea in George Balanchine's *Concerto Barocco*. *Photo: George Platt Lynes (Dance Collection, The New York Public Library)*

Some Balanchine ballerinas of the early years in America. Left to right, standing: Mary Ellen Moylan, Maria Tallchief, Marie-Jeanne, Ruthanna Boris. Seated: Tanaquil LeClercq. *Photo: Larry Colwell*

Ballet Society (1946–1948). Nicholas Magallanes and Maria Tallchief in George Balanchine's *Orpheus*, created for the company in 1948. *Photo: George Platt Lynes (Dance Collection, The New York Public Library)*

New York City Ballet (founded in 1948). Arthur Mitchell and
Diana Adams, for whom George Balanchine created the pas
de deux in his *Agon,* choreographed for the company in 1957.
Mitchell studied at the School and went on to become one of
the City Ballet's most popular dancers. Adams was the coordinator of studies at the School from 1963 to 1971. *Photo:
Martha Swope*

New York City Ballet. Edward Villella and Karin von Aroldingen in George Balanchine's *Prodigal Son,* first performed by the company in 1950, twenty-one years after Balanchine created it for Serge Diaghilev's Ballets Russes. Villella, a noted interpreter of the title role, was one of the first boys to study at the School, and von Aroldingen was later one of the many company performers to teach at the School. *Photo: Martha Swope*

exercises in academic ballet for students with some previous training and for those in need of corrective work. Classes in character dancing and contemporary- or modern-dance technique were optional.

Intermediate Division students, or those who had been promoted from Beginners' or received an adequate foundation in other schools, were offered academic ballet and classes in character dancing, contemporary technique, and dance composition, as well as beginning work in toe for girls and participation for the boys in the men's class held twice a week. By the Advanced Division, students were offered additional classes in partnering and variations. And the Professional Division offered all these courses as "preparation of the advanced student for theatrical ballet, developing style, precision, brilliance, projection and deftness of execution," according to the School catalogue for the fall-winter term of 1942–43.

Character classes included dances from Russia, Poland, Italy, Hungary, and Spain. And Contemporary Technique offered dance based on the styles of Martha Graham, Mary Wigman, and "other great innovators." "Exercises in this course render the body more supple and flowing and strengthen the torso and back," the catalogue explained. Dance Composition was designed to offer the new choreographer a chance to create dances and to learn about the fundamentals of composition and the structure of a dance in relation to its musical score. The School of American Ballet had become an actual academy of dance.

Class placement auditions were required for all students with previous training, and students between twelve and eighteen were advised to engage in a concentrated study of the complete curriculum over two to three consecutive years. Rates ranged from four hundred dollars for the complete course, including ten lessons a week for ten months, to two dollars for a single class. There was a summer session of six weeks in July and August designed for intermediate and advanced students, professionals and dance teachers unable to attend the School during the winter. The catalogue listed local representatives of the School in Boston, Rochester, Chicago, Denver, Louisville, and Dallas.

Balanchine suffered another disappointment, of possibly more symbolic value than anything else, in 1939, ironically the year in which he became an American citizen. He was the only prominent choreographer not to be included in plans for a repertory for Ballet Theatre, founded that year in New York City, though it has been said that his insistence on bringing with him a corps de ballet composed of School dancers helped to lessen his appeal to the founders of the new American ballet company. But two developments at the School the following year promised much for its future.

Kirstein bought out Dimitriew's shares in the School in the spring of 1940, and Dimitriew resigned in June, leaving Kirstein as president and director of the School and Ouroussow as its executive secretary. ("Dimitriew was so sure the School couldn't survive without him that one of the last things he did was to dictate letters of recommendation for Eugenie and myself so we would be able to get new jobs," Molostwoff recalls.) Soon Kirstein began to institute reforms. He incorporated the School as a non-profit educational institution and persuaded Balanchine to take a greater interest in the School. When classes resumed in September, Kirstein announced the School's first competition for scholarships. Three were supposed to be awarded, but the level of talent was so high among the 130 students who applied that Kirstein gave scholarships to five children.

One of the five was a small, skinny, solemnly determined-looking eleven-year-old named Tanaquil LeClercq. "She looks like a real ballerina already, only very small, as if you were looking at her through the wrong end of a telescope," Balanchine, chief competition judge, said at the time.[16] LeClercq became an unusually versatile dancer, able to move fluently through her roles, whether they demanded simple elegance, extraordinary musicality, or comic or tragic acting.

Her subsequent career on stage was cut short by polio in 1956, though she later taught ballet. But no one who saw LeClercq dance could forget her long, tapering legs, proud carriage, and vivid physical acuity. Carefully developed by Balanchine, whom she married in 1952, LeClercq was a prototype for the kind of performer popularly identified as the "Balanchine dancer" and an ideal interpreter of his choreography. A "brilliant, capable and strangely personal ballerina of wit," as Kirstein described her, LeClercq "was the epitome of Balanchine's lyrically athletic American criterion."[17]

Her first professional solo, performed in 1946 at seventeen, was the remarkable Choleric Variation in Balanchine's new *The Four Temperaments*, a violent but astringent dance for a lunging body and legs that slice the upper air. Created for LeClercq, the dance celebrated her clean technique and bold stage presence. But the entire evening had the air of an occasion, for the premiere occurred on the opening night of a new and important venture called Ballet Society.

A Balanchine-Kirstein company had been resurrected briefly as American Ballet Caravan in 1941 with a good-will tour of South America undertaken at the invitation of Kirstein's old friend Nelson Rockefeller, who had recently been appointed Coordinator of Inter-American Affairs at the State Department. Designed to reveal the United States as a cultured country, the tour drew from Balanchine *Ballet Imperial* and *Concerto Barocco*, two new ballets that proved to be among his most popular and were important extensions of his exploration of plotless dance and the classical canon. But the tour ended after four months and was only moderately successful, with the company facing audiences that had expected old-time Russian glitter.

American Ballet Caravan disbanded. World War II intervened, calling away a good many of the male dancers. (They returned, Muriel Stuart remembers, with very big feet.) But when Kirstein came home in 1945—making his way straight from the separation center to the School, as legend has it—he was filled with a new sense of self and not-so-new plans for the future. "I gained an illusion," Kirstein wrote of his time in the Army, "that I might do much as I wished so long as I knew what it was and analyzed the factors. A former weakness for the tentative, accidental, or improvisatory was sloughed off, and with it, much insecurity and doubt. In the service I behaved much *as if* what I wanted to do could be done."[18] It was an insight that might have surprised the friends whom Kirstein had enlisted in helping to found an American ballet school and company, as well as the dancers whom he squired across the country and back again during the Ballet Caravan days.

Balanchine had continued to place School dancers in the musicals and operettas he created, and the Ballet Russe de Monte Carlo received an infusion of young American dancers, most of them from the School. There had been opportunities for employment in the short-lived little American Concert Ballet of 1943, which was organized by and drew its performers from dancers from the School. That same year, forty-four students appeared in Bach's *Saint Matthew Passion*, produced by Balanchine and Leopold Stokowski at the Metropolitan Opera House. And eighty-five dancers from the School appeared in 1945 in a joint performance with the National Orchestral Society at Carnegie Hall, which brought the School some publicity and was the start of a successful partnership with Leon Barzin, the founder and conductor of the Society and City Ballet's music director for ten years.

But what was still needed, Kirstein saw, was an American company. Armed now with an inheritance of about $250,000, he was about to provide yet another one with Balanchine's help. The School had linked the two men during difficult and scattered times. Now working together again, they created Ballet Society, the direct precursor of the New York City Ballet and one of the most uncompromising and innovative ventures in the history of the arts in America.

Ballet Society was planned as a private subscription organization with a six-point program. Not only would it present new ballets and operas as well as solo concert dancers, but it would cooperate with other cultural and educational organizations to produce performances, complete with documentation, and documentary and experimental dance films. It would also award fellowships to gifted young choreographers and dancers to help them develop their own work. Critics would have to buy subscriptions to the Society's seasons, for only artists and impoverished dance enthusiasts would receive free tickets.

It was, of course, sheer elitism and madly improbable. But eight hundred people responded to a first mailing. And some had a sense of the Society's importance for the future. "I have here reported on the Society's lucky beginning at quite disproportional length," Edwin Denby wrote prophetically of its amateurishly produced first programs, "partly because it is a new, much talked of enterprise, partly because it may well, after several years of trial and error, turn out to have been the origin and foundation of the sensibly organized, exciting American ballet company we need now so badly."[19]

Members received everything but the promised record albums, and in the first season subscribers also received a yearbook, invitations to films, demonstrations, and rehearsals, and subscriptions to the scholarly *Dance Index*. Ballet Society presented Merce Cunningham's *The Seasons*, his first major production, and Gian-Carlo Menotti's *The Medium*. It screened the Jean Cocteau film *Beauty and the Beast* for its subscribers. But most of all Ballet Society provided Balanchine with a company and a showcase for his work.

It was for Ballet Society that Balanchine created *The Four Temperaments*, through whose plain-wrought classicism wound the roots of such Balanchine signature works as *Agon* and *Episodes*, as well as *Orpheus*, a stunningly simple evocation of the legend of Orpheus and Eurydice, created by Balanchine, Stravinsky, and the artist Isamu Noguchi. Maria Tallchief, then recently of the Ballet Russe, was in effect the Society's ballerina, and LeClercq its leading soloist, in a company that included apprentice performers from the School of American Ballet. But this was a company without stars. And critics who wrote about the performance did so nervously, with a sense of writing at the company's sufferance. Ballet Society was not a commercial venture, and it remained steadfastly so. The company did not even have a home base, but appeared in a number of unlikely houses after its opening at the Central High School of Needle Trades in New York City. Eventually, Frances Hawkins, manager of Ballet Society, was able to talk Kirstein into settling into a single theater late in 1947 and, with new awareness building, adding a few open performances for the general public.

The theater that Hawkins chose was City Center, which the city had acquired and designated as a popular-priced house, with the New York City Opera and Drama companies installed as residents. Ballet Society opened there on April 28, 1948, for three public performances in programs that included the premiere of *Orpheus* and *Symphony in C*, a hit when the company had first presented it a month before as a revised version of *Le Palais de Cristal*, created by Balanchine for the Paris Opéra Ballet and performed by the French dancers in 1947. Morton Baum, City Center's astute and sensitive director of finances, was in the audience one night, and shortly afterward he approached Kirstein to talk of Ballet Society's possible future as a resident of City Center.

Deeply impressed with what he'd seen, Baum had succeeded in winning over his colleagues, though they included Edward Warburg's brother Gerald, who warned Baum against getting involved in ballet. But Baum was greeted angrily by Kirstein, who, juggling the Society's rapidly dwindling financial resources, realized that he and Balanchine were on the brink of another disaster. Kirstein raged at Baum about the state of ballet in America. He paused for a moment, and Baum responded with a question. "Mr. Kirstein," he asked, "how would you like the idea of having Ballet Society become the New York City Ballet?" Kirstein was stunned. "If you do that for us," he said at last, "I will give you in three years the finest ballet company in America!"[20] And so, in October 1948, Ballet Society became the New York City Ballet, the first American ballet company to be granted status as a public institution.

The company remained at City Center for sixteen years. But the City Ballet's first season there, shared with the City Opera and a matter of only two performances a week for six weeks in the fall of 1948, was not a success. Headed by Tallchief, Marie-Jeanne, and LeClercq, the company opened with *Orpheus* and *Symphony in C* as well as a revival of *Concerto Barocco*, which, with Todd Bolender's *Mother Goose Suite*, were the season's new productions in a repertory of ten ballets. The ballet played to only half-full houses and incurred a forty-seven-thousand-dollar deficit, which Kirstein paid out of pocket, though there had been no more than an oral agreement between him and Baum to the effect that City Center would not be responsible for any company losses.

The initial arrangement had been that City Ballet would perform concurrently with the City Opera, which it supplied with dancers in an attempt to give the ballet-company members more employment. But City Ballet had performed on Mondays and Tuesdays, traditionally dead nights in the theater. And its engagement had followed a tenth-anniversary Ballet Russe season at the Metropolitan that had been replete with reassuring Russianized glamour.

Balanchine, whom a friend had once described as gently ruthless, was not disturbed. "To him profit or loss rarely meant much," Kirstein observed. "He would contrive to busy himself; if one theater seemed shut to him, there was, or always had been, another that was open. Maintenance and continuity would be someone else's job; his was to weld a company and furnish it with new works. If our repertory was itself a failure, if we did not now possess negotiable properties, if our artistic planning had not justified itself (none of which we believed), then and only then might there be cause for suicide." [21]

For Kirstein, the star system was a "negotiable security." "What we offer is not negotiable," he said many years later. [22] But City

Ballet's first audiences at City Center proved themselves not just ripe for molding in the determinedly elitist hands of Balanchine and Kirstein, but a public with a mind of its own, expressing some annoyance that the company had imported two guest artists, John Kriza and André Eglevsky, to dance at some performances of *Symphony in C.*

Baum now suggested that City Ballet sever itself from City Opera and play ten performances in January 1949, over consecutive Thursdays through Sundays. City Center would assume the company's expenses; the ballet company would be responsible only for the costs of its new productions. And so City Ballet became autonomous. At the same time, it began to draw the attention of the kinds of socialites who had traditionally supported the Metropolitan Opera and Philharmonic Orchestra, which eased fund raising and gave City Ballet "an air of somewhat raffish respectability and a bit of extratheatrical glamor," as Kirstein put it.[23]

By its third season at City Center, late in 1949, the company had its smallest deficit, had jumped to 75-percent attendance, and was attracting a younger and increasingly devoted audience. It also had a box-office hit that season in Balanchine's new *Firebird*, a ballet that filled the stage with exotic color and pageantry. Maria Tallchief danced in it with a febrile intensity and strong, clear technique that made her a star in the title role and brought her increased fame as the century's first American ballerina of international status to be trained in her own country.

City Ballet's first international appearance, in a summer season at London's Covent Garden in 1950, was on balance an artistic success that was discussed long after the company departed. "These fresh young Americans bring no mystery or sentiment to their dancing," Paul Holt wrote in the *Daily Herald*, in a perceptive view of these ambassadors of unexpected culture. "They are rugged, tough and gay. The men attack feats of grace as a sport and the girls make almost a miracle of their execution of the classical routine. That is the strangest thing about their visit. They are not so much interested in the folksy style. They are pure classicists absorbed by the perfection of the old Imperial Russian Ballet."[24]

Regular tours abroad to Europe and the Orient would follow. But that first London season set a new seal of approval on the New York City Ballet, pulling the still-doubting John Martin firmly into the ranks of its admirers. The company had outdistanced its reputation as a "dilettante's delight."[25] No longer did the dancers feel compelled to distribute leaflets around the city to announce performances. The company broke even for the first time and actually made a small profit in 1951 in its February season at City Center.

The next ten years were a time of extraordinary creativity for Balanchine, during which he choreographed some fifteen ballets that have become stylistic signature works or great popular successes. There were evocations of hauntingly romantic or morbid atmosphere and fiendish virtuosic challenges to his dancers. His one-act *Swan Lake* has come to seem a statement of intent, a reworking of the traditional that drew on nineteenth-century classical vocabulary and style while it exploited the lengths beyond which Balanchine and his dancers had taken them. In *Square Dance*, on the other hand, he produced a smooth and witty display of classical pyrotechnics delivered, improbably, in an American vernacular.

Within a mere five years, between 1954 and 1959, Balanchine not only explored both the legend and spirit of his adopted country, but also ventured into territory equivalent to outer space. In their mood and American music, *Western Symphony* and *Stars and Stripes* were amusingly folksy portraits of America, and *Ivesiana* captured the anomie of urban American life. *Agon* and *Episodes* were statements of the uncompromising dance "abstractions" that were Balanchine's province alone, though vastly influential, and the kind of dance that would come to distinguish him in the public mind.

"Balanchine was interested in making his style in ballet the

American style," Arlene Croce has written. "To do this, he would have to persuade the public that an authentic American dance tradition existed on which he—and he alone—could build. He had for years fought the inclination of Americans to regard ballet as ever and exclusively Russian. (Kirstein complained that 'ballet-russe' was one word.) He seems to have projected the winter of 1957–58 as his make-or-break season." *Square Dance, Agon, Stars and Stripes* and a major revival of *Apollo* "weren't designed with the sole intention of displaying Balanchine's versatility. Their apparent differences were transcended by the singular aim of clarifying and forwarding American classicism. Yes, it was a "campaign"; Balanchine even used the word to designate the separate sections of *Stars and Stripes*. And, to a great extent, this campaign of his succeeded. . . . Balanchine's message to his 1957–58 public was succinct. *Apollo* predicted the classical style that he would develop in America and consolidate in *Agon, Square Dance* demonstrated the Americanism of classicism, and *Stars and Stripes* outrageously celebrated it."[26]

But the decade also produced a box-office hit that not only tided the company through financially difficult periods, as it has countless other troupes, but signaled two important developments in the relationship of the School of American Ballet to the performing company for which its students were being trained.

The postwar years were good ones for ballet, which grew popular as a form of entertainment. Baum's invitation to the New York City Ballet was brave but timely. And with it, the company acquired a new independence. If the City Ballet was clearly an artistic entity in and of itself, the School was also an increasingly independent institution. So established was it by its second decade of existence that it was able to produce not just young dancers but the thirty-nine child performers needed for *The Nutcracker* in 1954. The children who appeared as party guests, toy soldiers, tiny angels, candy canes, and assorted fairy-tale attendants might flock to City Center each afternoon by subway, bus, or family station wagon, but they could trace their lineage to the children who had arrived at the Maryinsky in the coach-and-four provided by the Tsar forty years earlier in St. Petersburg.

The New York City Ballet uses children in its repertory as frequently as the Royal Danish, Kirov, and Bolshoi ballets do. By his death in 1983, Balanchine had created seven works containing substantial choreography for children. And students from the School appeared in a number of other ballets. In some, their childishness has been capitalized upon—most delightfully, perhaps, in Jerome Robbins's *Circus Polka,* created for the City Ballet's 1972 Stravinsky Festival. In other ballets the children serve as piquant ornament, as, for example, the Costermongers' two children in Balanchine's *Union Jack,* Hop o' My Thumb in Robbins's *Ma Mère l'Oye,* and the fireflies and rowdies of Balanchine's *A Midsummer Night's Dream* and the Balanchine-Robbins *Pulcinella.*

Balanchine used a few children as elements in a shifting nightmare landscape in *Don Quixote.* But perhaps nowhere was his use of children darker than in *Symphony No. 6—Pathétique: Fourth Movement, Adagio Lamentoso,* created as a closing ballet for the Tchaikovsky Festival in 1981, in which a small boy carrying a candle, the only child in the ballet and seemingly a symbol of hope, extinguishes the flame to bring the dark dance of mourning to its end.

Most distinctively, however, Balanchine treats the children as dancers. The choreography never condescends to its performers, who are dressed in costumes as finely made as those of the adults, but is as sufficient to its own needs as are the simple opening balancés, arabesques, and grands battements of the corps to the lucid nobility of Balanchine's "Diamonds." The directness and simplicity of his approach is epitomized in the dance for the eight little polichinelles in the second act of *The Nutcracker.* The balancés, emboîtés, skips, and arabesques and passés—simply, their fund of steps—are woven together with such artless ingenuity that the dance is an unmistakably professional divertissement.

Performed in soft shoes, the children's roles in such ballets as

Harlequinade and *Coppélia*, which has a corps of twenty-four little girls, require them to dance the ballet vocabulary they know as boldly and with as much unaffected style and finish as the grown dancers with whom they share the stage. Neither coy baby ballerinas nor miniature adults, they are naturally themselves, very young dancers-in-training, being used to their utmost by the choreographer.

Balanchine looks directly to his past in the Ivanov-inspired Candy Canes section of *The Nutcracker*, whose variation is similar to the Dance of the Buffoons, in which he won attention in *The Nutcracker* at the Maryinsky shortly after his graduation. But the eight adolescent boys and girls serve not as foils to the male soloist with whom they dance, but to frame, extend, and burnish his leaping, spinning variation.

The New York City Ballet may be the only American company to have its own children's ballet master, a job created by David Richardson. Richardson studied with Georgia Hiden and others, but received most of his training at the School of American Ballet and played the Little Prince in *The Nutcracker* in 1956 and 1957. He joined the City Ballet as a corps dancer in 1963. "*Nutcracker* was *it* for me," Richardson recalls. Playing Mother Ginger in the ballet in the late 1960s, he looked around him and felt that the atmosphere was less colorful than he remembered. "I wanted to relive that feeling, so I asked if I could help with the children. And it sort of progressed." Previously the children had been chosen by Balanchine and company members and ballet mistresses, who rehearsed them. Now they worked with Balanchine and Richardson alone.

Richardson retired from performing and left the City Ballet in 1983 to become a ballet master at the American Ballet Theatre. The dancer Garielle Whittle took over his duties, which included auditioning the children, directing rehearsals, and giving the young performers coaching in acting, dance, and pantomime techniques, as well as such mundane tasks as coordinating costume fittings and collecting Internal Revenue Service forms from the children, who are paid a flat fee of ten dollars per performance. But Richardson had a reputation for special gentleness and involvement with the young dancers, though he was as businesslike as any company director.

"I did a miniature version of how I thought a company director would cast," he says of the audition process. "I'd look for the exotic or pretty, the talented, the unusual children. I always thought that was what Mr. B. tried to do—give everybody special a chance. If they had something special to offer, not necessarily a strong technique, I wanted to see what they'd do on stage." Many of the children are repeaters. "I'd keep my eye on the whole group from year to year. Some got better. Some were over the hill. Some were eating too much. But some kids who were having trouble in school started to do better there because they'd received this attention from me and the School. It was really a whole little society."

By the School's fifth decade, the composition of that select society began to change. Berets had long served to hide the fact that most of the little boys in the first-act party scene were actually little girls with their hair pinned up under the hats. In 1979, with the increasing enrollment of boys in the School, the berets were retired, though a few reappeared in 1984.

In Richardson's last *Nutcracker* season, 1983, fifty children between eight to thirteen years of age were selected to fill the ballet's seventy roles.[27] Having played the Little Prince himself helped Richardson to work with the children. "I knew what it felt like," he says. "The kids get really scared and nervous, in *Nutcracker* more than the other ballets. That's the ballet everyone knows about—all their school friends. And it's such a big part of the holiday season."

The children begin rehearsals for *The Nutcracker* a month before the first performances. In the quietly but intensely competitive atmosphere of the School, that month is a particularly charged time. "What we have managed to do is that now anybody in Children II has the opportunity to be in *The Nutcracker*," says Nathalie Gleboff, associate director of the School, referring to the second level in the Children's Division. "The company is committed to take any child who wants to be in the ballet. I wanted to remain alive! Then, after that, we can explain to the parents and children that being chosen for the ballet is up to the company and doesn't mean anything as far as the child's talent is concerned. It has to do with size, and how quickly they learn. There are wonderful dancers who've never been in any children's roles." Auditions are held at the School for the more demanding children's roles in the ballet, and the children's ballet master also watches classes at the School to spot likely performers. The children are told immediately after the audition whether or not they have been chosen to dance.

But it is still a trying time. Costumes have been outgrown. Most of the little girls are sure that this year they'll play Marie, whose dream of a nutcracker prince serves as a pretext for the ballet. But the role, played in alternation by two little girls each year, invariably goes to someone not nearly so deserving.

Playing the lead children's roles has not usually led to later stardom in the City Ballet, though Judith Fugate, a New York City Ballet soloist, did play Marie and grew up to dance the Sugar Plum Fairy. Among the Little Princes who later joined the company were Robert Weiss, who became the director of the Pennsylvania Ballet; Robert Maiorano, Richardson, Jean-Pierre Frohlich, Christopher d'Amboise, and Peter Boal. The choreographer Eliot Feld remembers Balanchine's teaching him the Little Prince's mime by writing out the character's important second-act mime sequence and having Feld, then an eleven-year-old student at the School, learn it by singing out the action to the music that accompanied the passage.

In the 1950s, dancers who had had careers with other companies began to come over to the New York City Ballet. Noted European and American dancers had been turning up at the School in greater number for some time, which gave the students a stronger sense of their classroom work as training for a profession. The students could learn by new example and get a realistic idea of standards in the field. In close proximity with the older students were stars from Ballet Theatre and the Ballet Russe de Monte Carlo. "Top dancers would stand at the barre with us," Taras recalls, looking back to the earliest influx of dancers. "[Tatiana] Riabouchinska, [Irina] Baronova, Toumanova, Danilova. Eglevsky always. I don't think he ever studied anywhere else. It was an incredible atmosphere. Professionals do come to take class at the School now, but the classes are for the students." Within another two decades, dancers of the public stature of Mikhail Baryshnikov and Rudolf Nureyev were taking classes at the School. New York City Ballet dancers dropped by for class. What is surprising, perhaps, is the students' sustained concentration and focused hard work in the presence of such performers. But time, they know, is short. Their training days will soon be over, and a dancer's life on stage is brief. Classes are not for stargazing.

It was in the School's second decade that more boys began to attend, and the curriculum included a "men's class" for "developing strength and brilliance of execution, stressing leaps, turns and other technical points important to male dancers."[28] D'Amboise started his training there in 1942. Edward Villella began three years later and was the inspiration for a ballet long before he reached the stage. "One day in class, little Eddie Villella, who was standing next to me as a kid, suddenly began to stretch his body in a very odd way, almost like he was trying to get something out of it," Jerome Robbins recalled. The gesture remained with the choreographer, intriguing in its conscious "animalism," and gave him the germ of *Afternoon of a Faun*, an evocation of the sensuality and innocence of young ballet students.[29]

"There were not that many boys," says d'Amboise, who moved onto the stage in his early teens with Ballet Society. "I only remember three my age. I used to slip into Balanchine's class. I remember him grabbing me and telling me to take adagio class. I was thirteen or fourteen—too young to partner. I said, 'But no one will dance with me. I'm too little.' 'Take your sister,' Balanchine said." The prominence of d'Amboise and Villella, who were classmates, as American male star dancers is considered an important factor in the continuing increase in the enrollment of young boys at the School during its third decade.

Enlarged during the 1946–47 school year, the Children's Division offered three sections, for beginning, intermediate, and advanced-intermediate-level students, with attendance required at two classes a week in the first two groups and three in the third. A catalogue for that year advised that the girls were required to wear color-coded practice clothes to class and all but the youngest males were required to wear tights. A fourth section was added to the Children's Division by 1954, when the School was issuing even sterner notice of its status as a vocational institution unlike any other dance school in the city.

"The School of American Ballet is interested primarily in students capable of becoming professional dancers," a note in that year's catalogue read.

> Such students must be young enough to ensure satisfactory progress and possess the necessary physical qualifications of good proportions, coordination, normal weight and development, and musical aptitude. The School is not interested in students who enroll merely for physical exercise or in order to reduce. To spare their children the disappointment of a refusal, parents are asked not to bring them to the School if they are overweight or in need of corrective exercises, but to enter them instead in one of the gymnasiums or nonprofessional dancing schools in the city. A physical check-up is recommended to all beginners.
>
> An age limit of 18 is established for the Beginners' and First Intermediate Divisions. The first month of instruction is considered a trial period at the end of which the Faculty decides whether or not the new students should be encouraged to continue. Children and adolescents change so much that this decision may be subject to revision at various stages of the student's development, most often

with those reaching the Third and Fourth Children's Divisions and the Intermediate Divisions.

Classes in music and dance composition were no longer advertised, and from six to nine classes a week were recommended for intermediate and advanced students.

Emblazoned with a photograph of Eglevsky and Tallchief in *Swan Lake*, the catalogue also offered views of current and future company members in class. Arthur Mitchell may be spotted in a photograph of an adagio class conducted by a sharp-eyed Oboukhoff. (Mitchell, the first and only black dancer to become a star at City Ballet, which he joined in 1956, is partnering a smiling white woman. Considering the state of race relations in the United States at the time, the inclusion of the photograph seems a remarkably forthright gesture.)

The permanent faculty gained three important members during the School's second decade. Elise Reiman, recruited in 1945 to teach junior students, was the first School-trained dancer to join the staff. A veteran of the American Ballet, Ballet Society, and musical comedy, films, and television dance, she brought a touch of wry, home-grown pragmatism to the School (which she left in 1953 and returned to eleven years later).

Known for the vigor and warmth of her teaching, the Soviet-trained Antonina Tumkovsky, who joined the staff in 1949, was a former soloist with the Kiev State Theater of Opera and Ballet and had postgraduate training at the Leningrad State School of Ballet under the Soviet ballet pedagogue Agrippina Vaganova. Tumkovsky in turn brought Helene Dudin, a fellow soloist in the Kiev company, into the School in 1954.

Tumkovsky had just arrived in the United States in 1949 and spoke almost no English. "Someone told me Balanchine was here," she recalls. "I didn't know him, but I heard he spoke Russian." She arrived at the School and talked with Ouroussow and Molostwoff and, later, Balanchine, who watched her teach a children's class. "I had taught a little in Russia for the last six years. He took me immediately." Ouroussow wrote out useful English phrases for Tumkovsky, and the new teacher soon enrolled in night school to learn the language, which she now speaks with colorful elisions.

Beginning with children's and intermediate toe classes, Tumkovsky has taught everything at the School but adagio or partnering classes, including men's classes. Among her star pupils were Fernando Bujones and John Clifford, formerly a City Ballet principal and the director of the Los Angeles Ballet, who has cited Tumkovsky as his favorite teacher. One of Tumkovsky's favorite students was Gelsey Kirkland, noted for a stubborn sense of self-direction from her earliest years at the School. "I loved Gelsey," Tumkovsky says simply. "She was not naughty with me. She trust me." Tumkovsky is noted for her concern, if briskly expressed, for her students. "When they get into the company, she bursts into tears of joy," Molostwoff says. "I teach," Tumkovsky responds firmly. "They grow. They go away."

The addition to the faculty of Felia Doubrovska, who joined it in 1948 and taught until 1980, a year before her death, was a major event in the life of the School. Like Oboukhoff, Doubrovska is remembered as one of the most demanding and yet endearing of teachers. At five feet six, Doubrovska was thought too tall for major roles at the Maryinsky Theater, which she joined in 1913 on her graduation from the Imperial School. But after she and Vladimiroff, her husband, joined Diaghilev's Ballets Russes, she became the dancer on whom Balanchine tried out strange new steps and configurations.

It was she who originated the role of the Siren in *Le Fils Prodigue*, which gave full play to her "witty, graceful, brutal, burlesquing, intellectual legs," as Janet Flanner put it.[30] After Diaghilev's death, Doubrovska danced with Anna Pavlova and, briefly, with the Metropolitan Opera Ballet. She had appeared with the Balanchine-Kirstein American Ballet in a single, festival performance of Balanchine's *Magic* in 1936. But she seemed not to enjoy performing, and retired happily to live with her husband and her mother, who died in 1947. It was then that Balanchine approached her, as he had before, about joining the School faculty, and she accepted.

She began teaching advanced classes at Balanchine's request, and he later assigned her company classes and a special course for gifted, advanced women students. The class disbanded early in the 1960s. "Balanchine canceled it," Gleboff says. "The class was nice, but it provoked a lot of resentment and jealousy. If you weren't in special class, it was the end of the world."

Doubrovska found her first teaching assignment daunting, filled as the class was with Balanchine's ex-wives—a fact that drove him quickly from the studio, to which he'd escorted her. But she soon became a much-admired teacher of women. Her students remember her as serene, elegant, and authoritative. She was a teacher who gave her students a sense of the past by bringing in photographs of herself and other dancers of her generation. Speaking always in a soft voice, she brought "an aura of mauve and memory," in the words of Joseph Gale in *Behind Barres*, into the classroom along with her little Yorkshire terrier, Lala. Usually well behaved, the dog precipitated a small crisis one day that has become a favorite legend of the School. As Doubrovska taught her class that day, Balanchine appeared at the top of the stairs, looked over the students, and began to descend into the classroom. It suddenly became apparent to everyone but him that Lala had had an accident just at the foot of the stairs. Doubrovska danced over and sank, surprisingly, into a gracious bow to the master, her flowered teaching skirt spread over the puddle. Balanchine bowed back, turned, and left the classroom.

Doubrovska's eloquent legs, flexible feet, and long back served as examples. Nothing in class was to be done without quality, and Doubrovska tended to be very strict. "She was pitiless," Molostwoff says. "She'd criticize the professionals in class, and she wasn't popular for that." Nonetheless, she had a following in the company, where she taught some classes for women. Doubrovska was also known for the quiet personal attention she lavished on students during class. She might also confide her worry to the younger women about their personal appearance and lack of sufficient charm. It was important, after all, to be noticed by Mr. Balanchine, she pointed out. "Balanchine used to teach before and after her at the School," Schorer recalls. "Some of us would take her class to warm up for him, and she'd tell us to leave fifteen minutes early to get into fresh leotards and put on a little perfume for Balanchine's class."

But class itself was endless, exhausting developpés, a barre that started slowly, then built to dizzyingly fast exercises for the legs, perfectly placed turns and balances, and expansive jumps, all of which felt like dancing and being beautiful, the City Ballet dancer Toni Bentley observed, after the sheer technical exigencies of other classes. Doubrovska's corrections, though rare, were apt to seem astonishingly acute. Where one teacher might offer a suggestion about something that you were working on, a student remembered, Doubrovska often spotted a problem you were on the brink of discovering on your own. Most of all, there was constant attention to the way in which her students presented themselves in space. To see her enter the studio, always ten minutes late and tiptoeing across delicately with a shy smile, heavily but elegantly made up and with a silky kerchief floating from the waistband of her teaching skirt, was to witness the kind of presence that made some students wonder why they'd ever imagined that they could be performers.

" 'We are performers,' Doubrovska would say," d'Amboise recalls. " 'The audience doesn't care whether we're old, tired, cold, or stiff.' " D'Amboise, who enjoyed a special, teasing relationship with Doubrovska, often took her classes. "She had an excessive modesty about her teaching and her right to say anything. She was always under the influence of her husband. But she never gave anything less than everything." Bodies must be pulled up and backs and arms unceasingly alert and regal, though graciously so. The point of turnout, she reiterated, was that it beautifully presented the dancer's leg and foot to the audience, like the flower Balanchine used as an example in his own classes. Doubrovska was responsible for passing on the art of performing to three generations of ballerinas at the New York City Ballet. Alexandra Danilova, who joined the School in 1964, would continue the tradition.

IV. ENTER THE
FORD FOUNDATION

P et names or diminutives tend to attach themselves to staff
members of the School of American Ballet. Natalie Molostwoff has become "Miss Molo" over the years, and she and Nathalie Gleboff are "the Natashas." Andrei Kramarevsky is
"Krammy," and Antonina Tumkovsky is "Tumey" to all but her
youngest charges. But Alexandra Danilova is simply "Danilova"
or "Madame," a title that is hers by virtue not just of her years
as an internationally known ballerina, but of the aura today of
chic, Old World distinction about her. A sparkling atmosphere
clings to her as she walks down the long corridors to the classroom, stands in the center of the studio scrutinizing a next generation of ballerinas, or perches at the barre, coaxing distinction
from the young dancers performing in the School's annual Spring
Workshops. Danilova's recruitment to the staff was an important
step for the School, as was that of Stanley Williams the same year.

The School moved to studios on New York's Upper West Side
during its third decade, and the New York City Ballet found a
home at the New York State Theater, designed by Philip Johnson

in consultation with George Balanchine and Lincoln Kirstein, as a prime constituent of the sprawling new Lincoln Center complex for the performing arts. But there also occurred during that third decade an event that would profoundly affect not only the development of the School of American Ballet but also the nature of ballet training and the status of ballet itself across the nation.

On December 16, 1963, the Ford Foundation announced a ten-year grant of $7,756,750 "to strengthen professional ballet in the United States," an amount unprecedented not just in the Foundation's own arts funding programs, but certainly in dance itself in America. Of that grant, $3.8 million went to seven American ballet companies: the New York City Ballet, the San Francisco Ballet, the National Ballet of Washington, the Pennsylvania Ballet, the Utah Ballet (later Ballet West) of Salt Lake City, the Houston Ballet, and the Boston Ballet. The balance of the grant went to the School of American Ballet—$3,925,000—with $2.4 million to be spent on the School itself and the remaining money allocated for regional projects, including 425 scholarships to students in communities across the country, in a program administered through the School and under Balanchine's direction. In this way, the Foundation reasoned, the ballet-training resources scattered throughout the United States, and of widely differing standards, would be centralized, and professional activity decentralized, so that well-trained dancers would have performing outlets outside New York City.

"Although mounting interest of new audiences for ballet as an American dance form is apparent, two great and almost universal problems are also clear," W. McNeil Lowry, director of the Foundation's Humanities and Arts program, said in announcing the grant. "The standards of instruction are dangerously low. And those dancers who are fortunate enough to receive thorough training at some stage in their careers often cannot be assimilated in the few companies having any sort of artistic and financial stability."[1]

If the charges of unfairness and elitism from local ballet teachers had seemed shrill to Kirstein when he sought, initially, to establish the School of American Ballet in Hartford, they were as nothing compared with the national uproar that greeted the announcement of the Ford Foundation grants. Not only had most of the money gone to two institutions directly connected to Balanchine, it was pointed out, but the newer companies had ties to the choreographer as well, from the fledgling Pennsylvania Ballet, created with the aid of the grant by Barbara Weisberger, an early child pupil at the School, to the established San Francisco Ballet, which was directed by Lew Christensen, who had taught at the School of American Ballet in the 1930s and been associated with all of the Balanchine-Kirstein companies but one.

The Foundation's grant to the School of American Ballet included money for 115 scholarships a year for local students. Would other New York teachers be left with inferior material? Would ballet companies and schools not given the Balanchine–Ford Foundation seal of approval be forced from the field? And why had the award gone exclusively to ballet institutions, bypassing modern dance?

"The facts of the dance world in this country as they existed last Sunday are no more, and they will never ever be the same again," Allen Hughes wrote in *The New York Times* on December 22, 1963. "The Ford Foundation has declared by the bestowal of nearly $6 million that the dance technique and style preferred by George Balanchine are so superior to any others existing in this country that they should be developed to the virtual exclusion of all others. Under the provision of the two grants given to the School of American Ballet, all roads lead to the studios at Broadway and 82d Street. The teaching is good there. In the 30 years of the School's existence its teachers have developed excellent dancers. So have other teachers who never set foot inside the School of American Ballet and never will."

Looking over the field twenty-one years later, Doris Hering, director of the National Association for Regional Ballet, feels that the Ford Foundation project did not cause an appreciable decline in the number of schools and regional and civic ballet companies outside the Foundation group. What was harmful, she suggests, was the splitting up of families and the destruction of career potential in some talented children who were brought to New York, she feels, before they were emotionally ready, and who subsequently left dancing.

As it happened, the Ford Foundation added funds for the Joffrey Ballet, which was not an independent entity at the time of the 1963 award, and the Dance Theatre of Harlem, formed in 1968. By 1984, the Foundation had awarded $42,578,552 to dance and dance-related programs, including $24.8 million to twelve ballet companies, among them American Ballet Theatre. It began support to modern dance in 1968, and by 1984 had given $3.1 million to modern-dance companies, including those of Alvin Ailey, Merce Cunningham, Alwin Nikolais, Murray Louis, Paul Taylor, Twyla Tharp, and Martha Graham, as well as assistance to a number of modern-dance production projects, among them the American Dance Festival.

Not all public opinion was against the 1963 grant. Some felt that this first major foundation award to dance in America, together with the emergence of Lincoln Center and the Kennedy Center for the Performing Arts as sponsors for dance, might open up new funding and performing opportunities for both ballet and modern dance. In the School of American Ballet's fiftieth year, the Joffrey Ballet and Dance Theatre of Harlem schools operate successfully. American Ballet Theatre closed its school in 1980, choosing to retain only a scholarship training program that was subsumed into the general operations of its second company. Students from the School of American Ballet are recruited for children's roles in Ballet Theatre's repertory, as they have been by many of the international companies visiting New York.

Ballet studios have proliferated in New York City and operate with generally sounder and more professional standards than those of much of the studio training available in the mid-1960s. But as the first program of aid to dance on a national scale, the Ford Foundation's pioneering grants to the field did, in effect, establish the School of American Ballet as the kind of national academy of dance that Kirstein had envisioned thirty years before.

The program was created by Lowry, who had begun to attend the ballet at City Center when he joined the Ford Foundation in 1953. He was impressed with what he saw, and in time received the ultimate compliment from Balanchine. "No, he is not a balletomane," Balanchine said of Lowry, correcting a young ballet student at a Ford Foundation luncheon in the mid-1960s. "A balletomane is a man of advanced years who sits in the front row and looks under the skirts of the dancers. Mr. Lowry likes dancing. That's what he is."

In 1957, Lowry proposed the Foundation's Humanities and Arts program through which he envisioned a systematic gathering of information from practitioners of all the arts. Its aim would be to amass a body of material that could lead to the establishment of an informed and organized philanthropic program of assistance on a national level, which would serve the actual needs of the writers, composers, painters, sculptors, choreographers, and performers themselves. There existed, in the late 1950s, no national program for the arts. With the Foundation behind him, Lowry felt, it might be possible to discover and meet such needs.

He began by traveling across the United States and questioning everyone he encountered, in an attempt to learn what led people in the arts to seek professional careers outside the active creative life of New York City, and to find out how they went about it. "I covered as many dance studios as I could around the country," recalls Lowry, who retired from his post as vice president for the humanities and the arts in 1975. "I knew I was never going to be able to become an expert, but I tried to learn as much as I could." He also consulted leading figures in New York and regional ballet.

American modern dance was a fragmented field, whose companies and styles differed with each innovator practicing the art. The motivating factor in the creation of modern dance was and had long been the expression of a personal point of view. To perform, the modern dancer had first to create a technique and a dance. Classical ballet, however, had a formal academic vocabulary established over three centuries, as well as a common world repertory. A system existed in ballet that promised at least the chance of a structure for broad philanthropic assistance.

By comparison with the great Soviet companies then just beginning to appear in the West, and the organized systems of training and recruitment through which dancers moved into those companies, the state of ballet teaching in this country was immensely disorganized, though dance activity had increased greatly. Barred by law from giving money to profit-making organizations, the Foundation commissioned Ballet Society, the parent organization of the New York City Ballet, to conduct a survey exploring both the professional standards of ballet schools in America and the ways in which teachers could be helped by some form of connection with other teachers and schools throughout the United States.

Out of a preliminary grant of $525,000 awarded by the Ford Foundation in 1959 to assist dancers, writers, and theater directors, architects, and designers, Ballet Society received $150,000 (later augmented by $12,500) to establish a three-year program of regional scholarships to be awarded to dance students outside New York and San Francisco. Auditioned by Balanchine, Christensen, and their representatives, the students would receive advanced training at the School of American Ballet and San Francisco Ballet School, with a view to their joining the companies.

One of those first fifteen students was Cynthia Gregory, then a student in Los Angeles, who trained and performed with the San Francisco Ballet before joining the American Ballet Theatre and achieving international fame. Another was Roberta Sue Ficker of Cincinnati, who came east to study at the School of American Ballet, joined the City Ballet after a year, and became the prima ballerina Suzanne Farrell. By 1964, Balanchine had the gifted teen-aged dancer herself serving as a Ford Foundation scholarship-program scout.

A good deal of the ballet produced by Americans at that time came out of local dance studios with their own small, nonprofessional civic performing companies. In 1960, Balanchine taught the first of eight annual summer Teachers' Seminars at the School, for ballet teachers from around the United States. Held in response to questions about teaching that had been put to him as he visited schools and auditioned students, these seminars allowed Balanchine to work with sixty to seventy teachers a summer on topics that included the components, process, and vocabulary of the ballet class. "We looked at the map—all fifty states," Balanchine said of the first seminars. "We asked, Is anybody there? We found a few people. What I showed them was all free: four hours a day, sometimes more. How the instep is developed. How to turn. All free. Some that couldn't even pay for transportation—we paid. And they got to ask questions. 'Why do you do that?' I answered, 'That's what I think it is. That's what I was taught in St. Petersburg.' "[2] The program was discontinued in 1969. "Balanchine came to feel that the teachers learned nothing, and that some went back and advertised themselves as Balanchine-trained," Molostwoff says.

By 1962, Ballet Society had produced a survey coordinated by Eugenie Ouroussow that set forth the conditions of ballet training in the United States, and the following year the Ford Foundation awarded the School a further $60,000 toward a program to assist in the national and regional development of ballet performing and training. Ballet studios had proliferated throughout the country during the 1950s, some of them opened by former Ballet Russe dancers who'd grown tired of touring and decided to settle down, many of the schools the work of students of the early Russian and Italian teachers active in the United States.

But much of the training was haphazard or even damaging to the children, and where the studios produced good dancers, those dancers were often not developed sufficiently or were overburdened with performing in amateur companies in their communities. The 1963 grant to the School, which as a nonprofit institution could serve as a conduit for the Foundation to the generally for-profit schools it wished to help, funded a three-tiered program of assistance. Local and regional scholarships were awarded (the latter covering travel, subsistence, and tuition); members of the School faculty and the New York City Ballet visited and taught at local schools; and a beginners' project was developed to locate and train children between eight and ten years of age who normally would not find their way into a ballet studio, being financially and culturally underprivileged, male, or members of ethnic minorities. The children could, through the program, receive free ballet instruction for up to two years and become eligible for local scholarships and the chance for advanced study or professional employment.

Recruited by the teachers in their communities and sponsored by the Foundation, the Beginners' Groups did bring more young boys into ballet through carefully structured all-male classes. The program, in which thirty-seven schools participated, failed to develop many dancers among underprivileged and minority children, and this was due, School representatives felt, to the families' lack of understanding or involvement in the program and, controversially, because certain ethnic body types and feet did not conform to standards set by this European art form. But the School continued to send out guest teachers and auditioners on its own after the Ford Foundation grant expired.

The element of the project that had the greatest effect on ballet training in America was the Local and Regional Scholarships program. Ingeniously designed so that the money went not to the schools themselves but to the students, it started at the local level with awards to talented and serious young dancers to enable them to continue and increase their lessons with teachers participating in the program. In the process, the studios were encouraged to offer more classes.

Chosen by members of the School of American Ballet faculty and the New York City Ballet, who often stayed to give class and confer with area teachers, the students were then eligible to be selected for summer study at the School. By the end of the ten-year Ford Foundation grant period, 127 schools had participated in the local and regional scholarships program and 712 local scholarships, 317 summer-course scholarships to the School, and 138 school-year scholarships had been awarded. The regional program was also open to students from schools not participating in the local program. Seventy-one students from non-participating schools received scholarships to the summer course and thirty-five attended the regular course, twenty-one of these having moved into it from the summer session. Professional employment was found by ninety-four scholarship students from schools participating in the local program, and twenty-one scholarship students from those that did not, over a period from January 1964 to January 1973—worrisome figures to Ouroussow, who felt they indicated a sad waste of graduates of the School. By its fiftieth year, from twenty to thirty advanced scholarship and regular students a year found employment as professional dancers. But, like Ouroussow, Gleboff worries. Will there come a time when companies are overstocked with dancers?

Another effect of the program was that the New York City Ballet expanded and became more of a nationally representative dance company. And the program had a profound effect on the teachers who participated. In 1972, the year the local scholarship program ended, a team of five experts in the field, selected by the Ford Foundation, inspected the schools involved and found a rise in their teaching standards. Some teachers noted changes in their approaches and attitudes toward their work. "It helped me to feel part of the real world of ballet," Sheila Rozann, cofounder of the Rozann-Zimmerman Ballet Center in Chatsworth, California, said of the program. "It helped our status with parents. It gave the children confidence. I would say that contact with SAB has given us more insight into our craft, an outlet for our top students, and a curriculum to model our school after. In short, it helped us to change from a studio to a school."[3]

The School, too, developed. It was able to hire more teachers, develop an administrative staff, and increase its own scholarships to students from the New York area and beyond. Balanchine had long tended to be selective. During her first years there, Muriel Stuart remembers, there was an audition for the School for which thirty or forty people turned up. "They'd maybe danced a little bit. But he said no to everybody." Ouroussow conferred with her after the audition. "You know, Miss Stuart," she said, "we'll have to take some of those people. We've got to pay the rent. We'll just put them into your class. You mustn't listen to him too much, dear. We know what we're going to do."

With the Foundation grants, the School could afford to limit itself to the teaching and training of selected, gifted students who were professional material. No longer so dependent on tuition fees, the School could now offer smaller and more classes, with finer gradations of advancement, for a refinement of the total curriculum. A fifth advanced children's section was added, as well as two intermediate and advanced sections, and variations classes in which dances from the traditional and modern classical repertories were taught. Enrollment hovered at 310 students in 1984. "It hasn't grown so much because we've kept it down after the Ford Foundation," Nathalie Gleboff says.

With the Foundation's largesse, the School entered into a period of relative ease. "The Ford Foundation paid for everything," an observer recalls. "There was no fund raising, because there was no necessity to raise money." The "two Natashas" played Ping-Pong daily at the School, with Stanley Williams and Peter Martins their most frequent partners. But that ease left the School ill-prepared for the realities of running an institution that the Foundation had helped to become a business. The expiration of the 1963 grant was a traumatic event. "We thought the School was at an end," Mary Porter, the School's director of development, says. "No one had ever heard of it outside ballet. We were all really scared." The Foundation agreed to continue its assistance. In 1974, it awarded the School two million dollars for professional training and operating reserve fund programs and the start of an endowment fund, and a capital grant of $250,000 was given to the School in 1983 for the establishment of a separate Ford Foundation scholarship fund.

The Foundation agreed to tide the School over with the 1974 grant on the condition that it begin to raise money on its own; under the terms of that grant, the School was required for the first time to match a Foundation award, with $1.5 million to be raised over five years. Also for the first time in its history, the School was forced to create a board of directors drawn from outside its rarefied, small world. Roswell B. Perkins, a lawyer and assistant secretary of Health, Education, and Welfare under President Eisenhower, was one of the first "outsiders" to be added to the board of eight staff members and friends of the School, and it was he who, as chairman, helped to expand the board in 1975. Porter began an apprenticeship with Perkins. "We started with foundations," she says. "With the exception of a visionary grant from the Morgan Guaranty Trust Company, corporations came later. The School had no visibility, so corporate money was harder to get." The donors that year included Balanchine, Kirstein, Alexander Grant & Company, (the School's accounting firm), Morgan Guaranty Trust, the Jerome Robbins, Shubert, Helena Rubinstein, and Mona Bronfman Sheckman foundations, and the Lassalle Fund, Inc., administered by Nancy Lassalle, an early student at the School of American Ballet. The board also voted that year to establish a national advisory council, which later expanded to become international.

In 1978, the School received a three-to-one matching, special pilot grant of $250,000 from the National Endowment for the Arts, which enabled it to establish an endowment fund. Two years later it was awarded another three-to-one matching grant of

Above: LINCOLN
KIRSTEIN, EUGENIE
OUROUSSOW, execu-
tive director of the School,
and NATALIE
MOLOSTWOFF, executive
secretary, 1950s. *Photo:
Frederick Melton*

Right: NATHALIE
GLEBOFF, associate di-
rector of the School,
1980s. *Photo: Carolyn
George*

Above: GEORGE BALANCHINE with students at the barre, 1930s. *Photo: Ralph Oggiano (Dance Collection, The New York Public Library)*

Below: DOROTHIE LITTLEFIELD, far right, 1930s. Littlefield taught at the School of American Ballet in its first year. Other American Ballet dancers, from left: Elise Reiman, Kathryn Mullowny, Gisella Caccialanza, and Holly Howard. Littlefield died in 1952. *Photo: Ralph Oggiano*

PIERRE VLADIMIROFF and student in 1959 at the School's second home at 2291 Broadway, at 83rd Street, where it remained from 1956 to 1969. A leading dancer at the Maryinsky Theater, Vladimiroff was a charter member of the faculty of the School of American Ballet. He taught there for thirty-one years, from the School's first days to 1967. Vladimiroff died in 1970. *Photo: Martha Swope*

MURIEL STUART in performance. Stuart, who trained and danced with Anna Pavlova, joined the staff of the School of American Ballet in 1935. Member of the faculty in 1984. *(Collection of Ballet Society)*

ANATOLE OBOUKHOFF teaches a partnering class in
1959. Oboukhoff was a leading dancer with the Maryinsky
Theater. He joined the staff of the School of American Ballet
in 1941 and became one of its fiercest but most beloved
teachers, remaining on the faculty until his death in 1962. In
the foreground, Gloria Govrin and Jacques d'Amboise. *Photo:
Martha Swope*

KYRA BLANC teaching a children's class at the School of American Ballet. Blanc trained and danced as a soloist with the Bolshoi Ballet. She also performed with Kasyan Goleizovsky in several Max Reinhardt productions, and with the Ballets Russes de Monte Carlo, Les Ballets 1933, and the American Ballet, and at the Metropolitan Opera. Blanc became a teacher at the School in 1939 and initiated the first children's class in 1941. She died in 1946. *(Collection of Ballet Society)*

ELISE REIMAN, 1940s. Reiman, who studied with Adolph Bolm and at the School of American Ballet, danced with the San Francisco Opera and the American Ballet and Ballet Society. She joined the staff of the School of American Ballet in 1945, left the School in 1953, and returned in 1964. Member of the faculty in 1984. *Photo: Leo Lieb*

Above: FELIA DOUBROVSKA, circa 1954. Doubrovska danced with the Maryinsky Theater and Serge Diaghilev's Ballets Russes. She joined the staff of the School of American Ballet in 1948 and continued to teach until 1980, the year before her death. Despite her misgivings about teaching, Doubrovska was one of the School's best known and most influential teachers, a living example of style and stage presence to several generations of American ballerinas. Performers also studied with her, and Melissa Hayden may be seen, second from the right. *Photo: Frederick Melton*

Left: JANET COLLINS, a solo dancer, who appeared in Cole Porter's *Out of This World* and was prima ballerina of the Metropolitan Opera Ballet for three years, was one of the guest teachers of modern dance at the School. *Photo: Carl Van Vechten*

Above: ANDRÉ EGLEVSKY teaching a men's class in 1964. Eglevsky, known as one of the great classicists of contemporary ballet, danced with many European ballet companies as well as American Ballet Theatre before joining the New York City Ballet in 1951. He became a teacher at the School of American Ballet in 1962 and taught there through 1970. Eglevsky died in 1977. The boy jumping in the foreground is Paul Mejia, who joined the City Ballet and later became artistic director with Maria Tallchief of the Chicago City Ballet. *Photo: Martha Swope*

Opposite, above: ANTONINA TUMKOVSKY, 1959. Tumkovsky, who danced with the Kiev State Theater of Opera and Ballet and the Bolshoi and Kirov Ballets, received postgraduate training at the Leningrad State School of Ballet under Agrippina Vaganova. Tumkovsky joined the staff of the School of American Ballet in 1949. The little boy she is correcting here is Robert Maiorano, who performed the role of the Little Prince in *The Nutcracker*, joined the New York City Ballet, and is a writer on dance. Member of the faculty in 1984. *Photo: Martha Swope*

Opposite, below: HELENE DUDIN, 1959. Dudin danced with the Kiev State Theater of Opera and Ballet, the Bolshoi and Kirov Ballets, and the New York City Opera. She joined the staff of the School of American Ballet in 1954. Member of the faculty in 1984. *Photo: Martha Swope*

ALEXANDRA DANILOVA in the early 1980s, rehearsing a student for the School of American Ballet's annual Workshop Performances, which she helped to initiate and for which she regularly stages ballets. Danilova danced with the State Academic Theater for Opera and Ballet (formerly Maryinsky Theater), the Diaghilev and Colonel de Basil companies, and the Ballet Russe de Monte Carlo. She became a teacher at the School in 1964. Member of the faculty in 1984. *Photo: Paul Kolnik*

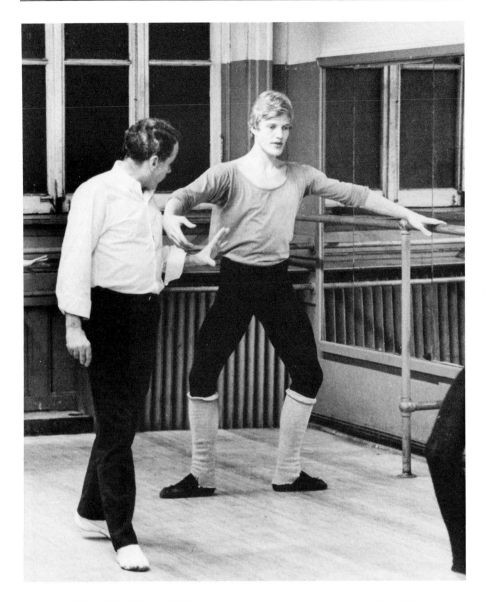

STANLEY WILLIAMS correcting a young dancer named Peter Martins in class at the School of American Ballet, 1968. Williams danced with the Royal Danish Ballet and taught at its school. He joined the staff of the School of American Ballet in 1964. Member of the faculty in 1984. Mr. Martins later joined the New York City Ballet and became its ballet master-in-chief, with Jerome Robbins, and chairman of the faculty at the School. *Photo: Martha Swope*

SUKI SCHORER makes an adjustment during a student rehearsal, 1970s, in a studio at the School of American Ballet's third home, at the Juilliard School, just north of Lincoln Center. The rehearsal is for an excerpt from George Balanchine's *The Four Temperaments*, to be performed at a New York City-area school as part of the New York City Ballet Education Department's lecture–demonstration program, in which the School participates. Schorer danced with the San Francisco and New York City Ballets. She joined the staff of the School of American Ballet in 1972. Member of the faculty and director of the lecture–demonstration program in 1984. *Photo: Carolyn George*

RICHARD RAPP teaching partnering, 1970s. A student at the School of American Ballet, he joined the New York City Ballet in 1956 and performed there until 1972, when he became a teacher at the School. Member of the faculty in 1984. *Photo: Carolyn George*

Above: ANDREI KRAMAREV-SKY teaching partnering, 1970s. The student with whom he is demonstrating is Darci Kistler, later a principal dancer with the New York City Ballet. Kramarevsky was a principal with the Bolshoi Ballet. He joined the staff of the School of American Ballet in 1976. Member of the faculty in 1984. *Photo: Carolyn George*

Center: KAY MAZZO, 1980s. Mazzo studied at the School of American Ballet and joined the New York City Ballet in 1962. She retired in 1980 and became a teacher at the School in 1982. Member of the faculty in 1984. *Photo: Carolyn George*

Below: SUSAN HENDL, a ballet mistress at the New York City Ballet, and Mary Porter, director of development at the School of American Ballet, conduct an audition for the School in Los Angeles in 1984. *Photo: George Reynolds, New York Daily News*

One third of the students enrolled in the winter course at the School of American Ballet in 1984 were on scholarship. Here Lincoln Kirstein and Marie-Jeanne congratulate the winners of the School's first scholarship competition, in 1940. One of the winners was Tanaquil LeClercq, standing next to Kirstein, who grew up to be a leading member of Ballet Society and the New York City Ballet, and a prototype of the "Balanchine ballerina." *(Collection of Ballet Society)*

TANAQUIL LeCLERCQ, a recipient of a Ballet Society fellowship for continuing study at the School. *Photo: Franz Lehman*

Above: Twenty years after the School of American Ballet's first scholarship competition, winners of the first Ford Foundation scholarships, awarded in 1960, gather in a studio at the School. The student jumping in the center is Suzanne Farrell. *Photo: Martha Swope*

Below: SUZANNE FARRELL, one of the New York City Ballet dancers who serve as guest teachers at the School of American Ballet, works with young students, 1980s. *Photo: Carolyn George*

The Ford Foundation helped the School to offer Teachers Seminars from 1960 to 1969. The seminars, which were open to ballet teachers from around the country, were taught by Balanchine, who used student and young company members as demonstrators. Those demonstrating in this seminar, in 1961, are, from left to right, Carol Sumner, Victoria Simon, and Patricia McBride. *Photo: Nancy Lassalle*

$250,000 from the Endowment, this time under that federal agency's prestigious "challenge grant" program. Both grants were matched, as was the Ford Foundation award. But the second had further-reaching effects.

Most dance training institutes in America are attached to dance companies. The School of American Ballet was the first dance training facility to receive a challenge grant, for which it was eligible as a separately incorporated entity. That placed the School in the category of a national cultural institution, a new identity that has helped in fund raising and other ways. Since the awarding of the challenge grant, for instance, Gleboff has for the first time been able to arrange for students with widowed mothers to be eligible for Social Security. Like the Ford Foundation award of 1963, the Endowment's challenge grant put a seal of legitimacy and approval on the School that signaled suitability for support from a new and much-expanded field of donors. And in 1984, the Endowment awarded the School a second challenge grant of $750,000, to be matched by 1987, which the School has earmarked for its endowment.

The School conducts separate campaigns to raise money for its endowment and for its operating budget. In 1984, with one-third of the students on full or partial scholarship, earned income accounted for only 20 percent of the School's $1.4 million budget. By 1981, three years after it began to raise money for an endowment, the School was drawing from the endowment to meet the widening gap between its budget and earned and raised income created by success and its desire to award as many scholarships as possible to talented students in need of support. The amount drawn annually from the endowment has risen from $75,000 that year to $434,000 in 1984. At the same time, it was realized that the School, despite its character as a performing-arts academy, must begin to see itself as an educational institution and raise funds accordingly. The number of board members has tripled since 1975, and 183 foundations and corporations contributed to its fund-raising campaigns in 1984.

In May 1982, the School began its fiftieth anniversary fund-raising campaign with a goal of $15 million—$5 million for a dormitory fund to establish facilities to house students, in the tradition of the Imperial School and European and Soviet state-run ballet academies, and $10 million to increase investments that function as endowment. In the latter amount, $3.2 million would be allocated for faculty salaries and benefits, $3 million for scholarships, $2 million for a permanently endowed George Balanchine Chair for Chairman of the Faculty and a Lincoln Kirstein Chair for Administration, $1 million for an operating reserve, $500,000 for an annual Workshop fund, and $300,000 for a national audition program.

Midway through 1984, $8.5 million had been raised in the campaign, with 40 percent given by foundations, 37 percent by individuals, 11 percent raised through benefit events, and 7 percent given by corporations. The School's fund-raising apparatus is the most highly developed—and admired and envied—in American dance, though Kirstein's pessimism about the future has not abated much. In its fiftieth year, the School also entered into an innovative project with Procter & Gamble, marking the first time that a corporation was sponsoring a specific program at the School: the School's National Audition Program will be underwritten by Secret deodorant, together with a performing workshop for the School's summer-course students. This sponsorship means that the School will be able to conduct auditions in more cities, and summer students will gain performance experience, some of it in ballets choreographed for the occasion. Although the School does not plan to endorse the product, its students will serve as models for the market of young consumers the company hopes to reach. In 1984, the School also was represented by one of New York City's best-known public-relations firms. "My worry is that we keep on expanding," one staff member says. "That needs more money, so the development department has to produce more money. And then we expand. And then there is no money. It's a vicious circle."

But such problems would have been beyond anyone's dreams before the first Ford Foundation grant to Ballet Society in 1959. Two years earlier, the School had been forced to move from its headquarters at 637 Madison Avenue, when the building was slated for demolition. Once more, the School's future had seemed threatened. Natalie Molostwoff and Ouroussow had been putting aside "a little money for emergencies." "We looked all over New York and couldn't find anything," Molostwoff recalls. Finally the School was able to purchase the President Theatre, at 247 West Forty-eighth Street, which had once housed Erwin Piscator's Dramatic Workshop as well as an all-midget theater company.

"We were going to renovate," Molostwoff says. "But it would have been too expensive, and very impractical. It was a very narrow building, so there would have been just one studio on each floor and we would have needed extra office help." The School sold the property to Mama Leone's Restaurant and moved instead to rented premises at 2291 Broadway, near Eighty-third Street, where it would remain until 1969, in a second-floor loft occupied previously by the scenery painter Eugene Dunkel. ("His mother-in-law was our pianist for many years," Molostwoff says, "but there was no connection.") Now the home of the New York School of Ballet—founded by Richard Thomas and the late Barbara Fallis, who had both danced with the New York City Ballet—the facility had one small studio and two large, sunken ones with high ceilings and big windows, as well as two dressing rooms and office space. "We did not do much reconstruction when we moved in, except to put in new floors," Molostwoff recalls. Soon, however, the new floors had to be replaced, this time by floors with springs under their newly raised surfaces, making them among the city's most resilient dance surfaces. "We had complaints from the stores downstairs," Molostwoff explains. One of the stores was a Florsheim shoe shop, still on the corner of Eighty-third Street in 1984. "They said the shoes fell off the shelves and the customers ran out of the store. That was when we discontinued charac-

119

ter classes. We paid the teacher to the end of the year and stopped. We had no choice. We could have lost the place."

During its fourth decade, the School had become unabashedly businesslike. "The principal aim of the School of American Ballet is to prepare its students for professional performing careers either in a company affiliated with the School such as the New York City Ballet, or in any professional ballet company in the United States and abroad," the 1970–71 School catalogue advised. "The School also maintains the premise that, with rare exceptions, a professional stage career is necessary for the development of distinguished choreographers and ballet teachers." The requirements to be met by the students were more specific, and included "a well-proportioned, flexible, coordinated body, legs that easily adopt the turned-out position, a high instep, etc., etc. They must possess musical aptitude, a natural gift for movement and determination." Race horses, the catalogue suggests, are trained here.

By the 1970–71 school year, eleven class levels were offered at the School. Courses of study for girls and boys were differentiated by the second intermediate levels, when the boys were required to take intermediate and advanced men's classes. Another indication that the School was attracting more male students was the announcement that beginners were now not accepted past the age of fourteen. The faculty, too, was coming to have a slightly different look. Members of the Balanchine-Kirstein companies had always taught at the School, among them Lew Christensen, William Dollar, Elise Reiman, and Beatrice Tompkins. Increasingly, however, the School drew on noted New York City Ballet dancers for its teachers. Two whose presence at the School marked its fourth decade were André Eglevsky and Diana Adams.

Acclaimed as the greatest male classical dancer of his age, Eglevsky was a popular principal with City Ballet from 1951 through 1958, when Balanchine created ballets for him that exploited his exciting pirouettes, jumps, and beats and his expert partnering. Among Eglevsky's own early teachers had been Nicolai Legat, an alumnus of the Imperial School and Maryinsky Theater in the late nineteenth century and a brilliant technician who approached the teaching of ballet as a science. He deeply influenced Eglevsky and Danilova, both of whom had studied with him in London in the 1920s. On Eglevsky's arrival in the United States in 1937, he made his way, penniless, to the School of American Ballet. "I understand you're the one who turns a lot," Balanchine said to him. Eglevsky agreed he was, and offered to do twelve pirouettes for a quarter. Balanchine accepted, and Eglevsky left the studio with lunch money.[4] The young Russian danced with the American Ballet briefly, then went from international company to company before settling at the City Ballet. In 1962, he joined the staff of the School, where he taught for eight years and became a noted teacher of male dancers.

Jumps and pirouettes were his forte in the classroom, too. "André taught a lovely class but it was extremely difficult and demanding, technically and in terms of stamina," Adams says. "As his own technique was extremely clean, that was what he taught." Eglevsky's corrections could be severe. "But they had reason," Suki Schorer recalls. "They were concrete. And he had a definite format or order for the class. It was solid and thought out. But you felt like you were dancing."

Adams was a purely American product, trained by Edward Caton, Agnes de Mille, and Antony Tudor. A member of Ballet Theatre, she joined the New York City Ballet in 1950 and became one of the leading interpreters of Balanchine's edgy, astringent modern classics of the late 1950s, creating roles in *Agon* and *Episodes*. But the woman who had earlier danced with as much distinction in De Mille's *Fall River Legend* and *Oklahoma!* was known, too, for her portrayal of the Siren in *Le Fils Prodigue*. And she danced Balanchine's more lyric ballets with the same physical authority. Long-legged, distant and intense on stage, Adams "could walk," as R. P. Blackmur put it in his essay "The Swan in Zurich." She had a gift for movement. On her retirement from City Ballet in 1963, Adams joined the permanent staff as an administrator, continuing to serve as an important recruiter of students. Among her earlier recruits had been Suzanne Farrell, in whom some saw Adams herself as a dancer.

Balanchine had gone out with Adams the first few times, before the major Ford Foundation grant, to audition nationally. "We did Buffalo together, I remember," Adams says. "You learned a lot. He had a better eye than anyone." Adams left the company when she became pregnant, and the position of coordinator of studies at the School was created for her by Balanchine. "I think a better title would have been 'head of admissions,' " Adams says. "I never ran the School. I was head of the scholarship program. I observed classes and checked the students' development and their programs. Balanchine was terrific about that. If there were any problems, he'd come over and observe, so I didn't feel such a dreadful responsibility." She tried to teach each class level, in the beginning, to get a better idea of the students. Her own teaching had been shaped by Balanchine in special technique classes he had given her in the mid-1950s. "His training was so beautifully and wonderfully worked out. So intelligent. And it was pretty clear to me, because we'd talked so much." Adams left her job at the School in 1971 to devote more attention to her young daughter.

There were eight guest teachers from the City Ballet at the School by 1971, including Schorer and Richard Rapp, who joined the permanent faculty in 1972 and were established teachers at the School in 1984. Peter Martins, who succeeded Balanchine as chairman of the faculty in 1983, served as a guest teacher for the first time during the 1975–76 school year. Jean-Pierre Bonnefous, another principal dancer, joined the faculty in 1977 and two years later initiated a separate Intermediate Boys' Division, to which were added boys' gymnastics classes as well as a daily "special" advanced men's class for chosen students. The Imperial School had long been the acknowledged source. But now the School had its own fully developed "American" tradition from which to feed, though not exclusively.

Another of the milestones of the School's fourth decade was the acquisition in 1964 of Danilova and Stanley Williams, two of its most popular teachers. Andrei Kramarevsky, a former principal dancer with the Bolshoi Ballet, followed them onto the faculty in 1976. Each represents a distinctive tradition.

Steeped in the Bournonville or Danish style of ballet from his years as a member of the Royal Danish Ballet and a teacher at its school, Williams was himself a student at the Danish school at a time when Bournonville's prescriptions were rigidly adhered to. In 1943 he joined the Danish company, where he was perceived as a Bournonville dancer of exceptional clarity and technical purity. Forced to retire from the stage due to injury, Williams, who had already taught at the Danish school, was invited to join its faculty in 1950. He served an apprenticeship there under Vera Volkova, a demanding but gifted and committed teacher who had trained at the Imperial School and with Vaganova, and had taught in England at the Sadler's Wells (now Royal) Ballet and its school before coming to Copenhagen in 1951.

"Volkova was a big influence on me," Williams says of the famed teacher. "I loved the steps: very simple, very logical. They just felt right. She used a lot of imagery. She created pictures, and that made me understand exactly what she was talking about. She never did any corrections."

Balanchine watched Williams teach during the long months he spent in Copenhagen, first with the touring City Ballet, then with LeClercq, who was too ill to be moved back to the United States after the onset of the polio that ended her performing career. "Balanchine would sit and watch me teach the children. He was not interested in the company classes. Just the children who were twelve, thirteen, and fourteen. I thought it must be boring, since he'd spend the whole day rehearsing. I never knew why, but he'd be there day after day." Remembering Williams as a teacher who "knows how to make people move,"[5] Balanchine later invited Williams to give classes to the City Ballet dancers and subsequently moved the influential teacher to the School permanently in 1964. Twenty years later, Williams teaches some company classes again. "But this is where my most important work is, in the School," he says. "It is no ballgame. It's really hard work."

As Bournonville had uniquely stressed male dancing in his time, so Williams became known for his teaching of male dancers, numbering Peter Martins among his early pupils. Martins, who began with Williams at twelve and continued studying with him until he graduated into the Royal Danish Ballet, refers to Williams simply as "my teacher." "When a dancer says, 'So-and-So is my teacher,' he means this is the one who determined my style, who gave me the clue to the art and to my way of performing. This is the teacher who set my goals, who set my standards of movement," Martins wrote in *Far from Denmark,* in a revealing tribute. "It was Stanley Williams who made me feel the challenge, the potential achievement, the *importance* of being a dancer."[6]

> Specifically, he taught me the importance of precision, of doing steps correctly, fully, so that each move is clear and accurate—the feet in first, second, fifth positions absolutely clear—no muddy approximations, no fuzziness—dancing in control, in shape, concentrating on proper form. Dance with responsibility to the steps. You couldn't just go out there and fly around and be extreme and dramatic, jump high and turn and turn. You had to know *how* to turn, how to land, how to present yourself, how to carry yourself, and you had to feel the relationship of one step to the other within the musical phrase. It always had to be pleasing to the eye, and never show strain; you did the most up to the point that strain entered. He emphasized turnout—the opening out of the legs, showing to the front as full an image of the body as possible. He concentrated on turning, the body shown all round, revolving around an announced center within. He demanded that the linking of steps, moving from position to position, have energy and point. The stress was on correctness and quality, not on extravagant virtuosity.[7]

A visitor to the School, pausing outside the studio door during a class taught by Williams, would likely hear nothing but a murmuring piano and perhaps the slightest scuffing of the students' feet against the floor. Intermittent laughter is likely to emanate from Danilova's classroom—quiet giggles from the students and a characteristic and infectious high coo of amusement from Danilova herself. "She's a real trouper," Reiman says admiringly. Kirstein describes Danilova as providing an "arcana of stage behavior and technique" to her women students.[8] She has survived with style. Classmate, early ballet partner, and common-law wife of Balanchine, Danilova was a soloist at the State Academic Theater for Opera and Ballet (formerly Maryinsky) when she left Russia with Balanchine and Dimitriew. Her first success in Diaghilev's Ballets Russes was in Balanchine's *The Triumph of Neptune*, and she danced Terpsichore in his *Apollon Musagète*; later she became ballerina of Colonel de Basil's Ballets Russes, prima ballerina of the Ballet Russe de Monte Carlo, and one of the most popular international ballet stars of the 1930s, 1940s, and 1950s.

Danilova's range of roles extended from Odette in *Swan Lake* and Swanilda in *Coppélia* to the Street Dancer in Léonide Massine's *Le Beau Danube* and the Glove Seller in his *Gaîté Parisienne*, all works in which she was celebrated. She staged ballets for the Metropolitan Opera House and productions for several ballet companies after her retirement from performing in 1958. Five years later, she began to teach at the School of American Ballet. "As usual, met Mr. Balanchine on street," Danilova recalls in her vivid English. "He asked what I doing. Then he said, 'Why not come and teach variations?' Then about one year trying, they invite me to faculty.

"I was always invited to teach everywhere I danced. Sometimes on Sunday. So interesting. You mold them. I enjoy." Gaiety seems the predominant mood in her classroom. "But it's nice. You can't be dry. Only exercises. Especially for talent—very boring. Must make lessons interesting. Pulse. Has to vibrate." Danilova stresses performance values and ballerina manners in her classes, starting her youngest students on dances from the classical repertory. "Polonaise for B1," she says, referring to the starting level of the Second Intermediate Division, a class of girls around twelve years old, "how to walk on the stage." And so it was fitting that it was she who, in 1965, directed the first of the School's annual Spring Workshop Performances, with a staging of dances from *Coppélia.*

The dances were included in a concert by the West End Symphony in which the School's advanced and graduating students had been invited to participate, in a program at the Joan of Arc Junior High School on West Ninety-third Street. "Mr. Balanchine, I think, decided," Danilova says. He had liked her variations class. "Do workshop like we had in Russia," he told her. "For me, it was very easy because I know what he talking about because we went to same school. Annual performance of graduating class at Imperial Ballet School. Take best of class and so on, descending.

"Think they got together with conductor of group. First in very small school. Tiny stage. Second time at Brandeis." She and the dancers had needed a bodyguard, she remembers, to get to the Louis D. Brandeis High School on West Eighty-fourth Street. "Such bad street. 'Murder mile.' Had to have police."

The excerpts from *Coppélia* included a prelude, waltz, and first-act "Ballad (four variations on a Slavic theme)," and second-act "Village wedding (galop and finale)." "Choreographers Petipa, Saint-Léon. Everyone had their paw in it. I did what Sergeyev put for me in Ballet Russe," Danilova says, referring to Marius Petipa and Arthur Saint-Léon and to Nicholas Grigorievich Sergeyev, a director of the Maryinsky Theater who left Russia after the October Revolution and was responsible for setting many Maryinsky ballet productions in the West. No dancers were listed in the program. "They are receiving their training at the School of American Ballet, under George Balanchine, here in our community," the program notes explain. "This is the first opportunity for these young people to dance publicly."

There had been other opportunities, of course, in sporadic early workshops. And by this time Balanchine had choreographed four ballets with roles for children: *The Nutcracker, A Midsummer*

Night's Dream (said to be the first full-evening ballet created in America), *Harlequinade*, and *Don Quixote*. But the Workshop tradition—one that, like *The Nutcracker*, has given visibility to the School as a productive vocational institution—began with the fledgling performance on May 9, 1965, an activity initiated under the Ford Foundation grant.

The Spring Workshop Performances have grown grander over the years. They are now fully produced programs that serve as a rite of passage for graduating dancers, a medium for neophyte choreographers, and, with representatives of dance companies in attendance from around the United States and abroad, virtually a public audition for School dancers who have not been chosen for the New York City Ballet. The Workshops also offer financial supporters of the School a chance to see the tangible results of their donations and to be courted in postperformance festivities.

The Workshop Performances have also become popular as entertainment, though the teachers stress that they are not finished performances, offering as they do merely accomplished technical work with a poignant extra dimension. "Attending SAB's Workshop is a little like being inside a bubble—everything's so clean, delicate, select," Robert Greskovic wrote of the 1982 Workshop Performances. "Realities of the outside world seem more distant than usual. The heightened effect we get comes from the remarkably accomplished dance articulation produced by undeniably innocent practitioners—mighty moments springing from fragile means."[9]

The second Workshop Performance, again on a program with the West End Symphony, took place at Brandeis on June 12, 1966, and consisted of excerpts from the first act of *Swan Lake*, choreographed by Danilova. The program lists young performers who went on to join the New York City Ballet, among them Robert Weiss, Linda Merrill (later Merrill Ashley), and Colleen Neary. The following year the Workshop was presented at the New York State Theater for two performances in addition to the traditional shared program with the West End Symphony at Brandeis. In 1971 the Workshop Performances were moved to the Juilliard Theater, where they have remained, with the Juilliard's student orchestra providing the accompaniment from 1972 on.

By 1984, the School was producing three performances with two different casts and a few new soloists in the third, conducted by Robert Irving, the City Ballet's music director, and reviewed by leading dance critics. The Workshop had become an event as important to many as the performances that weekend, a block south at Lincoln Center, by the New York City Ballet and American Ballet Theatre. And the Workshop served an important function in 1983, opening as it did on the day of Balanchine's death.

The company and its school would continue, the performance that evening suggested. Audience members, among them Mikhail Baryshnikov, director of American Ballet Theatre, raced from the Juilliard Theater mid-performance to watch the close of City Ballet's performance at the New York State Theater. At the railing in the left First Ring, traditionally reserved for City Ballet dancers not performing that night, stood a recent graduate of the School, his eyes glistening with tears as he watched a distant, exalted Suzanne Farrell move through Balanchine's *Symphony in C* as if she were dancing a prayer. "The future, I wouldn't know what it is," Balanchine once said. "Today is everything." [10]

Workshop Performances tend to include "something old, something new and something in between," as Greskovic put it. [11] The bulk of the first category is made of Danilova's stagings of ballet by Petipa and Michel Fokine [12] and stagings of Bournonville by Williams. [13] It has also included traditional and country dances from England and America, staged by Ronald Smedley and Robert Parker, and a 1974 setting by Michel Renault of the Paris Opéra Ballet, then a guest teacher at the School, of Albert Aveline's *Les Deux Pigeons*.

The "something in between" is usually a Balanchine work staged by Suki Schorer. [14] But the student dancers have also performed excerpts from Jerome Robbins's *Dances at a Gathering*, and they went right from the Workshop onto the New York City Ballet stage in the same year, 1978, in his *Interplay*. The students have performed in ballets created for the City Ballet's Stravinsky, Tchaikovsky, and Ravel Festivals, and Robbins's *Circus Polka* made a reverse trip from the New York State Theater, where the ballet was performed by the youngest children in the 1972 Stravinsky Festival, to the Juilliard Theater two years later. John Taras contributed *Polonaise and Ballabile* in 1980.

Balanchine may not have believed that choreographers could be made, but he behaved as if they could—and ought to—be nudged into creativity. Taras recalls Balanchine's early interest in his work and how Taras had used the score in the 1945 *Graziana*, a dance Taras created for Ballet Theatre. As was his wont, Balanchine suggested music for Taras's second ballet. The work was an immediate failure, but Balanchine was the first to call the next morning. "Don't pay attention to anyone," he told the young choreographer. "Just look at the ballet and see what you want to do to it. Look at it and work on it."

Balanchine encouraged Paul Mejia, a City Ballet soloist who became artistic director, with Maria Tallchief, of the Chicago City Ballet, to create dances while he was still in his mid-teens and a student at the School, even sending Mejia to a music teacher. And at times it has seemed that the Workshop is as much a testing ground for new choreographers as for new dancers. John Clifford was pressed into service at nineteen, contributing two ballets to the 1967 Workshop. Other new choreographers included Lorca Massine, Richard Tanner, and Kevin Higginbotham, who, while still a student at the School, created a rock ballet for the 1972 Workshop. Made for the 1971 Workshop, the Massine and Tanner ballets were taken into the City Ballet repertory that year, but received mixed reviews and were soon dropped.

The cast for the Higginbotham ballet included Wilhelmina Frankfurt, Daniel Duell, and Jean-Pierre Frohlich, who went on to become familiar City Ballet performers, and Hinton Battle, who became a Broadway star. In 1981, City Ballet principal dancer

Jacques d'Amboise created a work for Kramarevsky and the School's littlest dancers. And one of the most charming of new works by company members was Bonnefous's *Quadrille*, performed in the 1978 Workshop, a simple dance whose natural use of the children was comparable to Balanchine's way with them. It was also a dance that introduced Peter Boal, a promising young classicist who entered the City Ballet corps in 1983, to admiring balletomanes. Also in the cast were Julie Michael and Michael Byars, soloists in the 1984 Workshop, the latter an apprentice that year with the City Ballet.

Bonnefous created a second ballet for the Workshop, and young Joseph Duell, a principal at the New York City Ballet, choreographed two works, one of which went into the company repertory. *Ballet d'Isoline*, one of two Workshop pieces by the City Ballet principal dancer Helgi Tomasson, also made the jump to the stage of the State Theater, as did Peter Martins's *The Magic Flute* and *Delibes Divertissement*, created, like the d'Amboise, Duell, and Tomasson works, in the early 1980s.

Workshop programs carry the nostalgia of high-school yearbooks. Featured in all three of the 1968 Workshop ballets is Gelsey Kirkland, who entered City Ballet that year and became a principal dancer four years later, at eighteen. Marianna Tcherkassky and Fernando Bujones, like Kirkland, later principals at American Ballet Theatre, had important Workshop roles in 1969 and 1970, and Heather Watts, a leading City Ballet principal fourteen years later, may be found among the Nine Ladies in *Konservatoriet* in 1970. City Ballet's Victor Castelli, Bart Cook, and Daniel Duell are prominently mentioned the following year, as are Victor Barbee and Christine Spizzo of American Ballet Theatre.

By 1972, Bujones has become Siegfried in the Workshop *Swan Lake*. The names of three of City Ballet's most distinctive principal dancers may be found that year and the next, with Stephanie Saland in a lead in the Pas de Deux from *Flower Festival at Genzano* in 1972 and Maria Calegari and Lourdes Lopez among the Precious Stones in Danilova's 1973 staging of *Aurora's Wedding*. Calegari and Judith Fugate have leads in the Workshop's 1974 staging of *Serenade,* whose cast includes Roman Jasinski, the son of the dancer who starred in Balanchine's Les Ballets 1933 and who figured in Kirstein's first plans for an American ballet. Kyra Nichols, well on her way to becoming an important American ballerina ten years later, is listed as a lead in the 1974 *Les Deux Pigeons.* The program is decorated with a drawing by the artist Edward Gorey, a long-time admirer of the City Ballet and the School. It shows two rail-thin adolescents poised perilously in an absurd lift. "I can't imagine now why this ever seemed so difficult," the caption reads.

Christopher d'Amboise, the son of Jacques d'Amboise and later a principal with the City Ballet, bobs up as a Polovetsian warrior in 1976, and the following year Ballet Theatre's Patrick Bissell is dancing Zephyr in Danilova's *Les Saisons.* Both Darci Kistler and Stacy Caddell, striking young members of City Ballet in 1984, moved from ensemble roles in 1979 to leads in the following year's Workshop.

In the corps de ballet of the 1974 Workshop *Serenade* and dancing Aurora in *The Sleeping Beauty* the next year is Toni Bentley, later a corps member of City Ballet and the author, in 1982, of *Winter Season: A Dancer's Journal.* City Ballet dancers tend to write books. Like *Worlds Apart* by Robert Maiorano, one of the School's early *Nutcracker* princes and later a member of the company, Bentley's book is a perceptive classic, a portrait of life in the School and in the company.

What does the Workshop mean to the young dancer?

"She remained at the school for seven years and moved from the bottom of the class to the top," Bentley writes in *Winter Season.*

By her last year she was the only one left from her original class. All the rest had been weeded out. They had either grown too tall or fallen in love or gone to college. During her last year she injured her foot. It was her first injury, and it was more than a coincidence that it came at such a crucial point in her career. She could not dance for three months. The day she returned to class, George Balanchine, the director of the school and of the New York City Ballet, came to watch. He was choosing the girls who would dance the ballerina parts in the school's workshop performance. This performance would be the deciding factor in these young girls' careers. She was chosen along with two other girls to learn Princess Aurora in *The Sleeping Beauty*. Rehearsals lasted six months. The week before the performance she slipped—she came down badly from a pas de chat. She saw her performance, her Princess and her career disappear before her eyes. Her ankle turned black and blue and swelled. She sat for the last week of rehearsals in a chair, her foot packed in ice. On the morning of the performance, she got up and danced. She felt no pain at all. She was injured for a month afterwards. But she had danced, and she had triumphed. She was not going to give up the chance of a lifetime.[15]

Another chance came the next year, when Bentley starred in a Workshop performance of Balanchine's *Allegro Brillante*, a romantic, virtuoso ballet that the choreographer said contained all he knew of classical ballet in thirteen minutes. It was a distinct departure from *The Sleeping Beauty*. The point of the Workshop, Williams says, is for the young dancers to gain experience in performing and exposure to a wide variety of styles in ballet. With Schorer's stagings of Balanchine, the dancers get a taste of what the future may hold for them if they are lucky enough to get into "The Company" and to progress beyond corps roles, a feat that sometimes seemed, under Balanchine, as mysterious and miraculous a process as surviving the School's ongoing weeding-out of students.

A product of the San Francisco Ballet School and company, Schorer joined City Ballet in 1959, becoming a soloist in 1963 and a principal dancer six years later. Also the director of the School's lecture-demonstration group, Schorer began to set Balanchine ballets on the young dancers in 1973, a year after she joined the faculty. Her clean, brisk stagings are known for the way in which they seem to bring the ballets to fresh life in the students' bodies. And Schorer is widely perceived as articulator of the Balanchine canon of the final, Lincoln Center years. Kramarevsky, whose fast-moving, expansive classes serve as a perfect complement to the quiet logic practiced by Williams, is likely to be one of the last of the School's ballet teachers to come from outside the New York City Ballet. With Schorer and Rapp, a graduate of the School and a City Ballet soloist who retired from the company in 1972, the School's City Ballet connection was solidified.

V. THE "BALANCHINE STYLE"

The New York City Ballet came into its own coincidentally with the School of American Ballet's middle period, as George Balanchine and his dancers were shaping a new aesthetic. The ballets of those years suggest the extraordinary range of Balanchine's interests. And running like a thread through that diverse body of works was the developing "Balanchine style." There came to be the "Balanchine ballerina," a very tall, very young, very slender woman with long legs and supple feet, narrow hips, and a small head. With tall people, Balanchine once said, you could see more. And Kirstein is said to have observed that a long piece of string is needed for an elaborate knot. Balanchine's adopted land of lovely bodies had yielded cool, physically daring dancers who brought a peculiarly American tinge of athleticism to the classical vocabulary. The Balanchine dancer, a child of the twentieth century, moved fast and light and big, with an edge as sharp and clear as the facet of a diamond.

The young dancers in an advanced class taught by Suki Schorer are all sizes, as the dancers of the City Ballet are in reality, despite the legend of that piece of string. Schorer herself, a small dancer who became a City Ballet soloist, serves as a living refutation of the notion. But most look as if they might one day become the thoroughbreds for whom Balanchine choreographed. "Forty minutes in the room and you haven't put your shoes on yet?" Schorer exclaims as she strides into the studio. "You need a mother here." She is dressed functionally in a black turtleneck sweater, leotard, and short, filmy teaching skirt, and pink tights and flat-heeled shoes, with just the glint of small gold earrings to add piquancy to the heart-shaped face, which looks as young as it did when Schorer performed with the City Ballet.

The students put the final touches to the old scraps with which they bandage their bruised and gnarled feet. They ease into their toe shoes and tie them, then line up easily at the barre for the pliés that begin the class. "Head up, girls, and put your whole foot on the floor," Schorer calls out. "Show me the beginning of the phrase!" As the class continues she darts in and out among the students at the barre, flattening a hip, wrapping a foot, or opening out a knee. "I joined the company in 1959, and by 1961 I'd sometimes teach during layoff," she says later, referring to the time between seasons when ballet dancers are traditionally laid off from their jobs. Balanchine created a boys' class for her that she taught for a short time, and had her teach the Children's II and III classes. He and Kirstein came to watch. She smiles. "Mr. B. said he knew I'd get down on my hands and knees and fix their feet."

The barre in today's class is fast but fundamental, moving expertly through quick exercises for the feet and adagios to end with simple pliés and relevés facing the barre, with balances. "Stay over the supporting leg," Schorer tells one student during a sequence of tendus. "Don't jam the foot. No weight on it." During quick foot-brushes, she cautions the students to make sure their toes and insteps are pointed "all the way." "And pull up on the thighs in first," she adds.

More than the step is important. "Nice hands," Schorer suggests. "The fingers should have shapes up there, and the elbows are out, not in." She coaxes flow and presence from the students as they work. "Don't be staying in the plié at all," she calls out. "Don't sit there. Present that heel. Your arms belong to you." All of the body must be used. "Pick something up off the floor and watch it," she tells a student during the ports de bras. "And your face relates to the movement, too. You want the whole thing to relate."

As cogent as a wink, Schorer is never still, moving at least as much as any of her charges and with far more exuberance. But there is often a teasing, almost indulgent tone to her admonitions. "Try not to keep correcting yourself," she counsels one tensely serious student. "On the way, do the maximum you can so there's no room for correction. Otherwise you never feel the position. And feel pretty inside. Don't stare. It's good—you look terrific—but this is what I see." She stiffens her body and face, looking as if she's about to stalk out from the grave.

There is a rush to the sides to put on harder toe shoes for the center work. Schorer gives a running push to the piano, helping the accompanist move it to the corner to allow the maximum space for dancing. This portion of the class begins with tendu combinations that test the agility of the feet and degree of pull-up in the body and call for easy, flowing épaulements. The students move on to pirouettes, adagios, and a waltz. "Make it big and juicy," Schorer says. That is a frequent instruction from her. "Toes alive," she orders.

One of the students makes a timid sortie into the pirouettes. "You can't just pray to turn," Schorer tells her. "Your legs do it, and your upper body should participate. A lot of it is your upper body." The class ends with combinations that call for precise, very fast footwork that takes the dancers back and forth across the floor, bodies pulled up and poised in flight, as eager as runners nearing the finish line ahead of the rest. Still, attention must be paid to the look of it all. "A beautiful effacé," Schorer calls, coaxing them to shape, though never to pose in, the stance. "Model your-self in the step so your mother can be happy she spent all that money on ballet."

Early in the School's history, the students were trained to serve as the material with which Balanchine created his ballets. Those days ended with the major Ford Foundation grant, which en-abled the student body to become larger and more diverse and the training to become more stringently professional. "Essentially what the school does is teach the kids how to learn, as prepara-tion for the New York City Ballet or some other company," Kir-stein has said.[1] For Balanchine, too, the "eternal student" made an ideal dancer.[2] What the students learn at the School, however, is not just a solid classical base but the fine adjustments Balan-chine made to the Russian schooling of his youth, adjustments that characterize the "American style"—or neoclassicism, as it has been called, embodied in the Balanchine canon.

The hallmarks of that style are clear. The head was important to Balanchine, and it, the neck, and the shoulders must move in precise articulation, the bend of the head making the dancer's presence more vivid on stage. He seldom arranged or choreo-graphed for the arms, which were to follow the body naturally into a correct position. A port de bras should involve the lungs and not the arms alone. "You were to take that breath and go into the port de bras," Schorer told the Dance Critics Association at its annual conference in 1983, in a lecture-demonstration on the Balanchine style. "He used to say that when you open your arms it's like parting some curtains. A nice spring day. Slowly the elbows, finally the wrists."

For Balanchine, the elbows were part of the arms, as were the thumbs of the hands. Each element of the body, like every ele-ment of the step, was of importance. And so the elbows and thumbs were not to be rounded or softened into invisibility. The line of the hands was particularly important to him. In company classes in the early 1960s, the dancers held balls in their hands the size of small tennis balls. As they danced, they learned to achieve the right curving but controlled look. But the fingers were always to be separate and alive.

"The fingers reach and move out through each position as you move to the arabesque," Schorer told the dance critics. "And sometimes when you moved the hands over the head he would say, 'Your hand is like a paintbrush.' The bristles on the brush move, and that's what happens with the hands. It's not a static thing." That line of the hand, she says, was a fixed point comparable to one of ballet's five basic positions for the feet.

The dance writer Robert Greskovic suggests that, with Balanchine, those positions are distinctively ones for the legs as well as the feet, given the choreographer's use of the entire limb. Some dancers coming from other companies into the New York City Ballet in the 1950s reported that, after they had worked with Balanchine, the shape of their legs changed, leaving the thighs looking longer and leaner. He may have habitually overcrossed the legs, Schorer suggests. But his "conscious focus on the full length of the leg not only acts to elongate and enlarge an open ballet movement, it also causes closed positions to have their own certain definition," Greskovic observed. In the développé, "every increment of the leg works clearly and cleanly through to ultimate, physical possibility. The entire length of leg is also dramatized in Balanchine's signature fourth position."

The position is open, and grounded, but "unmistakably tall, not because the space between the feet is narrower than we expect (if anything it's wider), but because the thighs appear more actively keen in holding the position than the feet. (The legs determine the position, the feet finish it.) . . . This pulled-extra-tall accent through the thigh that so distinguishes the fifth and fourth positions of Balanchine's ballerinas accounts not only for this crisp stillness in posing, it also allows a peculiar lightness and freedom for their pointwork. . . . By concentrating energy throughout the leg with special accent in the thigh, the dancers leave their feet virtually more free to move delicately and intricately."[3]

Perhaps the greatest controversy about the Balanchine style has been the question of the raised heel. Did Balanchine break with tradition and sound anatomic principles and instruct his dancers in the late 1950s not to put their heels down but to land on half point from jumps—a tactic that increases speed and readiness but can also increase the dancer's chance of getting tendinitis? "I think the whole heel business is a question of semantics," John Taras says. "There was always a language problem. I'm not sure he was making things clear. It was **not to not** put the heel down, landing on half point and going down. It was a question of not landing on the heels." There should not, at least, be any weight on the heels in motion. "I never heard Balanchine say to land on demi-pointe," Richard Rapp says. "You go through demi-pointe through the foot into the floor. Look at runners, boxers—any sport. You can't move from a flat-footed position." Kay Mazzo recalls that a piece of paper was about all that should slip between the heels and the floor.

Moving off the heel, with its resultant lightness and cross-stage speed and momentum, may have had something to do with the increasingly streamlined look of the leg and thigh. But the feet had to be put "into" the floor to take off into the big jumps of Balanchine's ballets. And a good, resilient plié was necessary in order for the dancer to spring up and grab the mid-air position of the jump. "He wanted you to be in control all the time," Schorer recalls. "He used to say to pretend, in jumping, that you were landing on eggs—not hard-boiled eggs even—to be that controlled. To be 'like the pussycat.' It was up to you when and how you put the heel down. But the plié could never die. You descended in order to come back up. And to move fast you can't have your weight on the four points of the feet."

The idea of placement, as an analytical tool, bored Balanchine the teacher. His dancers were to be poised to move. They must emphasize the step rather than any preparation for it. But transitional moments must be clearly stated, without breaking the momentum. And the dancer must make of any preparatory move a beautiful if brief pose, rather than a functional one.

Rapp uses Balanchine's piqué arabesque as an example of this flow, with the dancer moving not into the step and then up into arabesque but through the step and into the stretching-up of the leg in a single, unbroken movement.[4] Not only must the standing or supporting leg always be alert, but the legs in plié must be elastic. And to keep dancers from sinking into the demi-plié that had always been the preparation for a pirouette from fourth position, Balanchine had the then iconoclastic notion of holding the back leg straight, a change that has now been generally accepted as giving the dancer a much lighter look than the traditional squat, which weakened the sense of a strong center and reminded Balanchine of laying an egg.[5]

There is, too, the open Balanchine arabesque. His use of the effacé stance, in which the dancer is at an angle to the audience with the upstage, working leg extended away from the body rather than crossing it, exposes the line of the body and presents the dancer clearly and expansively. It is a peculiarly open pose, and in the arabesque Balanchine similarly opened out the hip, with shoulders and hips tilting slightly out of a more traditional, squared arrangement of the body that shortened its line in arabesque.

Balanchine's musicality developed his dancers in a distinctive way. The complex rhythms of the scores of Igor Stravinsky, most obviously of the composers with whose music Balanchine worked, demanded musically expressive dancers with an acute sensitivity to the nuances of accent. A Balanchine dancer had to be able to count the beat while moving through what the dance critic Edwin Denby called Balanchine's "overarching musical phrases." "Mr. B. doesn't like monotony," Schorer once said. "He wants to accent the beginning of the slow movement. When you reach the end, you don't stop; you're not settled. It's like breathing when you're still. He wants you to be inside your own body."[6]

His manner of transmitting these stylistic tenets and adjustments at the School was as changeable as Balanchine's relationship to that institution came to be. As City Ballet grew, Balanchine visited the School frequently and even taught occasionally when he was well, in later years, and free of the business of the company. But his mere existence was felt as a motivating force whether he was physically present or not, and students strained to attention when he visited class or watched a rehearsal at the School. Stacy Caddell remembers widening her eyes at him during one visit, in the belief that he favored women dancers with big eyes. "If he even noticed, he probably thought I'd lost a contact lens," she said later, laughing. And new teachers quickly learned not to recommend a promising student to him. "That was a fatal mistake," Natalie Molostwoff recalls. "If you began to push someone, he'd become disinterested." Balanchine knew, he once said, "the few people I am waiting for."[7] And he was willing to wait almost indefinitely for potential to develop or the desire to dance to be manifested.

His motivation for choosing teachers was always clearest to himself. "I hadn't taught then," Schorer says of her early years with the City Ballet, when Balanchine pressed her into service in the classroom. "But I had had to learn a lot when I came into the company. I could move fairly quickly, but I couldn't lift my legs. I had a teeny jump. I couldn't do entrechat six. I looked fifteen or sixteen instead of nineteen, though, and Balanchine didn't know how old I was. So I worked really hard. I had to. I had to put everything consciously into my body. I was fascinated by what he had to say and always listened. I learned in class. I understood. And I put it on."

Company classes with Balanchine influenced Schorer deeply. "He taught us everything—what plié was about, what tendu was about. Sometimes we would spend a half hour just on port de bras. And there was no rush; we seemed to have endless time then. . . . He talked a lot in class. He talked about how he cooked, how he gardened in the country—what it was like in Russia. Some of the anecdotes would relate to a step; others were just to give us a break from jumping. . . . Balanchine always said, 'You have to listen, you have to want it. Be starving.' I guess I was hungry, and he helped me to stay hungry and feast at the same time."[8]

The teaching staff at the School became a body of individuals with increasingly varied backgrounds, personal physical types, and ways of moving, all of which communicate themselves subliminally to the students. For Muriel Stuart, this leads to a richness of training in which the same technique is taught with differing emphases. "I stress musicality and ports de bras," she says. "The Danish school is marvelous for men's feet. Kramarevsky is all movement." Outside observers have worried that with City Ballet performers filling the ranks in the future and students molded by outside teachers who are, increasingly, influenced by the Balanchine style, teaching at the School may become blandly homogeneous. "The variety and diversity of America has been too much for that French-Russian meld," Jacques d'Amboise says. "It's like a very pure chemical you throw into the ocean." "I think you teach everything you've grasped in your schooling," Kay Mazzo responds. "I've had a conglomerate. Mainly Balanchine, because he's my mentor. That's what I know best. But there was Danilova with her Petipa variations, and the strict classicism of Tumkovsky."

"Somehow, without knowing, we have same idea," Alexandra Danilova observes. "I think somehow, you know, we never go and see each other. I think it's bad. I think teachers should come to each other. Never. When they come first they are afraid but now everybody trusts everybody more. More amiable." The teachers do work together on the content of the children's classes, which are more uniform, and Antonina Tumkovsky's handwritten notes have served many a new teacher at the School.

The Balanchine canon was typically communicated by indirection, though not always. Elise Reiman remembers once incurring untypical wrath. "He came in to watch class just a few minutes one day and scared the hell out of me," she says. "He waited to talk to me. 'I never want to see you do that again,' he said. I was terribly offended. He was in a bad mood. He wanted the leg kept straight for turns. I'd said little pliés to the children. He was very particular about small things. He wanted battement tendu done a certain way. He had ways of doing glissade that he liked.

I used to go to Balanchine with questions. But you couldn't teach young children exactly that way. His counts are so difficult. You have to get them ready to become able to do that."

Getting the students ready often means relying on the pure classical foundation. "This is third arabesque," Rapp says in an intermediate men's class. "If it's going to be here"—he pushes his arm back out of position—"it has to be special." And "special," he adds, "means anything goes." For Danilova, "classical way is correct way." "Other way stylized. Balanchine has his arms. Jerry Robbins has his arms. But I always say in class we purify ourselves. We do correct classical way. Then I explain why this way and not other way, so they understand. Because in classical way, port de bras like a flower . . . in bloom, not wilt. Once when I was in Japan, I was asked what was the difference between the way Orientals and we dance. Here we dance and we open like flowers. Orientals go inside. Drooping flowers, like wisteria. Also beautiful. But they hang inside. All the Japanese when they dance, and the modern dancers, too, all down. But we are unearthly. We all go up. A vanishing in the sky."

The teachers had many ways of discovering what Balanchine wanted in the students, since his notions sometimes changed as challenging new dancers came into the company or ballets had to be reworked for different dancers or for the large stage of the New York State Theater, which demanded space-covering movement. When she was first asked to teach at the School, Reiman asked Balanchine how to put together a class. " 'How do you think up all these steps?' I asked him. 'Well, with children you do a glissade, jeté, assemblé,' he said. 'Do it this way first, then this.' He almost did a little ballet right there."

For most of the teachers, coming to the School much later, Balanchine's guidance seemed elliptical. Rapp recalls that Balanchine poked his head into the classroom a few times after he started teaching at the School, and occasionally stayed briefly to observe, but never talked to him about his teaching. "Clean, with the music, exact steps to move with the music," Balanchine explained to

Helene Dudin when she joined the staff and asked what she should emphasize in working with the children. "Just have them do it, dear," he told Schorer. And "Do what you know" was his instruction to Mazzo. "Balanchine absolutely left me alone," Stanley Williams says. "Except he had a wonderful way. I'd watch his company class and he'd say, 'You know, some people teach like this.' Sometimes it was a hint about me, to show the way he didn't want it."

Many of the teachers made a point of watching Balanchine teach. Peter Martins got private lessons. "Several times Balanchine came to me and said I had to teach girls and teach point in order to understand more," Peter Martins recalls, looking back to the mid-1970s. "But he didn't give me any instructions. One day during layoff I told him that his teaching made zero sense to me. 'Can you explain it? Is there a reason?' I asked him. 'Of course there is a reason,' he said. So we spent every morning in a practice room in the theater with Colleen Neary and Heather Watts, working four or five days a week. He tore down the essentials of the whole vocabulary. I sat and watched. At the end he said, 'Now you teach.' It was wonderful. There was no music. Just two people."

Balanchine's pedagogy could serve as a peculiar model to the uninitiated. "As a teacher he was a great theorist," Taras says. "A choreographer. He liked few people. Lots of things bored him. But he'd explain everything he wanted to do. He'd analyze steps. You could spend the whole class learning three hundred ways to use a step. The way his mind worked was fascinating. He'd do a lot of talking. Very often you'd get very cold in class. The awful thing is that if it had been recorded you wouldn't understand what he meant at all. You had to see it as he spoke."

Schorer recalls that Balanchine was a very physical teacher and his analyses tended to be simple. "He'd pick things apart," she says. "But he wouldn't say, 'Use this muscle.' He'd take your arm, hit your butt, and say, 'This should be like a rock.' His combinations were usually simple—not very long ones—that you could perfect. He taught the finesse of movement."

Dancers in his company classes had to be prepared for repetition. One way Balanchine instilled a sense of dynamics and the essence of the step in his dancers was by repeating the same step almost impossibly slow, then almost impossibly fast. "He'd concentrate on one thing," Martins says. "One day hands; you could hardly lift your arms after. Other days jumps; you'd get the barre over in ten minutes and start jumping. He'd watch the performance every night and see things creep in or disappear. Then he'd drill that in for a whole class. It was the most unprecedented class. You never knew what you were going to get."

Balanchine was apt to tease new company members about their training. "Where did you learn *that?*" he'd exclaim. "SAB? Ah, that's what they teach you. SAB is the worst." Despite lapses in communication, Balanchine usually managed to convey his desires for changes and additions to the School's unwritten syllabus to the teachers. "It never changed that Balanchine wanted the students to move a lot," Nathalie Gleboff says. "He had very definite ideas on the ways he wanted some steps. He'd discuss them directly with the teachers. Or he'd come watch class and tell the teacher that he wanted to do something in a different way. He watched all along—almost to the very end. And this is such a dressing-room community. Nothing could go by. Teachers would even be demonstrating in the hallway."

And yet, Schorer stresses, the School does not teach mannerisms. And the elements of what is taught are inextricably a part of work beyond steps or the establishment of a technique. "Once I saw a balletmaster teaching another company 'Serenade,'" Schorer said. "There are a series of arabesques he said to make à la seconde. But Mr. B. is looking for the long turned-out line in the back leg, not a specific position. Later on, the balletmaster said, 'Balanchine wants the arms crossed.' But it's not that the arms are crossed, it's that the elbows bend. The arms should look free and supple, not stiff."[9] The Balanchine style embodied in the School's teaching is, in the end, far more an aesthetic or a way of approaching dance than a technique or even a style or manner of expression.

Balanchine had many affinities, from August Bournonville's ballet to the Broadway musical theater. He took his dancers, preferably unformed, as his inspiration. Felia Doubrovska's magnificently vivid legs and feet were likely a strong influence early on, as were Maria Tallchief's bold immediacy of presence and Tanaquil LeClercq's physique and lack of mannerism. Balanchine was, he said, "staging ballets for today's bodies." "For people who are here now. And you admire the way he or she looks and how they move. It's this person today—not just *anybody*."[10] The physical and personal characteristics of his dancers suggested new dimensions as Balanchine adapted dance to them. He created new ballets or cast old ones with an eye to enlarging the dancers' capabilities and sense of self by expecting them to do what was, for them, impossible-seeming. "Balanchine would often take someone we would say was ugly and not good at all," Taras says. "He always used to say you have to have an ugly girl in the corps so the others will look beautiful. What intrigued him very often was what he could do with that. And he often brought out things that were more interesting than his style. It made his mind work differently."

Music and its relationship to movement were the greatest spurs to his creativity. "I occupy myself with how not to interfere with the music," he once said.[11] The dance must move with the flow of the music, as impossible to capture in essence in any arrested single pose or grouping as its score would be to dissect as metaphor. "Balanchine wants the dancer to have as much flexibility with his body as the musician has with piano or violin," Nancy Goldner wrote. "When done with Balanchinian dynamics, movements are easy to see and exciting to watch. But I think the crucial factor is their imitation of musical stress. It has been said many times now that watching Balanchine ballet is like seeing the music. His 'eye music' is usually attributed to choreography, but the fact is that the musicality of his ballets is built right into the technique, just as the drama of Graham's ballets is built right into her technique."[12]

Protean, Balanchine's dance was in the end a reflection of an intense lifelong interest in movement as the subject and object of the dance, providing, with the music, both form and content, and capable of expressing all that needed to be expressed. "He wanted emotion," Mazzo said of Balanchine's work with her on *Duo Concertant*, "not with the face, but with a turn of the hand."[13] Unflagging energy and controlled physicality are hallmarks of the Balanchine ballets and a goal for the students at the School of American Ballet. The dancers must move through the steps and music, presenting themselves and the dance all the while.

A simple tendu could be a complete and individual movement, but there had to be a reason for it and a sense of its inherent worth. For Balanchine, as Williams saw it, the point was "the truth of the movement."[14] And that truth was available only in the immediacy of the thing. Each step or pose must be the most it could be, a kind of heightened, vibrant distillation yet also riding with the momentum of the dance. The Balanchine dancer's body must, above all, be available to the moment, participating in it even in utter stillness, and aware of itself within that moment.

"Reach, get it, take it, go, so the whole body becomes long, extended, alive," Schorer said, describing the Balanchine aesthetic in her address to the Dance Critics Association. What are you saving it for? Balanchine habitually asked his dancers. "Everything was more. He demanded total extremes of the body. And then he said, 'And now we'll only use what we need.' You don't need all that. But you have it and you take what you need and use it where you need it. Some ballets may be more of something or less, like salt and pepper. He had us exaggerate a lot.

He'd say, 'If you have a lot of something, you can always do less. But if you have nothing, you can't get more. It doesn't matter what happens after. The point is for now. I want to see the now.' "

Balanchine was always searching for new ways to entertain, one suspects, not just the audience but himself as well. But there were constants. In his work, dancing is not about the smiling face, as Greskovic put it, but about the ecstatic body. And the controlled ecstasy of his dance is the lesson to be learned in daily class at the School of American Ballet.

VI. THE
SCHOOL TODAY

There is a moment of stillness in Studio 3. Rows of lean young dancers stand at attention, their neatly sculpted faces glowing in the afternoon light. The familiar opening notes of Tchaikovsky's Serenade in C Major sound from the piano in the corner; then suddenly the dancers break into motion as if freed from the constraint of that first pose. "Get your breath in the music so you're using your whole body," Suki Schorer calls from her perch at the top of the barre, marking "stage center" for them as they speed through the classroom. In two weeks, the student dancers will perform *Serenade* at the Spring Workshop Performances, fifty years after Balanchine created it for the first students of the School of American Ballet. At fifty feet by fifty feet, the studio is roughly the size of the Madison Avenue classroom where Balanchine began the ballet. But Avery Fisher Hall and the Metropolitan Opera House loom beyond the studio's high windows, visible reminders of the proximity of Lincoln Center and the glittering goal of the stage. And how different these sleek creatures look from the halfbacks puzzling their way through the ballet in the famous rehearsal photograph taken in White Plains just before the first performance. Dressed in oversized T-shirts, undersized leotards, and crinkly plastic pants designed to sweat out the last ounce of fat, these are the chic offspring of artistic privilege, hurtling with aristocratic ease through the tiny gaps in the ballet's fast-milling crowd of dancers and suddenly falling into perfect ranks again.

A breeze blows through, over the heads of the children who seem to congregate at every studio door in the School, endlessly watching their fellow students at work. The whispered comments are few and surprisingly generous, given the competitive nature of the life they share, a life for which they are selected by audition, bred to dance, then weeded out with gentle ruthlessness. The rooms in which they live that life are functionally spare, lined with barres and mirrors and filled only by a piano in each and a scattering of chairs for visitors, in lieu of the Maryinsky-style observation balcony that Balanchine had hoped to install in each studio. Huge, airy expanses of space yawn open to receive and disgorge the students ninety-six times a week from October through June. Beyond the glass doors that lead to the School, the third-floor hallways are alive with the student dancers, musicians, and actors of the Juilliard School. The everyday existence of the rest of the world seems very far away.

A half hour later, Schorer's rehearsal over and her performers replaced by students, a youngster will rush into Studio 3, as worried a latecomer as the one celebrated in *Serenade* half a century ago. She slips into place at the barre and advances her foot into a tendu with the rest of the class. Muriel Stuart moves toward her. "Wrists," she murmurs, extending her own long, lyrical arms in demonstration. Wrists round softly up and down the line, then stiffen just a little as Stuart coaxes the children to remove their hands from the barre to test their balance in relevé. In another five years, some will be dancing on the stage of the Juilliard Theater downstairs in their graduation Workshop Performance. Some have already danced children's roles with the New York City Ballet. And some will go on, after graduation, to join one of the thirty-five ballet companies around the world that have hired dancers trained at the School during the 1980s, a number of those companies created or directed by men and women who themselves studied at the School.[1] But at this moment, all the energy and purpose of their young lives is focused on achieving an instant of precarious balance, poised on the balls of their feet and straining upward.

Stuart is one of ten ballet teachers on the permanent faculty, which also includes guest teachers from the City Ballet, a gymnastics teacher for the younger boys,[2] two Juilliard music-theory teachers,[3] and two champion ballroom dancers[4] in charge of a pilot course in social dancing. In 1934, the School projected a full course of three years for the training of professional dancers with no previous schooling in ballet. By its fiftieth anniversary, the School offered a training program that could take ten years. The fluctuating twenty-four or so weekly classes of the School's first year has grown in 1984 to ninety-two a week, Mondays through Saturdays, with an additional sixty-seven classes offered during the five-week summer program designed for new students from outside New York, a program that serves as the School's principal source of new talent.

The curriculum for the winter or regular, full-year course is taught and developed in fourteen levels or divisions, all but the graduating classes identified by the color leotard the girls wear. Training starts, at eight to nine years of age, in the First Children's Division or Children I, from which girls are promoted into the next four levels of the Children's Division, or B and C classes. Training ends in the Graduating Division, or D class. Boys and girls aged ten through twelve who have had little or no previous ballet education start at the School in the Preparatory Division or A1 class, which is often also the next step in the training process for boys promoted from Children I. After Children I and II, with the exception of A1, there are separate technique classes for boys and girls, who meet only in classes that require partnering.

Students move from A1 into the First Intermediate or A-2 class, from which the boys progress to the Intermediate Men's class after from one to three years. The students then continue into the Advanced Divisions, which include the C1, C2, and graduating D classes for the girls and the Advanced Men's class. The number of required hours of study increases dramatically, starting with two one-hour classes a week for Children I, and increasing to three ninety-minute classes a week for Children III and A1, four a week for the students of A-2, and five a week for Children V, including an hour of toe each week.

The girls of B2 are expected to take eight lessons a week, including a variations class and two lessons in Intermediate Toe, while the intermediate-level boys are required to take six lessons, which must include a class in supported adagio or partnering. By the Advanced and Graduating Divisions, the minimum is nine lessons, which includes one class a week in partnering for the girls and two for the boys. The students are also expected to take such correlated courses as music theory and gymnastics, the latter for boys from Children I through the A-2 level. They must be prepared, too, to participate in rehearsals for the School's lecture-demonstration, Workshop, and professional performances, if they are chosen.

The summer course offers technique and toe classes on six levels to children from twelve years and up. Only the most advanced division, which is not usually filled, is open to students from the winter course. The 1984 summer program also offered classes for intermediate- and advanced-level boys, character dance, variations for boys and girls, and partnering, taught in 1984 by seven members of the permanent faculty,[5] as well as lectures in dance history and anatomy and the prevention of injury.

Classes spill over from the School to rehearsal studios at the New York State Theater during the winter course. But if its headquarters have come to seem cramped and wanting, the move to the new Juilliard School building in 1969 was an important event in the life of the School during its fourth decade. The Juilliard School is a conservatory complex with six constituents. With its own funding, faculty, and students, the School of American Ballet is the most autonomous of those constituents. It is located in a separate section of the ten-floor building, leased from Juilliard informally as a statutory tenant. The "Romanoff Empire," as a disgruntled member of the Juilliard staff once referred to the School,[6] maintains a discreetly independent and somewhat aristocratic existence behind glass doors that may be locked.

There is a pervasive sense of enclosure to the facility, which includes four studios, nine small offices,[7] two student dressing rooms, changing rooms for the male and female teachers, a minuscule faculty sitting room, and an even smaller shoe room, where students may purchase at a discount dance shoes ordered but not used by members of the City Ballet. One additional, large room serves a multitude of purposes as needed, from office space to music classroom. The School had planned on six studios. "The music room was supposed to be a lounge where students could do their homework," Nathalie Gleboff says. "But they've always done it on the floor in the hallway, anyway." At some point the teachers lost their spacious first lounge, and now occupy what was the file room. "Our filing cabinets are in the hall," Gleboff says with mock despair.

The four studios open onto the ends of a long, U-shaped corridor whose walls are covered with engravings, prints, plaques, and photographs of a variety that suggests most come from the attic holdings of an aesthete with wide interests; indeed, many belong to Lincoln Kirstein. Just inside the glass doors to the School hang paintings by David Langfitt of the studios in recent years, filled with familiar City Ballet dancers watched by George Balanchine and Peter Martins. Created and installed in 1984, they replaced engravings of ten views of old St. Petersburg.

Another face stares sweetly from the end of the next hall, past depictions of opera ballet, prints of a nineteenth-century mime, period views of the theater and architecture of other centuries and places, a few vivid photographs of Balanchine and Kirstein, costume and set sketches, and a proclamation from the New York State Legislature mourning the death of Balanchine. That second gaze belongs to a young dancer in a large and slightly tentative oil portrait. She is Edna von Breyman, a gifted soloist with the American Ballet under the stage name of Annia Breyman, who died of tuberculosis after leaving the company.

The children lolling on the couch below the painting know nothing of her, nor do the young administrative staff members who walk past the portrait every day. "She was a dancer who died of anorexia," one ventures amiably, referring to anorexia nervosa, the psychosomatic disease of self-starvation, which is popularly supposed to afflict all female students at the School and most ballerinas of the 1980s. "She dieted a lot," an older teacher says firmly. "She didn't eat properly."

All is serene bustle in the corridor. A girl hoists her leg up onto the drinking fountain to wet and soften her hard new pink toe shoes. Leaning against a wall, two giggling teen-aged girls flirt with two serious teen-aged boys. A youngster barges into the cubbyhole office of Mari Cornell, one of the School secretaries, to impress her with news of a mathematical discovery he's made at school in abstruse terms she greets with affectionate, teasing approbation. The halls are filled with people waiting for the next class to begin. Small children, neat as straight pins in their dance clothes, play at a safe distance from the slightly haggard parents and patient maids ranged on benches near the door—meek attendants who will be there when the children emerge from the studio after class, ready to be taken home. There is laughter from the offices. The student manning the long reception desk stretches his legs expertly between rings of the telephone, and a small, cheerful accompanist[8] shuffles cards for a game of solitaire. The studios lie beyond, pristine with their gray floors, high windows, and white walls.

Tucked into the back of a labyrinthine series of offices is the impersonal but comfortable little inner sanctum where Lincoln Kirstein works, suffering fools ungladly and worrying about the School's future through most of its moments of success. "A ballet school is the most undemocratic thing there is, and there are three things they have to learn about this one," he once growled, referring to the students at the School of American Ballet. "One is that there's no justice. The second is that they must never complain. The third is that they must shut up."[9]

Walking the halls, Kirstein is an imposing figure who is both the School's moral authority, as one administrator puts it, and a kind of Drosselmeyer to the smallest children. He may stop to congratulate a student, or shoo "the mice," as he refers to the littlest students, away from a studio but then relent and allow them back to watch the class. Accompanying a visitor about the School or staring into a classroom on his own, eyes glittering like an eagle's, Kirstein will pick out some promising student and quietly enumerate her gifts, or gloat over the latest young classicist to join the Special Men's Class.

The offices of Gleboff and Natalie Molostwoff are, on the other hand, accessible and spacious, airy oases at either end of the central block of administrative offices. Stanley Williams may glide in and swoop into a teasing révérence, mid-conference with a board member. Antonina Tumkovsky often bursts in, exploding in a torrent of exclamatory Russian. But little fazes the two administrators, who have been through more at the School than momentary interruptions to their day. Chic, with a languid air that masks a sharp eye for the telling detail, Molostwoff came to the School in 1938, after a job as personal secretary to "a rich young man" suddenly fell through. "He decided to change his way of living," she recalls. "I was a very good friend of Eugenie Ouroussow. We lunched together often. 'If you hear of anything,' I told her, 'I'm desperately in need of a job.' The School needed a replacement, she said. She didn't want me to be disappointed. But at the end of the week I was asked to stay, and my salary was raised from twenty dollars to twenty-five." Possessed of an equally astute eye, Gleboff has a more matronly air and an invincible calm about her. She arrived at the School in 1959, after working with the international Young Men's Christian Association and the American Embassy in Paris, to help with the pilot study for the Ford

Foundation. "Our jobs really have to do with the running of the School," she says. "Whatever needs to be done with students, teachers, and parents. The scheduling of classes. The budget. With the Workshop Performances, we get into scenery and costumes."

The School has the aura of a light-filled cocoon, spun and overseen with an attitude of laissez-faire pragmatism. William Blake's observation that "damn braces, bless relaxes" is a favorite saying of Kirstein's. If blessings are not abundant in the studios of the School of American Ballet, the damns are administered, for the most part, in a tone that implies regret at the unseemliness of warranting damnation. There is the sense of a community of equals, though the line of demarcation is clear between teachers and administration and the students. There are no surrogate parents among the teachers, or even aunts or uncles or older siblings. Both teachers and students are there to work for the common goal of producing dancers.

That work begins with the audition, in which the School selects the most promising new students. General auditions are held at the School in September for admission to the winter course. Auditions for the summer course are held throughout the country. In a holdover from the Ford Foundation days, representatives from the School and the City Ballet travel outside New York each year to conduct auditions in ballet schools, theaters, and universities across the United States and wherever the company is touring abroad. In 1984, twenty-three cities[10] were visited by auditioners who included Karin von Aroldingen, then a teacher at the School and City Ballet principal dancer; Susan Hendl, an assistant ballet mistress at the company; City Ballet principal Heather Watts; and Richard Rapp, a member of the School's permanent faculty.

Auditions are also held at the School on Wednesdays from January through the spring term, jumping to three or four a week in March and April, during spring vacations from academic schools. Out of 1,500 applicants for the 1984 summer course, 198 were accepted, from the United States and six foreign countries. Once accepted, they are assigned to one of the program's divisions on the basis of age and degree of training, in placement auditions held on the first day of the summer course. About 25 percent of the summer students are on full or partial scholarship, a figure that jumps to 33 percent in the winter course, with nearly three-quarters of the advanced-level students on scholarship.

Ten to fifteen students are invited to remain each year for the winter course. The School has six or seven families who board the students, and it recommends residences around the city. Some boys room at the Young Men's Christian Association residence near Lincoln Center. Older students cram into apartments together. Parents may feel their children are just too young to live on their own in New York. "Sometimes the parents are shell-shocked and feel they need another year to think," Gleboff says. With a dormitory, the School will be able to enroll those students at young ages.

"We must have a place for the kids to stay so that we don't lose the best ones," Kirstein says. "All over the country they are being formed. We must de-form them. It takes six to eight years to adapt to what we think is right. The critical ages are twelve to fourteen. We lose a lot of very good kids." During its fiftieth year, the School was involved with Lincoln Center in plans to build a multipurpose facility at the west end of the block on which the Juilliard School stands. The building will be used by constituents of Lincoln Center for rehearsal space, and will include a small film theater, classrooms for Lincoln Center's educational program, additional office space, and dormitories for two to three hundred students at Juilliard and the School of American Ballet. The sale of rights to build residential units above the space claimed by Lincoln Center was expected to help offset the costs of construction. But the School was to raise funds for its own dormitory quarters and to help to buy the site and construct the new building. One reason the School was eager to move to Juilliard was the possibility that such facilities might one day be available. But talk has ceased of the earlier goal of housing a student residence, studios, academic classrooms, offices, and health services for the School under one roof. And the dream of a free, state-supported national ballet academy has faded.

Auditions for the winter course focus on the body rather than any technical skills in the case of children under ten, most of whom are from the New York area. The audition proceeds along the lines of the examination given George Balanchine as a child entering the Imperial School and is comparable to those conducted by the state ballet schools of Europe. Tumkovsky and Helene Dudin, who conduct these auditions, first examine the child's instep to see if it is pliant and shows promise of a good arch. They note the degree to which the children's upper legs are able to turn outward from a natural standing position facing front. "I usually decide right away," Tumkovsky says. "From first sight sometimes. They grow. I'm sorry for them. Sometimes no place to put them. But good surprises."

The proportions of the body are extremely important. "There is no such thing as a 'Balanchine dancer,' " Gleboff says. "We don't care if a child is tall or short, but the proportions have to be good. If the legs are very short, chances are they will remain that way. You can sometimes get the feel of how a child will grow even at eight." The accompanist then begins a march or a waltz and, as Stuart was encouraged by Pavlova to do, the children are asked to move freely in the center of the studio.

"That we really look at carefully, too," Gleboff says. "Someone who doesn't have very good feet or proportions may have such a terrific sense of movement that we decide to try them anyway. And those are ways we look at the students all through their years at the School." An abbreviated ballet class is conducted as an audition for the older children, who are likely to be disqualified by short legs or a short neck, a big head, or heavy thighs. Age and technical level are considered here. Beginners older than twelve years are very rarely accepted. "If they have an extraordinary body, we might take them at thirteen, but even that is pushing it," Gleboff says. "But as long as the children are there at the audition, we do try to go through the whole thing."

Some question the School's emphasis on physique and apparent skill. "The School gets wonderful material," one former teacher says. "But sometimes it collapses. Many of the great dancers had great faults. They fought to do what they wanted. They worked hard. The School takes people who have a facility for dancing. Things often come easily to them. If you're born with an instep, for example, you don't have to work to strengthen your feet. But if you work on them, the feet are much more efficient."

Seven girls and two boys, all teen-agers, have arrived in Studio 1 for an audition, this one for the summer course. Tumkovsky moves around the room as they stand at the barre. Gleboff follows behind her, writing comments in a large record book of the sort attendance is taken in throughout the year. Tumkovsky stretches each leg up as high as it will go, prodding backs and hips, and asking the students to take off outer layers of practice clothes so she can see their bodies more clearly. The girls must point and stretch their feet to the sides and front. The boys simply point theirs. The room is almost silent as the two women move from one student to another, murmuring in Russian as they go.

"Not ideal professional material," Gleboff writes beside the name of one frightened-looking, chubby girl. "Nice extension," she writes beside another name. "A little stocky in hips," "sickling foot," and "pretty body" are other comments. The youngsters move with assurance at the barre through pliés, tendus, ronds de jambe on the ground and in the air, and développés. "Come on, dears," Tumkovsky barks kindly, and the girls move to the center for a glissade-assemblé combination and a variety of small jumps with quick shifts in direction that test coordination, mental agility, and previous training. One tall, thin adolescent soon gives up, her cheeks flushed in embarrassment, and stands shyly in the middle of the studio as the other girls dance on around her. Then the boys move center for their turn, biting their lips and hunching their shoulders as they begin to dance.

Two of the girls are asked to put on toe shoes. One, who has come from Rome for the audition, does not speak English and is mystified at first. She and Tumkovsky communicate in sign language. The two are led through a few steps that test their technique on point and the strength of their feet. The rest stand leaning against the barre, some worried, some relieved. Then Tumkovsky and Gleboff turn away for another murmured conference at the piano. The word "intermediate" starts out from the flow of Russian, and a girl smiles covertly at another. Then Tumkovsky turns to the students. "The lesson is finished," she announces. The studio empties quickly.

One boy and three girls are picked to enter the School next term. One of them is the Italian. A fifth girl will be taken if there is room. "She tries out every year," Gleboff says. "But her body keeps changing. The hips and buttocks keep growing bigger." All will be notified by mail. "There are so many people auditioning now that we can no longer tell them immediately," she explains. "So we send out a form letter, like a college letter. We talk to the foreign students right away, because they must make arrangements to stay or not to stay. And I talk to some of the others. There was a boy, for example, about seventeen, who'd studied only six months and kept auditioning here. He just didn't understand." The School has never charged audition fees, though a charge has been considered. "Mainly to stop people who aren't serious," Molostwoff says. Tuition for the five-week summer course ranged in 1984 from $250 for the first division to $310 for the fourth through sixth or Advanced Divisions. Tuition for the full nine-month winter course started at $525 for the two weekly classes of the First Children's Division and climbed to $1,350 for twelve lessons a week.

The children learn a standard Russian technique rooted in the ballet taught to Balanchine—and Vladimiroff, Oboukhoff, Doubrovska, and Danilova—early in the twentieth century at the Imperial School in St. Petersburg, the cradle of professional ballet in Russia and, by extension, of ballet in the twentieth century, given the pre-eminence of the Russian ballet.

The modifications of Russian technique as taught at the School of American Ballet are those of the Danish, Soviet, and American styles. The Danish school developed by the mid-nineteenth-century choreographer August Bournonville has its effect most clearly, if indirectly, in the teaching of Williams, starting in the School's third decade, and in his settings of Bournonville ballets for Workshop Performances. Tumkovsky and Dudin are exponents of the Soviet style expressed in the system devised and refined in Leningrad by Agrippina Vaganova, from 1921 to her death in 1951.

Vaganova drew on the Soviet stylistic innovations of her own time as well as the teaching of Enrico Cecchetti, whose attention to the head, neck, shoulders, and arms distinguished his classes at the Imperial School during the 1890s. Her codified teaching stressed control and accuracy, and a strong, body-centering back that gave her students a look of poised alertness and enabled them to spring quickly up and move through the air, contributing to the distinctive Soviet look of "space-conquering amplitude of movement," as the Russian ballet historian Natalia Roslavleva describes it.[11] That bold amplitude and appetite for space are features, too, of the American style developed by Balanchine and exemplified in the teaching of the City Ballet generation of faculty members. It is a style marked by a speed and clarity that render vividly legible not only step and gesture, as in the Soviet style, but also the fleeting interstitial moments and the path the dancer travels across the stage. Balanchine may have done away with plot line, but a signature of his American style of classical ballet is its linearity.

The fund of steps and positions unveiled in the first year at the School offers a surprisingly complete foundation that will be built upon up through the Graduating Division. That first year, steps at the barre, the opening segment of the dance class in which the dancer warms up through exercises done with one or both hands holding on to a wooden bar or barre, include demi-plié, rond de jambe on the ground, dégagé, frappé with the foot pointing rather than brushing to the position, and développé. The children learn passé and coupé, and acquire a whole vocabulary of battements alone, including petit and grand battement and battement tendu, tendu jeté, fondu, frappé, soutenu, and relevé, all identified as such to the children. They pivot like small soldiers to such commands as "en face" or "effacé," and know the difference between "en dedans" and "en dehors." There are very simple ports de bras at the barre and in the center, with épaulements stressed at every moment. And the children begin to work on placing the foot "sur le cou de pied," an element in their training that Balanchine stressed, by moving one foot from first position to rest against the ankle of the other. Steps in the center include the sauté, jeté, balancé, échappé, assemblé, glissade, pas de bourrée, temps lié, and changement de pieds. All must be "very clean and very slow," as Balanchine told Tumkovsky. And the class ends with the age-old révérence or bow to the teacher.

By the second year, in Children II, the students are expected to do everything with greater strength. There are more repetitions of steps in more directions, so that steps begin to emerge as elements in a combination or sequence. Tendus, for example, now point to the front, side, and back in one sequence. All five positions of the feet are used. Different steps are put together in combinations for the first time, and the children are given their first, small adagios—combinations of slow and flowing movements intended to develop line and strength. Steps are held, giving the children a clearer sense of the complexities of rhythm and phrasing. The grand plié and rond de jambe en l'air are added to the students' vocabulary, with sissonnes, assemblés, and pas de bourrées now being done to the front and the back. The children also learn the pas de chat, as well as simple emboîtés and a slow pas de basque. Another acquisition is the chassé—"famous step for Children II and III," Tumkovsky says laughingly of a step Balanchine gave the children in each ballet—with a stress on its components of a jump into the ground and a slide. And the children are taught that not only the feet but the arms figure in the steps, and that both must be put together for the proper effect.

Third-year children begin pirouettes and entrechats trois and quatres at the barre. By their seventh year, they will have mastered the entrechat six. Barre combinations are repeated more times and executed with few stops to break the flow. The formal positions of the arms in classical ballet are learned and added to the steps, and center exercises are longer and include more of the steps done at the barre. The ballonné is added to the children's repertory, and the working foot now wraps around the ankle of the standing foot, as prescribed by Balanchine in "sur le cou de pied." "Balanchine cared about the 'sur le cou de pied' position because the way feet leave the floor is very important," Suki Schorer says. "There are two ways the foot can leave the floor: by brushing out, and by picking up. In the right cou de pied, the toes start to wrap around the ankle, which releases the heel and moves it in front of the toes. That shapes the foot and develops a little bit of beveledness. The foot won't sickle. Then, when the student is more advanced, the heel will automatically be presented and the toes start back." This, in turn, also fans the thigh and knee out and back for a correct but often unachieved stance. There are more jumps in Children III, and the students learn to do changements en tournant and piqué turns. Class is now likely to end with a waltz across the floor.

Pirouettes have moved to center in Children IV and are done "en dedans" and "en dehors." Frappés are done with a brush now. The young dancers learn to do failli and tour jeté. There is increasing emphasis on the coupé, as Balanchine demanded. More time is spent working in the center of the studio, away from the supporting barre, and phrasing becomes a little more intricate. By the fifth year, the children are learning brisés, with cabrioles to follow in the Advanced Divisions. Double pirouettes are expected now, though not always required, and work on fouetté turns has begun at the barre. Fewer and fewer steps need to be added to the vocabulary, but steps must be repeated more times and with greater control, in combinations of increasing complexity, a process that continues through the Graduating Division. There are more turns in B1 and bigger jetés in B2. Steps may be acquired sooner or later, depending on the overall level of strength and talent in each year's class, but one thing remains constant: by the Advanced and Graduating Divisions, the slow exercises have gotten slower and the fast ones faster, as the dance writer Nancy Goldner, a former student at the School, put it.[12]

Only 5 percent of the children who begin at the School at the age of eight or nine, in the Children I class, complete the training process. As Kirstein puts it, "Mice become giants, nicely formed eight-year-olds suddenly become monsters."[13] It is nearly impossible to predict the child's physical development at so early an age. "And the children are brought in by their parents and may decide they hate it," Gleboff says. "Or we may realize the child has a nice body but no talent, motivation, or interest."

Children I is, according to Tumkovsky, the hardest of all the classes to teach. "Gelsey knew what we wanted," she recalls, speaking of Gelsey Kirkland. "She was excellent student. There are people who really want to do. But some children are not interested. 'Show me, darling,' I say. 'I don't know,' they say. 'Then for what you came?' I ask. In Children II, they know what it is. They want to dance in *Nutcracker*. To teach them to understand. To study discipline. That they cannot jump when teacher explains something. At first many not like. But afterwards it is all right."

The classroom existence of the mice of Children I seems one of an almost unmitigated drudgery that would test the patience of far more sophisticated older children or adults. Here, two hours a week, Tumkovsky and Dudin lay the foundation on which the children will draw for the rest of their training in classical ballet. Few concessions are made to age and the fact that the classes occur after a day at school. The red leotards that are the required uniform of the girls of Children I—the boys wear white T-shirts and black tights throughout their years at the School—are a deceptive spot of brightness. The frequently unintelligible commands and the French ballet terminology that serves as the medium of communication in the ballet class are delivered in a tone of brisk cheerfulness by Tumkovsky, whose classes are ranged in neat ranks of small bodies, and in a soothing, rushing murmur by Dudin, who seems to gather the children around her from moment to moment like a slightly distant version of the sweet-voiced Glinda in *The Wizard of Oz*. But no attempt is made to palliate the rather grim dose of basic technique with standard beginning ballet games like jumping over imaginary piles of coats.

A plié is not a "knee bend" here, but involves the exact placement of a straight back over the knees and of a rounded arm and a hand upon the barre. Steps are broken into logical components, with the children marking the front, side, and back of the circle described by the foot in a rond de jambe, through which that foot will slide in one smooth action in the years to come. Swaybacked, potbellied little bodies are steadier in the jumps after practicing them first facing the barre. With the polka that takes them coursing across the studio's long diagonal, the children get a small reward in the form of a near skip. But already the girls, at any rate, are conscious of their entry into a special world, eyeing the paunchiest of visitors with hopeful interest—could he or she be a famous dancer?—and affecting a look of blasé world-weariness as the boys are galvanized by a sudden burst of familiar popular music from the accompanist.

The girls will spend the next year in Children II, with the boys usually leaving them to move into the Preparatory Division, or A1 class, a more sophisticated beginners' class for children who have had some ballet classes.[14] One aim of A1 is to clean up mannerisms or counter poor previous training in children with potential. The girls are dressed in regulation black leotards. Many of the wispy little ballerina buns of hair are adorned with crocheted snoods and sprigs of artificial flowers. But a slightly more humane atmosphere prevails here among these students, whose preclass conversation is often a little less studiously bright, and who occasionally must keep a babysitting eye on younger siblings lounging quietly at the side.

Many of the children will not move into the School's more advanced classes, but that is not reflected in the teaching. "Let's put a little more juice into it," Elise Reiman calls out as she talks the students through a barre combination.[15] From time to time she asks them to identify a step. Small and slight but sturdy-looking, Reiman is dressed for the day's class in slacks, a jersey top, and soft ballet slippers, with the bangs she has worn since the 1930s parted like sleeves rolled up for work. She walks the length of the barre, adjusting a wrist, a head, or a foot as she goes. Basics are stressed here, as they are throughout the students' training. "The most important thing is to stand well," Reiman tells the children of A1. "Pull yourselves up. Chin up, shoulders down, and tight fanny."

The barre and center combinations are faster and more strenuous than those of the Children I class[16] and are comparable to what is being taught to the students in Children III. Balanchine tenets are consciously addressed. "Let's have a round hand, girls and Timothy," Reiman instructs the one boy and eleven girls in the class, coaxing fingers to become unglued and separated, and hands like small flags in a stiff wind to relax into an open curve. "Bolder," she tells a girl as the children do single pirouettes in the center. She corrects another student's épaulement, tilting the child's cheek up toward the light in a port de bras. "Like someone kissing you?" the girl inquires. "Did you hear that or did you think of it?" Reiman responds, once the exercise is finished, her usual matter-of-factness softened by surprise. "Because that's what Mr. Balanchine said."

The first year's confusion of details, whose resolution makes for a dancer's look of superior coordination, starts to be absorbed a little more readily in Children II.[17] The students are beginning to acquire more of the physical control that will mark them as dancers. By Children III,[18] when students are required to take three classes a week, a look of greater discipline marks the girls, who now wear pink leotards with their pink tights and ballet slippers. They may loll a little against the barre, whisper, scratch themselves, and point out a cockroach scurrying across the floor when Dudin turns to work with someone else.[19] But those are the only lapses of attention among these ten- and eleven-year-olds. Mere alertness is a given now. Her cap of black hair fluffed firmly into place, dressed in a neat navy skirt and leotard with pink T-strap shoes and a pearl necklace, Dudin is a tiny, firm figure of adulthood in that sea of small bodies. Feet, head, carriage, and épaulement are still focal points for correction as Dudin moves from child to child at the barre, touching faces and patting heads or taking all the children in with a single gaze as they stand center, listening to her rapid instructions.

"Very quiet, very clean," she murmurs as the children begin six free-standing ronds de jambe à terre or on the ground, their arms held low. An entrechat quatre facing the barre is achieved with a good deal of energetic thumping and a gentle admonition or two from Dudin about neat finishes. Then the combinations—which grow as complicated as a sequence of sissonnes, assemblés, and changements—are repeated in the center. The exercises have become only a little longer, and the combinations only slightly more complex. But Children III is almost more demanding psychologically than the first year's work.

Dancing is still by rote and slow, with very few moments when the children are given a chance to feel pretty or consciously challenged, as in the waltzing pas de bourrées en tournant near the end of class. But there is a sense of the glories to come. One girl whips off a wobbly triple pirouette that ends in an improbable arabesque penché when Dudin isn't looking, a conspiratorial smile on the child's face as her eyes meet those of her neighbor at the barre. Dudin herself grasps one girl's leg and raises it a good twelve inches higher in an extension at the barre, giving the child an idea of possibilities. And next year, the children know, they will be allowed to take the last fifteen minutes of Children IV in glistening pink toe shoes. That was a rite of passage that concerned Balanchine, who designed a special shoe for them. Built and distributed by Capezio, the "Balanchine shoe" was created with a box softer than those of ordinary point shoes and less likely to bruise the young toes of the students who have worn them in Children IV.

There is a continual emphasis at the School on feet, particularly their degree of turnout and pliancy, and the neatness of the fifth position. The girls of Children IV,[20] now graduated to moss-green leotards, learn quickly and will go on learning, in the separate, hour-long Toe I classes to come,[21] that the foot must be as flexible in its boxed and pointed shoe as it is in a soft ballet slipper. Turnout and a pliable arch must be developed. The feet must not jerk up on point, however expert that may feel, but must roll up onto the toes, as if joint by joint, passing through the demi-pointe or ball of the foot as deliberately as the younger students pass through a tendu on their way into a grand battement. It is a lesson they will continue absorbing through Toe II and III, for without that knowledge and skill the girls will not be able to work on point with the ease demanded for the brisk, acute footwork of Balanchine ballets. At his suggestion, students are required to take all ballet classes from the Second Intermediate Division or B level on in point shoes, at first soft or old, but hard by C2 classes.

The girls of Children V[22] and A-2[23] take class together once a week in the elementary toe class, which is required for the first group and taken on the teachers' recommendation by students in the latter group. Four technique lessons a week are required by the Children V and A-2 level. Here the training has become more analytical, with the students expected to present the steps with an understanding of why and how the details are to be accomplished with precision. Classroom exercises stress such refinements as rhythmic accent and the dynamics of sustaining the energy of a step, as, for example, in the accent out of the frappé or the fast rise and slow but vital fall of a leg in a grand battement.

At each level the students are exposed to more than one teacher, and by Children V they are being taught by four teachers with different bodies, ways of teaching, and ideas of what must be emphasized. The most analytical of these is Stuart,[24] whose class is a blend of poetic example and crisp English determination charged with kindliness. Here the children learn about such things as musical phrasing, soft landings, and making the most of their ports de bras.

The girls of Children V have survived to the brink of notable advancement into the Second Intermediate Division, and are proud and more realistically ambitious. On the verge, too, of full adolescence, they sit about the floor of Studio 3, late in the darkening afternoon, tickling one another and making earrings of their barrettes, like giggling younger versions of the girl in Jerome Robbins's *Afternoon of a Faun.* Their raspberry-colored leotards are pulled open across their strong, slightly plump backs. The School allows the students to wear leg warmers and other extra layers of practice clothing, though they must be peeled off for the center work. But these children do not wear leg warmers here, even at the barre, possibly the better to savor the long, tapering line of their legs in newly acquired toe shoes, which several of the girls are wearing for class.

Dressed in a navy leotard and skirt, a red scarf tied around her long neck and dark, laced-up soft ballet shoes on her feet, Stuart moves through their midst with splendid dignity. Her bearing is imperious, the arc of her torso and arms suggesting what a fluid performer she must have been. Her back is erect at all moments. At eighty-one she is still able to demonstrate a well-turned grand battement. "Let's go," she commands softly at the end of each demonstration. She strides across the classroom to tilt a head or round an arm, and often reminds the children to pull up their stomachs and buttocks and drop their shoulders, for a poised but easy look.

Small, fleeting corrections will suddenly offer a key to solid achievement. Stuart suggests a minor adjustment to the free arm in a relevé at the barre, bringing it a little forward of the body. "That makes it easier," she says plainly, and, trying it, the student achieves a firm balance. "Go through both feet into demi-plié," Stuart says, still working with the girls on their relevés. "Be careful to center the weight on the foot first. Don't go way over on the joint of the big toe." No "stiff rods" for arms, she tells them as they work in the center, tension visible in their shoulders and arms, and brought to their attention. "Darling child," Stuart exclaims as one girl, her back tilting behind her, starts to fall a little out of a développé combination. "Don't stand that way. And let me see a nice passé."

Simplicity is another key to the look Stuart tries to get from her dancers. "Don't do everything fifty times badly," she counsels a child who pushes herself through multiple turns in a pirouette combination. "Better to do it two times well." Another girl stumbles. "Never mind," Stuart calls out, and the child rights herself, smiles, and keeps on dancing. At one point, Stuart grabs the hands of two children near her and, as the others fall into a long single line outward, begins to dance with her charges, moving forward with them at the same time she keeps a stern eye on all. But it is almost time for the class to end. Stuart pulls away and looks at them appraisingly for a moment. "Come along," she says briskly, "because I know you're going to enjoy this."

They do, for it is a long combination of small jumps with quick-changing épaulements that takes them across the floor in an exhilarating sweep. They race back to start again, but she claps her hands to signal that time is up. A groan rises, then the children encircle her. "Please, could we have fouettés?" they beg. "Please?" Stuart shakes her head but finally relents, and the children wrap their arms around her in a hug, suddenly babyish for a moment. They begin the turns, which are not a frequent feature of classes at the School, and Stuart becomes sternly methodical once more.

Danilova is as formidable in her way.[25] Her classes are won with promotion into the Second Intermediate[26] and Advanced[27] Divisions. Now, at last, the girls are within reach of their goal, the stage. What they do in class—whether exercises, partnering, or dances or variations from actual ballets—may be interrupted and repeated just as often as the little steps performed by the youngest children. Like musicians, dancers learn their craft by repetition. But whereas the youngest may dream of "being" Suzanne Farrell or Patricia McBride, the girls of the Second Intermediate and Advanced Divisions can see themselves on stage as they dance across the classroom.

From the B1 class on, Danilova teaches technique and, in the advanced classes, variations from the classical repertory. (Dances from the Balanchine repertory are taught in Schorer's variations classes.) Her back a little hunched and her gait occasionally hesitant, Danilova is nonetheless a magical creature, with her coiffed hair, bits of glittering jewelry, and brightly colored chiffon skirts, leotards, and pumps. She is eighty, but her arms and still-slender, beautifully shaped legs recall the photographs taken of her in the Ballet Russe, as she demonstrates a classroom exercise with suggestive wit and grandeur.

Musicality and attention to details of style are hallmarks of Danilova's class, whether at the barre or in the center, where she often gives variations or repertory dances instead of the academic combinations that are the stuff of most ballet classes. It is as if a window has been opened to let a little breeze and sunlight in, once students have passed successfully through the dull fire of the beginning and early-intermediate classes, with their laborious insistence on the careful implanting of basics.

Students give in at their peril, even briefly, to inattention or sloppiness in Danilova's classes. Reproachful reprimands are quick to come in her celebrated English. "Why such a miserable leg?" she calls to one girl who beats a leg feebly against the other in a cabriole. Danilova is also a merciless, though not unkind, mimic. "Ahem: I hope you don't walk on street like that," she says, strolling with her head turned back in imitation of another girl's bourrée forward, eyes fixed on the receding mirror. "Or on stage. All kinds of trees. You bump head."

Finishing lessons of another sort are given in the social-dancing class, initiated by Martins in 1984 and taught by Pierre Dulaine and Yvonne Marceau, with the idea of alternating it each year with a class in character dancing. The social-dancing class is the envy of the School's administrators, who have been known to whirl down the hall arm in arm to strains of waltz music coming from Studio 2. "We wanted one of our own, but Peter said we'd have to take the class with the students," one says wistfully. "Balanchine always wanted social dancing," Peter Martins, a competition ballroom dancer in his childhood, explains. "It's an enormous help, and not just with the waltz ballets."

In traditional classical ballet, he says, the male dancer spends most of his time standing behind the ballerina, but not in the Balanchine repertory. "There's much more dancing, and a lot of it has to do with facing the girls. Social dancing has a lot to do with that, too: awareness of partner, how you treat your partner, how you hold and face a woman. The boys must learn how to take charge. The girls must look vulnerable and be able to be totally at the mercy of the boys." Martins knew Marceau and Dulaine, who operate a ballroom dancing school in New Jersey. "I told them, 'Let me look at what you'd teach.' Then I danced with Yvonne just to make sure we were talking about the same thing. And already the students look a little better."

The learning process is laborious, however, with the young dancers looking at ease only in the stylized tango. No tour jeté was ever so hard, it seems, as a simple change of direction in the Viennese waltz. No fouetté could ever have been so mind-boggling as learning to dance on the entire sole of the foot. For one thing, the thrust of the weight is down, in direct opposition to the upward accent of the body in ballet. "Muscles working toward the floor," Dulaine calls out. "Relax into the floor. Work with gravity. And take two steps to cover eight yards. Ladies, you can get up on your toes. That is hard for Joe in the street. What's hard for you is not to go high onto your feet. And, gentlemen, feel the natural weight of your partner."

Some of the girls have let down their long hair and put on little short, flowered wisps of chiffon skirts. Somehow they look waiflike and vulnerable out of their ordinary practice clothes. One boy, the School's most gifted Advanced Division classical dancer, asks intent and probing questions of Dulaine about the reasons for several of the ballroom-dancing conventions. But most of the couples have the look of people at the controls of a jet plane for the first time in their lives. "Oh, shit," a boy groans as he steps squarely on his partner's foot.

Danilova watches it all from a chair in the studio doorway, during a pause between classes, whispering animatedly in Russian with one of the accompanists. There is little doubt from the glint in her eyes and the pianist's muffled giggles that choice comments are being made and relished about the class or its dapper leader. Later, absorbed in an interview, she loses track of the hour until muffled scratches and whispers are heard at the door to the teachers' sitting room, where her B1 students have sought her out.

Classes tend to start late at the School, but Danilova carries off tardiness with panache. She moves through the door quickly, then sails down the corridor. Bowing slightly to the right and left, she enters the studio like a queen. "Sorry to be late," she says, pausing a little suspensefully. "But I was interviewed by *New York Times*." The children's obedient, teasing "ooh"s, "aah"s, and applause float out the classroom door. The girls fetch her the chair she seldom uses during class, for she prefers to move with them, eyes fixed on her charges, or to lean against the barre.

"I don't like when people stay like soldiers," Danilova says of her pupils. "I see they relax because they understand better. I think we work very hard but have good time." One of her favorite School rituals occurs on April Fool's Day, when, as if by unspoken agreement, some of the intermediate and advanced children may engage in little jokes. "Once all had witch hair," Danilova recalls. "Like young branches in hair. B1 dressed like Mickey Mouse with long tail. So I make them hold the tail at barre. Another time I come into class with nose and mustache like Marx Brothers. 'OK, girls, plié,' I say. They look at me. They couldn't believe. No one did anything last year. I was sort of disappointed. But then C2 squatted down in preparation for manège. I was very pleased. It is nice to be children."

Through the B1 level, the students may be full-time children. Classes begin at 4:00 P.M., at the end of the regular school day, though some take more than the required number of classes. Ballet training can still be sustained as a simple adolescent passion, with its satisfying degree of physical activity, attention to the self, and calming and claiming discipline. But with promotion into B2, these fourteen- and fifteen-year-olds must make a decision that will affect their entire adult lives. The technical level increases dramatically, as does the number of required classes, adding up to a minimum of eleven hours weekly in the studio.

The girls begin classes at 2:30 P.M. By the C1 or next level they must arrive at the School at 10:30 A.M., and may not leave before 6:30 or 7:00 P.M. At the Russian or European state ballet schools the children board from an early age and so become used to a sequestered life in pursuit of narrow vocational goals. The children of the School of American Ballet lead some semblance of the life of a "normal" American child, with school friends, family, and casual, after-school pursuits, at the same time they are competing for a continuing place in the rarefied professional atmosphere of the School.

The School has long fed visibly into the City Ballet, and now into other ballet companies. Its goals are clear. With entry into B2, the choice must be made to devote the greater part of daily life to training for the ballet, with no guarantee the student will ever make it to the stage. An academic school, often New York's private Professional Children's School, must be found that will accommodate itself to such special hours. Sometimes the entire family moves to New York for the sake of the child's possible career in dance. The pressures of so life-determining a choice at such an early age are intense.

Those pressures make themselves felt in many ways. At the School, there are occasional minor contretemps with Juilliard personnel. Autocracy and arrogance are evident in some of the older students. But in the classroom the students are expected to display good manners to other students and to the teachers and support one another there with touching spontaneity and only an occasional hint, from the very talented, of noblesse oblige. Applause from fellow students for a well-executed combination in class is a not infrequent response.

Such behavior is encouraged, for, as Kirstein puts it, ballet is about how to behave.[28] A girl falls in a variations class taught by Danilova. "Do again right away," she tells the student. "Are you hurt?" Embarrassed, the girl shakes her head a little tentatively. Danilova moves to the girl's side and strokes and kneads the thigh and hip she fell on. The other students giggle. "Well," Danilova says, turning on them, "there is not one person who has not fallen here." The girl goes through the combination once again for Danilova, by herself, and dances it strongly and with inspiration, ending with an obvious thrill of pleasure at her accomplishment. The others cheer. "Something about falling," Danilova muses. "When you do next time, you do well."

Danilova describes the students as "very nice." "We teach them to be," she says. "If one girl in front all time, we put in back. They learn next time. Not long ago, slippery floor. One girl fell. Many pick her up and carry her." She mentions the ballet *La Sylphide*, in which a sylph goes into death throes, her wings dropping off, and is carried off by her companion spirits. "Six girls here. Like sylphs. So touching. They pick her up and carry her, like sylph with lost wings. One girl to go get ice. Very sweet." Told of this anecdote, a less generous observer of the School laughs. "One less dancer to get into the company," he says.

Getting into the New York City Ballet is a goal. And in May,

at the end of the winter course, there are always talented graduating students who are not invited to join the company. "Is she
still with Peter?" Schorer asks a group of girls sitting on the couch
in front of the reception desk. They are absorbed in making lists
of the Entenmann's cakes they are about to buy for a party that
afternoon, on the last day of the term, but not so absorbed they
have forgotten that Peter Martins and a graduating student are
engaged in a crucial career-planning conversation around the corner. Schorer has just emerged from a rehearsal for a lecture-
demonstration performance of Balanchine's *The Steadfast Tin
Soldier*. Work never seems to be over at the School, whose students often find part-time employment as fashion and commercial models and performers with the City Ballet, approved companies requesting their services, and the lecture-demonstration and
performing series presented by the School under the auspices of
the New York City Ballet Education Department at schools in the
tristate area. The girls nod worriedly. Schorer shakes her head,
concerned about the student, whose dreaming, introverted style
does not make her a good candidate for City Ballet. She has been
asked to join another leading ballet company, but her heart is set
on City Ballet.

Some students quit dancing if they do not make it into "The
Company." Others join other companies and leave them, discon-
tented, after a year or two. And some who are taken into City
Ballet cannot stand what is, after the first excitement, an exacting
demotion. Gifted regional students often find themselves starting
all over in the classrooms of the School of American Ballet, acclaimed at home but frightened and not even sure of what is expected of them here. In the same way, the girl and boy who danced
the leading Workshop roles tend to find themselves lowly members of the corps de ballet, where there is much, suddenly, to be
learned and unlearned, and where advancement may be a numb-
ing matter of years if it occurs at all.

Peter Martins was named chairman of the School faculty during Balanchine's last illness. In addition, he is ballet master in chief

of the City Ballet, a position he shares with Jerome Robbins. It is difficult to juggle both jobs, and Martins was hard put in 1984, the first full school year after Balanchine's death, to squeeze three weeks of concentrated teaching of advanced classes into his schedule. "The only way you really know the kids is when you teach," he says. "And I like to know them before they get into the company. But I haven't been able to set up a schedule at the School this year. I run over whenever I have free hours. I talk to Stanley over the phone all the time. I think I'll have more time and things will be less frantic as the company settles in, in the years to come. I can't use this year as a criterion."

One of the hardest tasks facing Martins is the talks with the students. Twenty minutes after Schorer's anxious question, Martins emerges from the quiet spot in a hallway at the back of the School, where he has been talking with the girl. "You want to hide," he says later. "I have gone through this with a lot of the graduating kids. I like and care for them. But you can't just be kind and take everybody into the company. We have to make sure the dancers we take are better than the last ones we took. Otherwise how can we keep or raise the company's standards? And sometimes I decide that it would be best for a student to remain in the School another six months. I talk with a few of the teachers. The transition into the company, where you rehearse all day long, can be tough after intense, rigid schooling. Sometimes that extra six months or year in the School is something the student can never get back. It's not that he'll stop learning in the company. But it's important he doesn't just get ripped away. I remember being seventeen, eighteen, too. If someone had taught me facts as that person saw them, it would have been a help."

VII. APPROACHING THE STAGE

The "facts" can be harsh. In the old days, before the 1963 Ford Foundation grant, the School could not afford to be as selective as it is today, and students could stay on as older and older preprofessionals. Children were sometimes asked to leave, or it was suggested to parents that their offspring might be happier elsewhere. That job occasionally fell to Muriel Stuart in her early years at the School. "I think Ouroussow thought of me because I spoke English, and she may have felt I could treat it in a nice way," Stuart says. "You can't just say a child has no talent, so you make it more of a suggestion. You say that possibly the child might take drama, or some other thing." Such conversations were a duty Diana Adams dreaded, despite her reputation for sternness. Now it is often Nathalie Gleboff who informs parents that the School does not consider their children professional material.

"Actually, I'm only a spokesman for the teachers," Gleboff says. "And ninety percent of the time the teachers agree. We always try to bend backward on the positive side. If even one teacher disagrees, we certainly keep the child." Aside from the natural weeding-out that occurs in the earliest years of training, often as much a matter of the children's waning interest as of their aptitude, the level at which most children drop out or are asked to leave is between the B1 and B2 classes. "By that time the child is thirteen or fourteen and the teachers feel they have a good idea of the student's potential," Gleboff says.

The smaller and more difficult the classes, the greater the sense of competition—with girls and boys with whom each day is spent. Often the competition is internalized. The eye continually checking the body and its line in the omnipresent mirror is usually more critical than admiring. In almost every advanced class, there are one or two gifted dancers whose drawn faces and tight bodies reflect a handicapping drive toward some unreachable perfection. There have been occasional emotional breakdowns, though these tend to occur after a student enters City Ballet.

The struggle can drive the young dancer into anorexia nervosa or bulimia, eating disorders to which, with amenorrhea, women dancers and dance students have been somewhat more prone than the general female population. Thinness can seem a more manageable and enhancing goal than artistic excellence. "I am sure at certain levels it must go on," Gleboff says, a few days after she has seen to it that a doctor's scale donated to the School has been moved into an obscure corner away from the students. "It's difficult to catch behind the scenes. The worst are the little ones, the eight-year-olds who tell their parents they can't eat dinner because they must be thin for the School of American Ballet. In terms of medical anorexia, there have been two cases in my years here. One was a child who apparently was having tremendous psychological problems at home. Some suddenly decide they are too heavy and start losing a tremendous amount of weight each week. They become bags of bones. I see it, or teachers come and tell me. There is a communal spirit here." In such cases, Gleboff will speak with the child, or talk with parents if the child is under eighteen or a student from outside New York.

Sometimes the unspoken concern reaches beyond the graduating class. Gleboff speaks of an apprentice dancer in the New York City Ballet who has been "on my mind." "She still kind of belongs to us, and we worry about her. So I've talked to some people in the company like Heather Watts and Joe Duell and asked them to talk to her." Contact with parents is immediate when a student from out of town, boarding in New York, starts to have behavior problems or miss class. "We are very careful about attendance," Gleboff says. "We don't want the children wandering around New York. Sometimes we'll call and ask the parents to take them home." Occasionally teachers have alerted parents to unsuspected physical problems in their children. And the School offers free office visits once a week with William G. Hamilton, M.D., orthopedic consultant to the School and City Ballet. The children also sneak over to the New York State Theater to visit Marika Molnar, officially physical therapist to the City Ballet dancers alone.

The teachers attempt, on the whole, to maintain a discreet distance between themselves and the students. "I think there has to be a separation," Kay Mazzo says. "I want what's right for them. But sometimes I think I get too involved. I don't want them to feel that I'm there as an Ann Landers." But a sharp watch is kept on the students, though they may not be aware of that. "I keep track of all students," Tumkovsky says. "I ask other teachers. When in company, finished. But in School they pay attention very much. No one will take them if they gain. But have to tell children to eat, too, sometimes. Cornell and Molo tell them."

Injuries are a dreaded fact of life at the School, as they are in every dancer's life. "I need to make an appointment with the doctor as soon as possible," a teen-aged boy says patiently but firmly, standing carefully at the pay phone near the reception desk. "No, you don't understand. I have a stress fracture in my leg. I can't walk. And I have to dance." The older students are expected to use their own, adult discretion about injuries once they have been examined by a doctor. "I've hurt my calf," a boy explains, sitting at the sides watching the last half of his advanced-intermediate

Above: Children pay special attention to the tendu from their earliest years at the School of American Ballet. *Photo: Carolyn George*

Below: GEORGE BALANCHINE demonstrates the all-important tendu in class, 1962. *Photo: Henri Cartier-Bresson*

Above: A young hand curls into a neatly rounded shape in a children's class at the School of American Ballet. *Photo: Ernst Haas*

Below: Girls take class in point shoes from the Second Intermediate Division on at the School of American Ballet, in order to adjust to moving easily and quickly on their toes. *Photo: Ernst Haas*

JACQUES D'AMBOISE remembers that there were only three other little boys in class when he began his studies at the School of American Ballet in the 1940s. Due in part to the popularity of American-born and America-trained male star dancers such as d'Amboise and his classmate, Edward Villella, there is more interest today in ballet training for boys. In 1984, the School offered twenty-three classes a week for its sixty male students. Here, in 1982, three boys jump, feet well pointed. *Photo: Paul Kolnik*

Linda Merrill (later MERRILL ASHLEY), GELSEY KIRKLAND, and COL-
LEEN NEARY in "Precious Stones" from *The Sleeping Beauty,* staged by Alexandra
Danilova in 1967 for the School of American Ballet's first full Workshop Performance.
Photo: Martha Swope

Master of the plotless
ballet, George Balan-
chine has said that
Michel Fokine's *Chopin-
iana* (reworked and
later retitled *Les Syl-
phides*) made him real-
ize that ballets need not
have plots. Alexandra
Danilova and Frederic
Franklin staged the bal-
let for the School's 1982
Workshop Performances.
Deidre Neal is the soloist.
Photo: Michael Leonard

Left: MARIANNA TCHERKASSKY and FERNANDO BUJONES, left, foreground, as student performers in August Bournonville's *Konservatoriet,* staged by Stanley Williams for the School of American Ballet's 1970 Workshop Performances. In 1984 they were principal dancers with American Ballet Theatre. *Photo: Martha Swope*

Below: HEATHER WATTS, far right, in 1984 a principal dancer with the New York City Ballet, performs in *Konservatoriet* in the 1970 Workshop. *Photo: Martha Swope*

Above: The corps de ballet in "Grand Pas Espagnol" from *Paquita,* staged by Alexandra Danilova for the School of American Ballet's 1974 Workshop Performances. Note Maria Calegari, fourth from left, and Kyra Nichols, second from right, principal dancers with the New York City Ballet in 1984, and Toni Bentley, first on left, in 1984 a corps dancer with the New York City Ballet and the author of *Winter Season. Photo: Martha Swope*

Opposite, above: JOSEPH DUELL and LESLIE BROWN in George Balanchine's *Concerto Barocco,* staged by Suki Schorer for the School of American Ballet's 1975 Workshop Performances. Duell subsequently joined the New York City Ballet, where he was a principal dancer in 1984. Brown joined American Ballet Theatre and was a soloist (as Leslie Browne) in the company in 1984. *Photo: Martha Swope*

Opposite, below: Jerome Robbins's *Dances at a Gathering,* staged by Sara Leland for the School of American Ballet's 1977 Workshop Performances. Note Patrick Bissell, a principal dancer with American Ballet Theatre in 1984, in the foreground. *Photo: Susan Cook*

The ensemble in Joseph Duell's *Jubilee,* created for the School of American Ballet's 1980 Workshop Performances. This was a first ballet by Duell, one of several company members to choreograph for the School. *Photo: Carolyn George*

PETER MARTINS and JOCK SOTO, a soloist with the New York City Ballet in 1984, rehearse for Martins's *The Magic Flute,* created for the School's 1981 Workshop Performances. The ballet later became part of the City Ballet repertory, where it was danced by Soto, then a company member, and included students in its cast. *Photo: Steven Caras*

JOHN TARAS rehearses ZIPPORA KARZ for Act III of *The Sleeping Beauty,* staged by Alexandra Danilova and Taras for the School's 1984 Workshop Performances. Karz joined the New York City Ballet and was a corps de ballet dancer in 1984. *Photo: Paul Kolnik*

A moment of anxiety before an audition at the School of American Ballet for children's roles in a New York City Ballet production. *Photo: Carolyn George*

DAVID RICHARDSON, the School of American Ballet's first children's ballet master, auditions children for *The Nutcracker* in 1980. *Photo: Carolyn George*

ALBERTA GRANT and ELIOT FELD in the New York City Ballet's first production of *The Nutcracker*, in 1954, choreographed by George Balanchine. It was this popular hit that brought the School of American Ballet to the public eye. *Photo: Frederick Melton*

GEORGE BALANCHINE teaches the art of stage swordplay to a child from the School of American Ballet in a rehearsal of Balanchine's *Don Quixote,* which he created for the New York City Ballet in 1965. Balanchine appeared in the title role several times. *Photo: Martha Swope*

The small creatures of Oberon's kingdom, played by the children of the School of American Ballet, in *A Midsummer Night's Dream*, created for the New York City Ballet by George Balanchine in 1962. *Photo: Martha Swope*

A host of little Pulcinellas storm the pot in the spaghetti orgy in *Pulcinella*, created for the 1972 Stravinsky Festival by George Balanchine and Jerome Robbins. Balanchine, as a Beggar, is in the center of the fray. *Photo: Martha Swope*

JEROME ROBBINS, as the Ringmaster, with three of the forty-eight children from the School of American Ballet who completed the cast of Robbins's *Circus Polka*, performed in the 1972 Stravinsky Festival. *Photo: Martha Swope*

JOCK SOTO, a member of the New York City Ballet, dances Peter Martins's *The Magic Flute* on the stage of the New York State Theater with two children from the School of American Ballet. *Photo: Paul Kolnik*

Children from the School of American Ballet, first two rows, and members of the New York City Ballet, behind them, in the "Garland Dance" from *The Sleeping Beauty*, in *Tempo di Valse*, created by George Balanchine for the City Ballet's Tchaikovsky Festival in 1981. *Photo: Paul Kolnik*

Three years later, in 1984, students from the School of American Ballet help Lincoln Kirstein blow out the candles on a birthday cake onstage at the New York State Theater, after a performance of "Garland Dance" at a gala celebrating the School's fiftieth anniversary. Standing at the back are, from left, Philip S. Winterer, chairman of the School's board of directors, Bess Myerson, Commissioner of Cultural Affairs in New York City, Matilda Cuomo, representing her husband, Mario Cuomo, Governor of New York State, and Mrs. Sid R. Bass, chairman of the School's Fiftieth Anniversary Campaign. *Photo: Paul Kolnik*

LINCOLN KIRSTEIN watches students in a classroom at
the School of American Ballet as the School approaches its
fiftieth anniversary. *Photo: Paul Kolnik*

class. "I have tendinitis. The doctor said to go back little by little, and the School lets you decide. But the School likes you to watch class while you're injured. And you can learn a lot by watching. But it's depressing."

Some students are unable to cope with that depression and, aware of time lost from class, push themselves physically in the time-honored way of dancers. "You miss so many," Alexandra Danilova says to a girl in B2 who has waffled through a barre combination with repeated relevés. "What is the matter?" The girl admits she has a sore foot. "Yes, but where?" Danilova asks, examining the foot. She tells the student not to go on half toe for the rest of the class. Two combinations later, however, the girl is wobbling covertly on the ball of the injured foot. The School reinforces that internalized press of goals with strict discipline. "No, it's too late," Sinikka Finn, a member of the administrative staff, hisses at a student as she checks attendance during an intermediate class. The girl remonstrates with her in an agitated whisper, but the roll taker turns on her heel and walks out, leaving the student to continue class abstractedly. A sterner judgment than any rebuff comes with the advancement of one's fellow students.

There have been times when the obvious talent or quality of a student galvanized the School, as was the case with Allegra Kent when she arrived as a scholarship student at the age of fourteen, in 1952, a year before Balanchine invited her to join the company. Vladimiroff and Oboukhoff were feverish with excitement. "Everyone knew," Molostwoff recalls. "It changes the atmosphere very much. Miss Stuart was exalted. It was immediate with Allegra. Or Suzanne. Or Darci." Most often the School's only open acknowledgment of special talent comes with grade skipping. "Darci didn't seem to be the talent of the century when she came to us at eleven," one staff member says dispassionately of Darci Kistler, widely seen as the last of Balanchine's hand-picked ballerinas. "But she was so strong we decided to put her right into the fourth group."

Such outdistancing tends to occur in small but noticeable increments. There are the few C1 students who are given roles in the Workshop Performances. Some are asked to demonstrate when visitors peer into a Variations Class. Others are invited to join the Special Men's Class or perform with the School's lecture-demonstration groups, a program that has been in effect for twelve years at the School and is directed by Suki Schorer. "They want the most talented," Gleboff says of the fifty to sixty performances a year, most of which take place at public schools, danced on the School's portable floor. "But conditions are sometimes rough. There may be cement floors. And some talented students we want to protect. They may not be strong enough, or they may be injury-prone." Then there are the early moves into choice roles in Workshop Performances, for which rehearsals begin, in Schorer's case, as early as November. It is, in a way, fitting preparation for the harsh realities of a dancer's life, and it starts early at the School, where children learn about survival of the fittest with their first auditions for *The Nutcracker*.

"The way you got a role in *Nutcracker* was if the costume fit," one former student, enrolled in the children's classes in the mid-1950s, recalls. "They assumed you could do the steps. But the mothers were so competitive. I remember one year I was supposed to dance a polichinelle, but a mother grabbed the costume from me. My mother worked. She didn't come to the School. The trauma of standing there, not knowing what to do! And I remember one ten-year-old girl who played the lead in *Nutcracker*. The mothers used to say that her mother dyed the girl's hair blond, and that the reason she got the role was that her mother slept with Mr. Balanchine.

"I didn't learn how to survive, because dancing didn't matter enough to me. At SAB, the only word out of anyone's mouth was 'dance.' But I'm glad I was there. It was fantastic training, and I got something from the experience of being a kid from the Bronx in such a concentrated world. Tumkovsky's legs, everyone said, had been broken by the Nazis. All those little ladies with big books. The dancers, who were so nice to us. Wilde, Hayden, Tallchief.

They'd sign their toe shoes for us. Eglevsky would pick us up and play with us. We got to watch them put on their makeup. But the only time I really liked the School was when there were articles written about us. My fifth-grade teacher suddenly liked me, I remember, because she read about us in *Life*."

"Are you casting a ballet?" a knowing ten-year-old asks, edging surreptitiously over to a visitor taking quiet notes during a children's class. "I don't know why I stay," a teen-ager weeps to a friend in the girls' dressing room, behind doors covered with messages and notices, where she has retreated mid-class.[1] "I had to begin all over again," an edgy adolescent says of her first year in the School as an advanced transfer student. She sighs: so much precious time was lost. "It took me a year just to figure out what they wanted here." She had been good enough to perform frequently with her home-town civic ballet, but here there was to be no performing to sweeten the dose of basics studied with dancers who seemed far better than she. Is the School breeding ground for neuroses? "Neuroses?" Kirstein once responded. "It's a nightmare. And the terrible maniacs, they're the angels, the ones who make it as dancers."[2]

From B2 on, however, the students begin to draw more consciously on their teachers' personalities and the traditions they represent, from Dudin's gentle firmness to the poetry of Stuart's bearing to Reiman's matter-of-fact attack on the vocabulary of classical ballet as filtered through Balanchine's American style. "Suki's class is slow, so you can work by yourself and also incorporate what she says," a youngster comments. "You can feel yourself improving. She won't let you get ahead until the simple things are perfected. She's very technical. Tumey gives you a lot of everything. She's funny, and hard, and you have to move in her class. For Rapp, you have to have a good mind. He gives strange combinations. You have to think. Krammy is so cheerful. He doesn't correct that much, but he's good for pirouettes if you can do them his way, which is staying up before you come down. Williams is very musical. His accents are different. Danilova expects everything to be light and airy. You have to know every-thing already. She won't tell you not to forget to point your toes."

"Pull up," Danilova says to the eighteen dancers, dressed in navy-blue leotards, in her B2 class. She still prods errant arms and legs into graceful lines, but now she gives more emphasis to ver-bal tips and instructions. "God give you two arms—use it!" she exclaims, as a girl's port de bras wilts with the growing complex-ity of a variation from *Raymonda*. ("Such a big ballet," Danilova says lovingly of the work, created by Marius Petipa in 1898 and produced by Danilova and Balanchine in a shortened version for the Ballet Russe de Monte Carlo. "So many beautiful variations. That one teach them to *walk*.") Grab a spot in space to fix on, she reminds the girls—"but not in the mirror!"—and their ara-besques will be steadier in long balances. There is a look here of students beginning to test themselves, rather than to rely on their teacher for challenges. Don't let ambitions go until they bless you, the teachers seem to be saying by this point, as the dance writer Mindy Aloff observed.[3] And Danilova reinforces independent thought. "Practice your memory," she says. "Learn it when the teacher show it to you." And practice in the head as well as at the edge of the studio. "Some people need it, to go through it in your mind."

With the end of the barre comes a moment of frivolity sur-prising to anyone familiar with the routine of classes at the School. "All right," Danilova calls, "jambe à la main, s'il vous plaît." The girls stretch up their legs into vertical splits, at a full 180-degree opening, slide into horizontal splits along the floor, then lunge into a standing position in a single, graceful sweep. They move on without a pause into a circle in the center of the studio, then swoop into a bow and suddenly swoop up again and raise their arms above their heads, snapping their fingers gaily. "One day they were being silly," Danilova explains. "I did. They liked. So exercise stayed." She curtseys back to the students at the end of class. "Amazing girls," she comments as she leaves class, half to an observer and half for the sake of the students themselves. "Aren't they good? Very good class."

"I think I pay a lot of attention on placement," Danilova says of her teaching. "On the balance. To be able to stay on one leg. Sustain. Then I stress ports de bras. Rhythm. It's difficult to say for oneself. You like to do everything. As I say, you have to see what your class need. Where really weak. Class is sometimes weak on développé. The leg doesn't go high enough. Make stretching and special. Work on that and then go on."

Stressing performance values and style as she does, Danilova gives variations in all her classes, starting with B1 or the youngest of her students right through the Graduating Division. Center work begins in this B2 class, for instance, with a minuet from *Raymonda* that is one of two variations she gives this age group. A matter of presentation, the dance is clearly a favorite among the students. Its balancés and bourrées give the girls a chance to feel confident enough in the relative simplicity of its choreography to let go and expand a little, becoming more consciously themselves as they learn and savor the feeling of going beyond the conscious execution of steps and gestures, as performers must.

In the three years to come between B2 and graduation, they will become imbued with that sensation in the variations class.[4] "They can express themselves there," Danilova says of the class. "And it also gives them stamina. In class you do this, this, then rest. In Variations, you start and have to do until you finish. We want them performing. Straight exercises are for technique. But when they come on stage, they have to perform and interpret the mood of the variation and what they are."

Are they ready for "the killer"? Danilova asks a C1 variations class. "Straightaway the killer?" Cries of "yes" and "no" rise up in equal strength. And so the students warm up on an easier dance from *Paquita*, in which most of her corrections have to do with line and elegance of presentation. They then move on to the killer, also from *Paquita*, whose surviving Petipa choreography was restaged by Danilova for the Ballet Russe de Monte Carlo. This variation demands quick, subtle changes in direction and quick beats and jumps, all to unfold proudly in one smooth filament of dance. The students cannot pause in confusion or right themselves for fear of collision. With repetition of such dances, both the hallmarks and the niceties of differing styles become ingrained and burnish all their dancing.

From time to time, Danilova stops the students, demonstrating in such a way that the full, dramatic shapes of the upper body, the footwork, and the rhythmic accent are all indicated in a few stiffish steps and gestures. The girls watch carefully, then begin to move. In several, Danilova seems suddenly to have bloomed in these teen-aged dancers. She is averse to displays of acrobatics and sheer pyrotechnics. But these are the dancers of the 1980s, the products of Balanchine's experiments in space. "Part of dancing is also to put the movement on stage," Danilova calls to one undersized amazon. "Two steps and you are off."

Outside and down the hallway, Stacy Caddell works a new pair of toe shoes into a softness she can dance in by poking them into the crack behind a door, then pulling the door laboriously shut on them. In a few minutes she will begin working on passages from Jerome Robbins's *The Goldberg Variations,* which she will perform later in the week at City Ballet. Girls from C2 cluster around the door to the studio, watching her as she rehearses. Five years ago, Caddell was a student in that class. In the girls' dressing room, students in their early teens pin together their fashionably slit leotards. ("Your mother buy and you cut," Danilova will cluck at them another day. "You have beautiful back. But do not need to cut so low. I even see your tights. You want me to see your tights?") They slip into the loose-fitting tops that are popular this year, and fluff their bangs. They are ready for class.

The older girls of C1, waiting quietly one morning for their teacher to arrive, look considerably more sober in their black leotards and crisp pink toe shoes. They are almost at attention as they lean against the barre, and require very little adjustment to stand up tall and straight as Tumkovsky speeds in, ready with a little joke about oversleeping.⁵ "What!" she exclaims in mock horror, pointing to a student nursing a sore ankle at the side. "Yes, rest," she adds. She tells one of the students to check the thermometer on one wall of the overheated studio. "It's eighty-five degrees," the girl calls back. "What?" Tumkovsky says. "Beach!" Then she turns back to the class. "One, tuh," she commands, ready for action in her black sweater and skirt and pink T-strap shoes, her blond hair swept into a small bun. And the class begins.

If Danilova adds color to the curriculum, Tumkovsky reinforces it with steel. John Clifford referred to Tumkovsky, his favorite teacher at the School, as "the most demanding, the toughest, the strongest."⁶ A more recent pupil describes her as the "most Russian" of the teachers. "Danilova is logical and really into music," she says. "Tumey is technical. Sometimes she makes the kids feel like they can't do anything. Not often. But the people who do well in this class are those with a lot of natural ability. And you need stamina and technique for it."

The class builds that stamina and technique. Combinations are spit out in a mix of Russian, French, and English that at first sounds harsh. Tumkovsky is hawk-eyed, somehow noting mistakes that occur behind her back and across the studio. But there is a glint of humor in her scrutiny of legs moving fast through tendus, heels barely skimming the floor, of grands battements, and of ronds de jambe at the barre. She takes hold of a foot and bends it into an exaggerated arch to give the student a sense of stretch. Sweat begins to pour from foreheads and necks, and there is hard breathing from a few tense and wide-eyed students right from the start.

Exact in her specifications of what each step in a sequence should and shouldn't be, Tumkovsky reels out demanding combination after combination in the center. The otherwise indistinguishable student who does the quick jumps and beats most cleanly, her body pulled up more than all the rest, is one of the few survivors of early children's classes at the School. A young Korean girl springs like a flea. Covert looks at the extreme arches of a Hispanic student, most evident in the entrechats six and little changements that follow big tours jetés across the floor to end the class, signal that these are "the feet" of the class and the object of some envy. Fellow students are objects of appraisal, in the way of dancers. But then, after the strain of combinations that involve held counts and abrupt, long balances in arabesque and attitude, a chorus of high-pitched voices cry out, "Thank you, Tumey," as class comes to an end.

"I want them very correct," Tumkovsky says of her students. "Every step they must understand what doing. Not just copy. Like moving. In the first children's class, when I give them polka, they must *move* nicely. Not 'one-two.' Dance has to be pretty, nice, elegant. That's hard to teach. For the advanced, what is important is technique, turns, jumps, beats. They have to know absolutely everything. Like in Russia. How to be on stage, how to bow, how to move. They are not machines. They must move. And be elegant. I also pay attention very much to arms. Technique is in the legs. With the arms and back, you present yourself." She springs from her chair in the teachers' lounge and mimes a stern tendu and rich and sweeping port de bras.

If Tumkovsky sends her students plunging deftly into space, a D class with Mazzo can be a process of cleaning and tidying loose ends.[7] Of a young professional level, these students must work on finishing their dancing. Dressed severely in a black leotard and black teaching skirt, a pair of small pearl earrings accentuating the neat contours of her small head, and a simple gold chain about her neck, Mazzo walks calmly into the midst of the dancing students to correct, adjust, or point out a good example to the others, without a trace of theatrics. Her mimicry of incorrect placement or execution of a step is more briskly illustrative than funny. Her instructions are explicit, talking of the position of the hips in a balance at the barre, or the placement of the heels in ronds de jambe. "The important thing is to have the leg straight," she says of one exercise with small, quick frappés. Then she demonstrates the sounds of the foot hitting the floor correctly and incorrectly. "Like a seesaw," Mazzo says of a swing-back of the leg in one barre combination. "Pull up. Don't sit on your leg." "Don't forget the demi-plié when you pirouette. No cheating. No skimping."

City Ballet dancers are allowed to take the D class, and three corps members and a soloist are scattered throughout the classroom, as well as one of the School's most gifted advanced boys. There is no attempt made by the professionals to stand at the front of the class, as there is in many ballet schools: this is the students' time. But Mazzo pays equal attention to all, suggesting changes in the placement of one corps dancer's arms for a pirouette in center, but including all in her suggestions about a clearer cast of the head as the épaulement changes in a simple tendu combination. "Nice and crisp," Mazzo stresses as the class moves through a flowing, lyrical exercise that ends in a luxuriant arabesque penché. A deceptively simple soutenu and pirouette combination has her insisting that greater attention be paid to working through the foot. But the neatly constructed class offers a chance to let loose with series of whipping multiple piqué turns across the floor in each direction, big jumps, and a space-covering waltz combination.

"I liked teaching when I was in the company," Mazzo recalls of her eighteen-year career with the City Ballet, which she left as a principal dancer in 1980. "I taught a few company classes. Mr. B. knew I had a very great interest, and he wanted me to teach at the School when I was performing. But there was no way I could do it. It was too hard. I've never been able to juggle things easily. I have to be there, wherever I'm at." She stopped dancing to have a baby, then found she couldn't come back. "Mr. B. said, 'OK, then, the School.' And actually I was missing dancing." She started by watching the children's classes but, like most other company members, had no interest in teaching them. "What do you give an eight-year-old?" Mazzo asks. "How do you begin? How can you be sure you're not hurting them?" When another teacher fell ill, Mazzo was asked to teach an older class. "Thank

God," she says. "It takes great patience to teach the children." She substituted for a year, then joined the permanent faculty in 1982 and began to be assigned classes of her own.

"I start with the bottom," Mazzo says of her teaching. "Good, pointed, correct, neat feet. A straight supporting leg. The very basics, and just about everything." Her look and approach remind Jacques d'Amboise of Kyra Blanc. "Neat and precise, like filigree," he says of both. As a recent principal with City Ballet, Mazzo finds herself being asked for advice on getting into the company. She understands the pull the students feel. "I started out in a small neighborhood school in Chicago. When I was nine, there was an audition for supers for *The Nutcracker*, which City Ballet was performing in Chicago. Three thousand auditioned, and I got in. Maria Tallchief and André Eglevsky danced. City Ballet was where I wanted to be. I lied and said I was eleven when I auditioned for the summer course at the School. I'd never even done certain steps. But at that time they took everyone into the School. After the next summer, they suggested I stay. But I was just in seventh grade, so my family moved here." At fifteen, in 1961, Mazzo was invited to tour with Robbins's Ballets: U.S.A., and the following year she joined City Ballet. "I don't think I realized what I was doing when I was at the School. It was just something you loved. Now that I'm older and teaching, I'm so impressed with how the students work and with their dedication."

If Mazzo brings an air of serene ordinariness to the classroom, Richard Rapp is so low-keyed and recognizably mortal as to seem, at first, exotic in comparison to his fellow teachers.[8] He is dressed in neat, nondescript fatigues of the sort office workers wear to work on days off. His voice is even, and quiet. "Those were such good tendus the sun is shining," he tells twelve boys in an intermediate men's class as the sun suddenly breaks through for a moment after four days of torrential rains.[9] The feet in this class are outstandingly supple and neatly placed. His own, as he demonstrates, are almost prehensile in their arch. Like Mazzo,

Rapp works on essentials, demonstrating combinations with a straightforward lack of flourish. It is a simplicity he expects from the students, too, telling one tall and long-haired preener in the class in certain terms that his leg is much too high in the extensions at the barre.

Rapp's combinations may be thought-provoking and sometimes tricky, but his hints are explicit. Concentrating on the toe and knee should help with the turnout of the leg in one step, he advises. Analysis tends to concentrate on the physical sensation of a step done right, and is often delivered in homely imagery. "Squeeze the toothpaste out of the tube," he suggests, trying to make clear the look and sensation of a leg stretching out in a développé at the barre. "Pie crust," he nods to one boy whose foot is slurring through the directions of a tendu exercise. The glissade, he suggests in one center combination, should be "like a hiccup." "But don't turn it into a sissonne," he adds. "You still have to slide." There is a good deal less self-scrutiny in the mirror here than in the girl's classes, and some of the boys go through the center work as if in a void. "You know the way they carry out the tray of corn on the cob in those big backyard barbecues at home?" Rapp asks suddenly. "Well, present yourselves."

His workmanlike approach, betrayed from time to time by an almost imperceptible, wry ghost of a smile, is particularly suitable for an adagio class in which he must guide the girls of C1 and the boys from the Intermediate and Advanced Men's Classes through the intricacies of partnering. In adagio class, too, it seems, the student has returned to basics, and it can be awkward going. Ballet has been up to this point a matter of individual effort and advancement. Now the young dancers must rely on one another, a lesson some performers never learn comfortably, although a ballet that requires no partnering is an anomaly. Lifts and ballet falls are impossible to do alone. A good partner can immeasurably enhance a ballerina's line and balance, and if he is very good he makes it seem as if she is doing it all without more than the slightest flick of support. Sometimes, rarely but excitingly, two performers are so well matched physically, temperamentally, and artistically that they dance as one. But it starts in a classroom.

It begins, in Rapp's class, with a simple walk together onto the floor and ends with a fast-moving combination of quick, sharp supported turns, stylized plunges, and high, floating lifts. A girl's step across the boy's body requires a shift in weight that is subtler but just as difficult to get as the shift involved when the boy must later catch her as she falls low into his arms. "How do you get the girl's arm *around* in promenade?" one puzzled boy asks as he and his partner end in a tangle of limbs.

Some of the girls tower over the boys when they rise up on point, though with a constant changing of couples, amazons get to be partnered occasionally by tall boys and petite girls by boys who haven't yet reached their full growth. The shortness and slightness of some of the best recent male graduates has limited their choice of partners in City Ballet. In the adagio classes here at the School, such considerations of weight and height are not attended to, and the small boys lift the large girls with the merest shaking of the knees to suggest strain. Sometimes, too, a step feels easier without a partner. But Rapp is unyielding. "Help her," he insists. "But careful with her points. Put her down lightly. And, girls, jump into that jeté. Follow your toe." If the boys and girls have looked forward to the class as their first real chance to be together at the School, there is no sign of it in the serious, occasionally grimacing faces.

A native of Milwaukee, Rapp trained in the Middle West and enrolled at the School in 1954, joining City Ballet in 1956 and rising to the position of soloist before he left the company and joined the School's permanent faculty in 1972. "I'd always wanted to teach," he recalls. "It was in the back of my mind. I started teaching at the School a few years before I retired from City Ballet. Eglevsky was sick and someone asked me to fill in for the summer and teach the Intermediate and Advanced Men's Classes." There was only one men's class a week in his first year as a student at the School. "I started with Doubrovska, then studied with Tumkovsky, Vladimiroff, and Oboukhoff."

Stuart was a favorite teacher. "She was teaching boys and girls then. She was a marvelous teacher and a great person to talk to when you felt a little unsure of yourself as a student. One of the nicest people." Eglevsky's classes were also influential. "He had a fantastic knowledge and range of knowledge of ballet technique. But you had to grab it. He was a little remote. But he gave wonderful combinations and steps and a very logically developed class."

Like choreographers, some teachers prepare classes in advance and others develop them as they go along. Rapp belongs to the latter group, but there is one element of the curriculum that he stresses in all his classes. "You have to get the basic technique correct, but I'm interested in better ports de bras, for men, especially. That's often thought to be unimportant, or is left out. But you can't do a double tour with your finger in your ear. It completes a dancer so much more when the arms are coordinated with the rest of the body and don't fight with what it's doing."

Rapp, Williams, and Kramarevsky share the teaching of the men's classes, embodying, in their very different styles, the School's philosophy of varied paths to a common end. "I teach basically Russian method, and take from my teachers in West," Kramarevsky says.[10] A member of the permanent faculty since 1976, the former Bolshoi Ballet principal had seen the City Ballet in Russia and came to the School two weeks after he'd arrived in New York. All he had as evidence of his former employment was a statue of himself dancing: none of his papers had survived.

"They said nothing available. But maybe once in a while teach." Kramarevsky was called soon after, when Martins was unable to teach a scheduled class at the School. "Phone call that night. Balanchine interested to see." Balanchine watched his second class but left early. Kramarevsky encountered him in the dressing room after class. "He tell me, 'I have been looking forty years for someone to teach like you,' " Kramarevsky recalls.

"It is an interesting story," Molostwoff says. "We were looking for a male teacher—Mr. Balanchine had the idea we needed
another—but there was no rush." Kramarevsky had asked to watch
a men's class at the School, and arrived with an interpreter. Kirstein came by to watch the same class and, fascinated by Kramarevsky's story, introduced the Russian dancer to Molostwoff.
As the conversation ended, it was discovered that the visitors'
leather coats had been stolen. "The School replaced them, of
course," Molostwoff says. Kirstein spoke to Balanchine, who
suggested Kramarevsky give a trial class. He asked Colleen Neary,
then a City Ballet soloist and teacher at the School, to inspect the
class. "She gave a glowing report, and Balanchine and Robbins
watched another class." Formed in the expressive and virile
"Moscow style" developed by Vassily Tikhomirov, like Balanchine
a pupil of Pavel Gerdt, and Asaf Messerer, Kramarevsky was the
"lion," as Balanchine put it, who would wake up his well-be-
haved American student dancers.

Kramarevsky's aim is to produce dancers who can perform in
any company. "Prepare for any styles. If I teach Russian, style
very narrow. For Bolshoi. I watch many, many kinds of teachers.
Take best principles. Every teacher has some good principles. Even
bad teacher has one moment. I take. Maybe a little transforma-
tion. Some Bolshoi, some Bournonville. Combine and transform,
and I try to teach my lovely students." Like Vladimiroff and
Oboukhoff, Kramarevsky has a shaky command of English. His
young son, Alexander, a former student at the School and a
promising young ballet choreographer who dances in musical
theater, often serves as an interpreter. But his father hasn't the
patience to wait for the translation. Words burst out in much the
same way as dance does from Kramarevsky and his students in
classes that are designed to make the dancers move, and move
with energy and stamina. Trained at the Bolshoi Ballet school,
Kramarevsky disliked taking class, though he occasionally taught
the Bolshoi's company class. But he loved performing, and later

tried everything from classical ballet to circus acts while touring with a concert group in the mid-1960s in the Soviet Union.

Kramarevsky's Special Men's Class is a standard though demanding one, with virtuosic combinations that require the physical strength to sustain flowing dynamic changes, while attending all the while to precise footwork. The Special Men's Class was created in 1982 by Balanchine, who chose the first students. The School had begun to develop a separate men's program in the 1960s. In 1984, sixty boys were enrolled in the winter course and fifty-one in the summer course. Taught by Kramarevsky and Williams, the Special Class is open now to promising male students between fourteen and eighteen on the advice of their teachers. So far the problem of jealousy has not been overriding, as was the case with the earlier Special Women's Class, though there is much wistful questioning of teachers by boys not in the class. In the wake of internationally celebrated male stars like Rudolf Nureyev and Mikhail Baryshnikov, dancing has become less frowned upon as a profession for men. More boys are auditioning for the School, some equipped with ambitious ballet parents, and young male students are no longer welcomed unconditionally. But ballet is still a far less competitive and crowded profession for men.

The emphasis in Kramarevsky's sessions is on expansive movement and technically challenging steps and combinations. But in the end it is his exuberant personality and gusto that give the class its distinctive flavor. Kramarevsky's net shirt, dark-green nylon trousers, and leather sandals set him off immediately from the crisply attired Rapp and Williams. A dancer who specialized in character roles, Kramarevsky has a face whose expressions shift wildly in mood from moment to moment. Leaning against the piano as the boys work through the first, warming-up exercises at the barre, he watches them, eyes filled with the brooding look sometimes caught by the camera in Vaslav Nijinsky's face. His eyes glitter with interest as he and the pianist engage in animated Russian conversation while she plays, a conversation briefly interrupted when he waves an arm or fingers at the boys, signaling a new exercise each time they finish. He speaks comparatively little to the class. For these are, after all, the preliminaries to the dancing that will follow. He combs his fringe of hair, wanders to the barre, and stretches a sandaled foot, singing brokenly with the music in a guttural hum. He eases into a chair in an earthy squat, absent-mindedly stroking one arm with the other, powerfully, to demonstrate the look he wants in a développé.

Oddly enough, the cheerful roars that issue from him most often during the center combinations have to do with curbing or restraining motion. "Slow . . . sl-o-o-ow, yah, yes!" he yells as the students arch into arabesques. "Eh-lah-stic, very deli-cat movement, yes," he croons as the boys launch into pirouettes in arabesque in a combination that requires extreme physical control. "Arms beautiful." But there is to be no timid or complacent dancing here. "One more time, last time," he calls out after a long series of pirouettes in second position. "Also one more time, last time," he adds again as they finish. The boys begin to laugh with Kramarevsky. He grins at a girl watching from the door but doesn't miss some scrappy sauts de basque across the floor. "Arms open while jump," he roars. "And too much. Too fast. SLOWLY!"

Some of the boys may be seen in Williams's[11] Advanced Men's Class,[12] but there they might be dancing on the surface of the moon. Williams comes closest to being the School's guru, working with company members in need of special corrective attention, and drawing noted dancers from outside the School and company to his classes. There is little demonstration of combinations in the class. His students seem to know what is required of them and the steps flow out in a mostly steady stream. "People ask me what it is I teach, and I don't know," Williams says softly. "It isn't a style. It's just what I see and hear."

The finely detailed footwork and ballon or buoyancy suggest the influence of Bournonville. "I give Bournonville steps for the boys at the end of class once in a while. There are some wonderful steps. But I never insist on putting things any certain way. It is for the students to discover and *feel*. You can see when they feel it. Of course, a teacher has to know what he's doing. But it is a discovery for the students themselves. It depends on their own minds, on their musicality."

He has noticed an overlay of mannerisms in some students who start late at the School. "A way has been put into them that is not them. It has nothing to do with the reality. It's almost phony. You can't say anything. They believe deeply. You have to wait. But you give them, and little by little you see the body just absorb. What's bad just goes." Williams was asked to teach when he was twenty-one, while a dancer with the Royal Danish Ballet. There, as at the School and the City Ballet, his teaching was slightly controversial. "There have been people who hated my class. They felt I exposed people, took their clothes off. But I don't care who people are. I have a certain purpose with every step."

There are a few teasing, murmured exclamations of "uh-oh" as Williams walks quietly into the classroom, dressed simply in a khaki shirt, gray trousers, and white shoes, with pipe in hand. The boys end their preparatory push-ups and stretches and move to the barre. Darci Kistler, a protégée of Williams, shifts her place in a corner so that she can more easily watch the class. The music begins, and there is an immediate sense of soft, velvety flow. A little sad-eyed and deliberate, Williams almost involuntarily softens into a demi-plié in the center of the studio as the boys begin theirs at the barre. His arms rise and spread slightly to the sides in a characteristic gesture that calls to mind an unusually elegant Petrouchka perched from the pegs of his puppet booth. Williams speaks so quietly as to be nearly inaudible. But the students know the class routine by heart, moving from one exercise to another in one long ripple of music, with sudden brief bursts of jazzy syncopation to accompany frequent brushings of the feet.

There is a pause for stretching, halfway through the long barre, and a student slips over to the door for a quick kiss and some whispered conversation with the girl watching him in class. Then the barre begins again, with continuing attention to the feet. In the center, Williams moves with the students, pouring like cream into an attitude turn. "You're holding, you see," he tells one boy who's having trouble. "You can't move."

The combination that follows, while typically understated, has the look of contrariness of the children's game of rubbing the belly while patting the head, as the feet flick through staccato tendus and the arms flow through ports de bras. "Never stop," Williams advises a student. "If you think about what comes next it's all gone." His corrections are few but succinct. They are hints whose precise acuity befits the limited palette of movement he gives the students. Here pirouettes are from fifth position and the jumps very small, neat ones with changing épaulements. It is a shock to see a very young and promising boy working his way through the technical complexities of sustaining Williams's combinations of jumps and beats coming forward across the floor—then hulk to the other side of the room as if on his way to football practice, or at least a marble-shoot.

The sudden appearance at the end of the class of Robert Irving, music director of the City Ballet, is also surprising. Towering over Williams, Irving is dressed in colorfully mussed clothes that end in an exclamation point of bright-green track shoes. Typically, he is in boomingly magnanimous spirits. He has arrived for a rehearsal of "Aurora's Wedding," which will be presented in two weeks at the Workshop Performance and which he will conduct. Students begin to fill Studio 3, where Schorer has rehearsed *Serenade*. Danilova and John Taras have staged this version of excerpts from *The Sleeping Beauty*, and they soon join Irving at the front of the studio. Three weeks remain till the performances. The pianist begins Tchaikovsky's gracious third-act music, with Irving beating time as the students move to the center of the studio and dance before the four adults, students in other casts dancing behind them like shadows.

"Big attitude," Taras calls. "Show your attitude." He and Irving trade wry comments. Perched at the barre, Danilova silently scrutinizes the students: their legs and feet, their hands, their torsos;

how Petipa's rich elegance informs their young bodies; and how they bow after their variations. She applauds for each. "Well, we hope applause," she says. "I will be in audience." Two of the ballet's fairy attendants wave covertly at each other from arabesques penchés at opposite sides of the studio.

Familiar classroom faces have become attached to aristocratic bodies and manners. A pale, rather primly nondescript girl suddenly and convincingly assumes nobility, poised while the pianist begins the familiar opening bars of Aurora's entrance music. "Do you know," Irving suddenly exclaims, "that's not in the score!" Intrigued, he studies the pages of music spread out before him. "I put it in," the pianist says. "The orchestra usually does." A chorus of "We did it that way" rises from Danilova and Taras in support of the accompanist. How did the music get to be rewritten? "I think it was Diaghilev who started it," Danilova says. An almost palpable sense of history hangs over the studio for a moment. Then, "No hoppety-hop," Danilova calls briskly out to a student practicing at the side, and it is back to the business of rehearsing for the Workshop.

With rehearsal four times a week, "the Workshop" takes on a nearly physical presence for the last five months of the school term. And the sense of occasion is great when the performances at last are near. "You going to all three?" a small, wiry man known only as Charlie, the School's unofficial mascot, asks a visitor as she passes by his post near the reception desk. "It's different casts, you know." One Aurora will become injured and will not dance. One or two Aurora's fairies will succumb to nerves but rally, at one performance or another. But at last the days come when the audience is met. "Aurora's Wedding" is pronounced charming. *Serenade* sweeps to a crisp, well-received climax. Williams's staging of excerpts from Bournonville's *Napoli* gives some promising younger dancers a chance to prove their mettle. All are greeted with tumultuous cheers and applause.

There are congratulatory telegrams from President Ronald Reagan and Mario Cuomo, governor of the state of New York, marking the School's fiftieth anniversary. A message from Edward Koch, mayor of New York City, somehow went unread at an earlier benefit for the School at the State Theater. His words are read here in a curtain speech by Philip S. Winterer, chairman of the School's board, who clearly savors the mayor's reference to the School as a "source of great pride to the city" and an institution that has enhanced the city's status as an international center of culture.

The greatest excitement comes from the students thronged with City Ballet dancers at the sides and back of the theater. Rudolf Nureyev is in the audience. A typically glum Kirstein and impassive Martins disappear unobtrusively during intermission, as board members greet and visit with one another. Dressed in elegant evening wear, Stuart and Reiman are transformed into distinguished stars as they move regally through the final night's gala audience, handed on by student ushers who suddenly look very young and innocent. Parents, balletomanes, critics, and company scouts jam the theater.

The critics will write of the program as "a touchstone of pure classicism, linking both the nineteenth-century classical traditions of Marius Petipa and August Bournonville with George Balanchine's twentieth-century Neo-Classicism," in the words of Anna Kisselgoff in *The New York Times*. "Suki Schorer's mounting of 'Serenade' was splendid, one of her best Balanchine stagings, showing off a flawless, poignantly youthful corps," Kisselgoff continued. "Mr. Taras did wonders with a mazurka, and Miss Danilova's ability to imbue all with the most refined classicism was breathtaking. There was an air of porcelain delicacy but also human warmth in each variation. . . . Stanley Williams's staging of the pas de six and tarantella from 'Napoli' is as spirited and meticulous as ever, although the dancers seem to be having more difficulty with the Bournonville 'style' every year."[13]

The day after the benefactors' closing gala party at the School, there are small traces of merriment in the studios where the party had been held. Some of the older girls sport thin red ribbons from party decorations on their ankles at the barre in Danilova's class. And a small boy stares, mesmerized as he bends and straightens at the barre, at a red party jelly bean that has rolled unnoticed into a crack in the studio floor. A few balloons float throughout the School. A gang of "mice" heave their ballet slippers and dance bags at one clinging to the high ceiling of the studio where their class is about to begin, then plead with a passing visitor to pull it down for them. "Oh, how beautiful! What is this? Somebody's heart?" Danilova cries, as a heart-shaped silver balloon wafts mysteriously through the door into Studio 4, then rises as she teaches.

She and Tumkovsky engage in desultory conversation at the reception desk—greeting, praising, consoling, and gently scolding Workshop performers as they drift by on their way to class. The girls kiss Danilova and hug Tumkovsky, who demonstrates a step for the benefit of a student who feels he performed it wrong the night before. "They should have a holiday today," Schorer says. And Mazzo congratulates the students before starting class. "You all should be so proud of yourselves," she says. "You looked so beautiful yesterday." The girls seem pleased, but moments later they are immersed in the intricacies of their daily barre. In the dressing room, two younger girls chat about the Workshop weekend. "I gained two pounds Sunday and four yesterday," one says cheerfully. "Will they do *Concerto Barocco* or *Stars and Stripes* at next year's Workshop?" her friend asks. "Suki says *Stars and Stripes*," the first girl answers. And they break into a high-kicking passage from the ballet, skirting benches, lockers, and piles of strewn clothing, singing the score at the top of their lungs.

There is little feeling of anticlimax. By the last day of the term, however, the air is flaccid and talk muted along the corridors. Graduating students who have gotten into companies are congratulated by younger dancers, and two new City Ballet apprentices discuss a rehearsal schedule with studied nonchalance.

Two days later, the nakedly hopeful children they once were will flood the School's halls and studios once more, this time for the summer course. Mothers and a few fathers will hover at the fringes. The mothers arrange their daughters' hair and smooth wrinkles from their leotards and practice skirts. Two fathers, one Japanese and one American, talk of summer homes and the rigors children of all nationalities face adjusting to the different atmosphere and demands of yet another ballet school.

During the summer, parents are allowed to watch class each day, and mothers cluster in the studio doorways, sitting and standing. One penetrates to the center of the classroom as the students wait for the teacher to arrive. She snaps away as her young daughter poses with slightly grim alacrity, swinging into tortured 180-degree extensions for the camera. Two other mothers discuss attractive stage names for their thirteen-year-old daughters. In its earliest days the School advertised itself as being an academy for American students. But the regular winter-course enrollment represents eight foreign countries as well as twenty-eight states, and foreign students are well represented in the summer session. "How long takes to fly from Turkey?" one of the School's Russian accompanists asks a pretty Turkish student. The girl giggles in incomprehension, then answers in halting English.

Baby carriages throng the hallways, and toddlers are barely restrained from plunging into the studios where their older siblings are taking class. The teachers thread their way obliviously through the clamor, past the line of students waiting anxiously at Gleboff's office, and toward the studio. "Tumey," a young woman says a little hesitantly. "Do you remember me?" Tumkovsky smiles broadly. "How are you?" she asks, smoothing back the former student's bangs. "I didn't recognize you!" They talk of others in the woman's class at the School. "I'm married now," she tells Tumkovsky, who exclaims proudly over this news. "And I'm teaching on Long Island. One of my students is in this class." She points to a beanpole clad in pink, who smiles back shyly. "I taught her just the way you taught me."

This year the summer students will attend lectures on anatomy and the prevention of injury, and on the history of dance. It has been a long time since the School attempted such ancillary activities. In the past, there were sporadic, mostly unsuccessful, attempts to coax them to theaters and museums. "I don't believe in it very much," Kirstein says. "We are interested in making professional dancers, not in turning out well-rounded gentlefolk. By law we must fulfill the truancy laws. But there is no more reason to teach the kids academic subjects than there is for West Pointers to learn art history. They aren't interested. They're very directed and limited. The idea of a well-rounded ballet student is not important. And it is the temperament of dancers that they don't require a great deal of intellectual stimulation." Young dancers tend to agree with him. "Dancers aren't dumb, but I'm afraid most of us have very one-track minds," Barbara Seibert, a thoughtful young graduate of the School and a City Ballet corps dancer in the late 1970s, explained.[14] "I don't miss the news if I don't hear it. I don't really care, because it doesn't affect us. You always hear things in the end."

Some worry about such blindered concentration. "In a way, it's a shame," Taras says. "I think it's a pity that they don't get involved with other things. A dancer's life is so short. You can't just train them for stage appearances. They must be able to go on and do something else. It's a great tragedy now. There are so few who do. There is that concentration on legs and feet and body, and the dancers are trained very well. But I'm not sure if the head is that well trained. Lincoln often tried things out. I think he gets discouraged. It takes an awful lot of energy, planning, and durability. You have to collar the students."

Some of the older summer pupils who have studied previously at the School treat the dance-history lectures as a recreation period, chatting and laughing as slides flash by in the auditorium of the New York Public Library at Lincoln Center, which housed a comprehensive exhibition on the School's history in 1983. A few boys ask thoughtful questions, but it is only when the lectures reach the ballet of their own time that the students become fully engaged. There are cheers as pictures of their teachers as performers appear on the screen. Roars of laughter greet the rehearsal photograph of the first performers of *Serenade*. And there are sad little intakes of breath as Balanchine and Kirstein are shown toasting Stravinsky together before the golden curtain of the State Theater.

"There is one country we have neglected so far," Robert Greskovic, the dance writer conducting the lectures, tells the students in the last session. "And the reason for that is that not a lot happened there until the twentieth century. The country is, of course, the United States. We start about 1933, when Lincoln Kirstein met George Balanchine. Well, we have a pretty big country with a lot of people, Kirstein said. But nobody has any understanding of ballet. Why don't you come there to work? There were no courts, no kings, no dukes to give Balanchine money, but there was a man named Edward Warburg. And soon Balanchine made a ballet called *Serenade* to show his students that the stuff they did in classrooms was part of something greater. The students in this picture are doing the best they can to take part in a Balanchine ballet. And when they could do something more than stand there with their arms in the air, Balanchine made something more for them."

The circle has come full. Fifty years later, the School is envied for a success beyond most dreams of Kirstein and Balanchine. Some admire the School for its professionalism. Others are disturbed by the autocratic single-mindedness of an American institution that is comparable to the state ballet academies of Europe and the Soviet Union. Asked if he looked forward to the School's growth over the next fifty years, Kirstein retorted that he would settle for five. With each of those years, the School will move further into a new history. It will be a history ungoverned by the direct influence of the motivating work, physical presence, and pragmatic idealism of Balanchine.

The School's place in the history of ballet is secure, for without its existence the look of an inevitably American style of classical ballet might have been very different. For Kirstein, the School's future lies in the maintenance of the Balanchine repertory and the extension of his ideas, as well as in the continuing development of classical dancing. Continuity was not an issue that troubled Balanchine. His school and company had come about, after all, in the most improbable of circumstances and persisted, at times, even more improbably. "Dancing doesn't exist," Balanchine once said. "It's the people that make it." [15]

APPENDIXES

COMMON TERMS IN BALLET INSTRUCTION

arabesque: A basic position in ballet in which the working leg extends up behind the standing leg, usually at a ninety-degree angle, with the arms stretched out. The body is in profile, with the standing leg straight out or bent into a plié, the foot flat or in relevé. There are many kinds of arabesques, but generally the aim is for a long, flowing line from the head and extended arms, hands, and fingers along the curve of the back and out to the toes. In an arabesque penché, the dancer's upper body bends low with a corresponding rise in the working leg.

assemblé: The working foot slides out from the supporting foot and stretches into the air as the dancer pushes off from the floor in a small jump, which ends with the feet "reassembling" themselves on the floor in a small plié in fifth position. The assemblé serves as a good training preparation for all jumps.

balancé: A waltz or rocking step from one foot to the other.

ballon: Lightness and ease in a jumping dancer, including the spring with which the dancer leaves the floor, a look of pausing in the air, and the softness and elasticity of the return to the floor.

ballonné: A bounce up as the working leg extends in a battement before the supporting leg returns to the floor in a demi-plié, when the foot of the working leg comes to rest at the ankle.

battement: A beating of the extended straight or bent leg.

brisé: A small beaten step in which the body springs up in a jump that is "broken" by one leg beating in front of or behind the other leg, which meets it in the air.

cabriole: A large beaten step that, like the brisé, may be done in a variety of manners. The dancer leaps up, legs at an angle in the air, with the lower leg beating against the upper one.

changement de pieds: A jump up in which the feet switch position, from fifth to fifth.

coupé: A transitional step, generally preparing for another, in which the working leg cuts into the standing leg with a transfer of the body's weight to the working leg.

dégagé: The "disengagement" of the working foot from a standing position in alignment with the supporting foot to an open position that prepares for the execution of a step.

développé: A flourishing scooping up and out of the working leg from the floor to the knee of the supporting leg and out into an open position in the air, where it is held. An exercise that builds control and balance.

échappé: A step in which the feet "escape" from each other, moving from a closed position to an open one and back into a closed position, as, for example, from fifth to second or fourth and into fifth position. At the barre, the échappé is an exercise that strengthens the feet and legs.

effacé: The bold, opened position of the body in which the dancer stands at an oblique angle to the observer, who sees the working leg extending away from the body rather than crossing it, as in the croisé position.

emboîté: A small, boxy jump forward, with the working leg bent forward into the air in front and returning as the dancer moves, beginning and ending in fifth position.

en dedans: In a step done en dedans, the leg moves in toward the body, or counterclockwise.

en dehors: In a step done en dehors, the leg moves away from the body, or clockwise.

en face: The position of the body in which the dancer faces the observer squarely.

en tournant: Turning.

entrechat: A spring straight up from fifth position, feet and legs criss-crossing into fifth position before the body lands once more in fifth.

épaulement: The carriage of the arms and upper torso and its relationship to the head and legs. The épaulement of the body, particularly in the line of the shoulders and head, serves to present or finish a step or movement.

extension: The ability to raise and hold the leg, usually at anywhere from a forty-five degree angle or hip level to ear level or a near-upright split.

failli: A connecting or preparatory step in one count in which the dancer springs up on both legs from fifth position, body in croisé (or at an oblique angle to the observer, working leg crossing the line of the body). The back leg opens out as the body springs, then comes front as the other leg lands in a demi-plié, moving through first and into fourth position.

fouetté: The leg whips up and out to the side, into the knee, and out again in a slight circle. The fouetté turn, of which there are a celebrated thirty-seven in the third act of *Swan Lake*, was once a test of the ballerina's technical skill.

frappé: The working foot, wrapped around the ankle of the supporting foot, beats against that ankle. In battement frappé, a common barre exercise that develops speed, coordination, and strength in the legs and feet, the foot beats to the ankle from a tendu to the side, then beats out again with the toe striking against the floor.

glissade: A sliding or gliding step in which one foot stretches away from the body along the floor and the other follows, beginning and ending with a fifth position.

jeté en tournant: A jeté is a jump from one leg to the other, with the working leg thrown into the air. There are many different kinds of jeté, including a turning jump or jeté en tournant.

manège: A wide circle around the edge of the stage; this term usually refers to a circle traveled by a dancer executing a series of turns.

pas de basque: A slight spring to the side, front, or back in three counts, beginning, to the front, with the front foot moving from fifth position to the side, followed by the second foot, which moves through first into fourth position, with a close in fifth position.

pas de bourrée: A small traveling step done in many different ways.

pas de chat: A catlike spring up into the air, feet beginning in fifth, pulling up under the body one after the other, and ending in fifth position.

passé: A transitional movement in which the leg transfers from one position to another, most commonly in the développé, when the foot moves up the leg to the knee before stretching out into an extension.

piqué: A step onto the toes of a straight leg.

pirouette: There are many kinds of pirouette, which is basically a turn on one foot, usually with the toe of the working leg touching the knee of the standing leg. Pirouettes may be done on a flat foot or in relevé.

plié; demi- and grand: A basic half or full bending of the knees, usually done as a warm-up exercise at the barre during class or at the start and end of jumps, turns, and most steps.

port de bras: The carriage or movement of the arms.

positions of the feet: The five positions into and out of which the feet move in classical ballet, developed in the seventeenth century, are: first, in which the heels touch and the feet form a straight line outward; second, in which the heels are separated but the feet still extend to form a straight line; third, in which the heel of the front foot moves into line with the instep of the back foot, touching it, with the feet ideally parallel; fourth, in which the front foot separates and moves forward and in front of the other, with both remaining turned out; fifth, in which the feet are parallel and touching, with the big toe protruding past the heel of the front foot.

promenade: A slow turn executed on one leg in arabesque or attitude (a bent-legged arabesque) by a single dancer or by a ballerina turned by her partner in a pas de deux or duet.

relevé: A raising of the body onto the ball or toe of one or both feet.

révérence: The curtsey or bow that ends the ballet class.

rond de jambe, à terre or en l'air: A circular path described by the working foot, moving front, side, and back and returning in alignment with the supporting foot. The rond de jambe is done either on the floor or with the working leg extended up to the side.

sauté: A jumping step.

sickling foot: A foot that points inward.

sissonne: A scissorlike jump to the side, front, or back that lands on both feet or only one.

sur le cou de pied: The placement of one foot on the ankle of the other.

temps levé: Whereas a pas is a step that involves a transfer of weight, a temps is a step or movement that is part of a pas but does not involve a weight shift. A temps levé is a small jump up from one foot that lands on one foot, or a hop.

temps lié: A temps lié is a connected movement of the arms and legs based on fourth, fifth, and second positions. In *Technical Manual and Dictionary of Classical Ballet,* Gail Grant describes it as a popular exercise in the Russian school of ballet, starting at the beginning level and increasing in difficulty, to develop a soft demi-plié and balance and control in transmitting weight smoothly.

tendu: "Stretched," as in "battement tendu," in which the foot of the working leg is extended to the front, side, or back, stretched with the heel off the floor and forward and the toe maintaining contact with the floor, before it returns to the starting position. The tendu develops the instep and flexibility of the foot.

tour jeté: An American corruption of the term grand jeté en tournant.

TEACHERS AT THE SCHOOL
OF AMERICAN BALLET *

1930s: George Balanchine
Kyra Blanc
Lew Christensen
Erick Hawkins
Berenice Holmes
Dorothie Littlefield
Ludmila Schollar
Muriel Stuart
Anatole Vilzak
Pierre Vladimiroff

1940s: George Balanchine
Kyra Blanc
Janet Collins
Merce Cunningham
Alexandra Danilova
William Dollar
Felia Doubrovska
José Fernandez
Frederic Franklin

* Including permanent, guest, and summer faculties.

Paul Haakon
Yurek Lazowsky
Anatole Oboukhoff
Elise Reiman
Trude Rittmann
Boris Romanoff
Ludmila Schollar
Muriel Stuart
Beatrice Tompkins
Anatole Vilzak
Pierre Vladimiroff

1950s: George Balanchine
Janet Collins
Felia Doubrovska
Helene Dudin
Ann Hutchinson
Yurek Lazowsky
Anatole Oboukhoff
Elise Reiman
Anna Sokolow
Muriel Stuart
Maria Tallchief
Antonina Tumkovsky
Pierre Vladimiroff

1960s: Diana Adams
George Balanchine
Ruthanna Boris
Marjorie Bresler
Mireille Briane
Esmée Bulnes
Lew Christensen
Janet Collins
Alexandra Danilova
Felia Doubrovska
Helene Dudin

André Eglevsky
Melissa Hayden
Jillana
Christa Long
Anatole Oboukhoff
Muriel Stuart
Maria Tallchief
Antonina Tumkovsky
Pierre Vladimiroff
Stanley Williams

1970s: Diana Adams
George Balanchine
Jean-Pierre Bonnefous
Alexandra Danilova
Felia Doubrovska
Helene Dudin
Suzanne Farrell
Gloria Govrin
Irina Kosmovska
Andrei Kramarevsky
Conrad Ludlow
Peter Martins
Colleen Neary
Richard Rapp
Elise Reiman
Michel Renault
David Richardson
Suki Schorer
Victoria Simon
Muriel Stuart
Carol Sumner
John Taras
Antonina Tumkovsky
Violette Verdy
Stanley Williams

1980s: Karin von Aroldingen
Merrill Ashley
George Balanchine
Jean-Pierre Bonnefous
Lisa Cain
Alexandra Danilova
Felia Doubrovska
Helene Dudin
Pierre Dulaine
Suzanne Farrell
Andrei Kramarevsky
Yvonne Marceau
Peter Martins
Kay Mazzo
Richard Rapp
Elise Reiman
Inka Rudnycka
Rebecca Schlieben-Scott
Suki Schorer
Muriel Stuart
John Taras
Helgi Tomasson
Antonina Tumkovsky
Stanley Williams

NOTES

INTRODUCTION

1. Willa Sibert Cather, "Training for the Ballet," *McClure's*, October 1913, p. 86.
2. Quoted in Margot Fonteyn, *The Magic of Dance* (New York: Alfred A. Knopf, 1979), p. 139.
3. Ann Barzel, "European Dance Teachers in the United States," *Dance Index*, April–June 1944, pp. 58–59.
4. Ibid., p. 57.
5. Quoted in ibid., p. 59.
6. Ibid., p. 61.
7. Ann Barzel, "Victorian Ballerina," *Dance Magazine*, March 1944, p. 30.
8. Cather, p. 87.
9. Ibid.
10. Ibid., p. 95.
11. Barzel, "European Dance Teachers," p. 80.
12. Ibid.
13. Ruth Page, *Notes on Dance Classes Around the World, 1915–1980* (Princeton, N.J.: Princeton Book Co., 1984), p. 14.
14. John Martin, "The Dance: The Ballet in America," *New York Times*, September 17, 1933.

I. 1933

1. Lincoln Kirstein, *Thirty Years: Lincoln Kirstein's The New York City Ballet* (New York: Alfred A. Knopf, 1978), p. 30.
2. Lincoln Kirstein, letter to A. Everett Austin, Jr., July 16, 1933. Contained in a scrapbook of material on the founding of the School and the American Ballet, presented to the Dance Collection of the New York Public Library by Lincoln Kirstein and the Wadsworth Atheneum.
3. Bernard Taper, *Balanchine* (New York: Times Books, 1984), p. 151.
4. Ibid., p. 152.
5. Anna Kisselgoff, "Kirstein—The Man Who Brought Us Balanchine," *New York Times*, May 8, 1977.
6. Kirstein, *Thirty Years*, p. 4.
7. Ibid., p. 15
8. Ibid., p. 14.
9. Ibid.
10. Ibid., p. 16.
11. Taper, *Balanchine*, p. 148.
12. Kirstein, *Thirty Years*, p. 8.
13. Ibid., p. 23.
14. Ibid., pp. 26–27.
15. John Gruen, *The Private World of Ballet* (New York: The Viking Press, 1975), p. 279.
16. Ibid., p. 280.
17. Zakhary L. McLove, "Russian Ballet Has Risen in Revolt," *New York Times Magazine*, November 15, 1925, p. 9.
18. Ibid.
19. Taper, *Balanchine*, p. 53.
20. Quoted in Yuri Slonimsky, "Balanchine: The Early Years," *Ballet Review* 5, no. 3 (1975–76), pp. 49–50.
21. Ibid., p. 50.
22. Ibid., p. 63.
23. Don McDonagh, *George Balanchine* (Boston: Twayne Publishers, 1983), p. 25.
24. Horst Koegler, *The Concise Oxford Dictionary of Ballet* (London: Oxford University Press, 1977), p. 203.

25. Quoted in Slonimsky, "The Early Years," p. 39.
26. Ibid., p. 42.
27. Ibid., p. 54.
28. Lincoln Kirstein, *Movement & Metaphor* (New York: Praeger Publishers, 1970), p. 218.
29. Taper, *Balanchine*, p. 61.
30. Gruen, *Private World of Ballet*, p. 279.
31. Slonimsky, "The Early Years," p. 38.
32. Quoted in ibid., p. 61.
33. Taper, *Balanchine*, p. 278.
34. Ibid., p. 99.
35. McDonagh, *George Balanchine*, p. 19.
36. Lincoln Kirstein, letter to A. Everett Austin, Jr., August 11, 1933. Contained in a scrapbook of material on the founding of the School and American Ballet, presented to the Dance Collection of the New York Public Library by Lincoln Kirstein and the Wadsworth Atheneum.
37. Edward M. M. Warburg, "Fifty Years Ago: The Beginning of the School of American Ballet," *Playbill*, New York City Ballet, winter season 1983–84, p. 4.
38. Ibid.
39. Anna Kisselgoff, "A 'Forgotten' Figure in U.S. Ballet History," *New York Times*, January 15, 1984.
40. Taper, *Balanchine*, p. 153.
41. Robert Tracy, *Balanchine's Ballerinas* (New York: Linden Press/Simon & Schuster, 1983), p. 66.

II. 1934

1. Lincoln Kirstein, introduction to School of American Ballet catalogue, 1944, p. 5.
2. *American Dancer*, January 1934.
3. Lincoln Kirstein, report on School of American Ballet, March 1934, p. 13.
4. Lincoln Kirstein, *Thirty Years: Lincoln Kirstein's The New York City Ballet* (New York: Alfred A. Knopf, 1978), p. 35.
5. Kirstein, report on School of American Ballet, p. 11.

6. Quoted in Bernard Taper, *Balanchine* (New York: Times Books, 1984), p. 157.
7. Ibid.
8. Kirstein, *Thirty Years*, p. 40.
9. Taper, *Balanchine*, pp. 156–57.
10. Quoted in Nancy Reynolds, *Repertory in Review* (New York: The Dial Press, 1977), p. 37.
11. Quoted in ibid.
12. Quoted in ibid., pp. 38–39.
13. Edward M. M. Warburg, "Fifty Years Ago: The Beginning of the School of American Ballet," *Playbill*, New York City Ballet, winter season 1983–84, pp. 8–9.

III. THE FIRST THIRTY YEARS

1. *"Thirty Years: Lincoln Kirstein's The New York City Ballet* (New York: Alfred A. Knopf, 1978), p. 67.
2. John Martin, *New York Times*, December 16, 1934.
3. Quoted in Nancy Reynolds, *Repertory in Review* (New York: The Dial Press, 1977), pp. 39–43.
4. John Martin, *New York Times*, August 18, 1935.
5. Lincoln Kirstein, *New York Times*, August 25, 1935.
6. Edward M. M. Warburg, "Fifty Years Ago: The Beginning of the School of American Ballet," *Playbill*, New York City Ballet, winter season 1983–84, p. 10.
7. Lincoln Kirstein, *Thirty Years: Lincoln Kirstein's The New York City Ballet* (New York: Alfred A. Knopf, 1978), p. 57.
8. Quoted in Bernard Taper, *Balanchine* (New York: Times Books, 1984), p. 177.
9. Quoted in ibid., p. 181.
10. Ibid., pp. 195–196.
11. Lincoln Kirstein, "Ballet: Record and Augury," *Theatre Arts*, September 1940, pp. 653, 657.
12. George Amberg, *Ballet: The Emergence of an American Art* (New York: Mentor Books, 1949), p. 80.
13. Warburg, "Fifty Years Ago: The Beginning of the School of American Ballet," *Playbill*, p. 10.

14. Kirstein, "Ballet: Record and Augury," p. 653.
15. Kirstein, *Thirty Years*, p. 108.
16. Taper, *Balanchine*, p. 205.
17. Kirstein, *Thirty Years*, p. 109.
18. Ibid., p. 89.
19. Quoted in Taper, *Balanchine*, p. 212.
20. Ibid., p. 227.
21. Kirstein, *Thirty Years*, p. 104.
22. Anna Kisselgoff, *New York Times*, June 17, 1971.
23. Kirstein, *Thirty Years*, p. 106.
24. Quoted in Anatole Chujoy, *The New York City Ballet* (New York: Alfred A. Knopf, 1953), p. 254.
25. Emily Coleman, "How Balanchine & Co. Changed the Ballet," *New York Times Magazine*, November 30, 1958, p. 18.
26. Arlene Croce, "An American in Paris," *The New Yorker*, February 25, 1985, pp. 89–90.
27. Robert Greskovic, "Thinking Small for 'Nutcracker,' " *New York Times*, December 4, 1983.
28. School of American Ballet catalogue, 1947–48.
29. Reynolds, *Repertory in Review*, p. 147.
30. Janet Flanner, *Paris Was Yesterday* (New York: Penguin Books, 1981), p. 55.

IV. ENTER THE FORD FOUNDATION

1. Allen Hughes, *New York Times*, December 16, 1963.
2. Elizabeth Kendall, "Dancing: A Ford Foundation Report," New York: Ford Foundation, December 1983, p. 67.
3. Ibid., p. 65.
4. Anna Kisselgoff, "The Nijinsky of Massapequa," *New York Times*, April 11, 1976.
5. Tobi Tobias, "The Quality of the Moment: Stanley Williams," *Dance Magazine*, March 1981, p. 79.
6. Peter Martins, *Far from Denmark* (Boston: Little, Brown and Company, 1982), p. 6.
7. Ibid., pp. 13–14.

8. Lincoln Kirstein, *Thirty Years: Lincoln Kirstein's The New York City Ballet* (New York: Alfred A. Knopf, 1978), p. 207.

9. Robert Greskovic, *Ballet News*, August 1982, pp. 32–33.

10. "Balanchine," *Dance in America*, Part I, PBS-TV, May 28, 1984.

11. Greskovic, *Ballet News*, pp. 32–33.

12. Among the works staged by Danilova for the Workshop Performances are excerpts from *Coppélia*, in 1965; excerpts from Act I of *Swan Lake*, in 1966; excerpts from Act III of *The Sleeping Beauty*, after Marius Petipa, in 1967; the Grand Pas Espagnol from *Paquita*, after Petipa, in 1968 and 1974; Dance of the Mermaids from Petipa's *The Humpbacked Horse*, Les Fileuses from Act III of *Coppélia*, the Dance of the Pages from Act I of *The Sleeping Beauty*, after Petipa, and *Les Sylphides*, after Michel Fokine, in 1969; excerpts from *Coppélia*, in 1970; excerpts from Act III of *Raymonda*, after Petipa, in 1971; excerpts from Act I of *Swan Lake*, after Petipa, in 1972; *Aurora's Wedding* (a staging of Act III of *The Sleeping Beauty*), after Petipa, in 1973 and 1984, the latter with John Taras; excerpts from Act I of *The Sleeping Beauty*, after Petipa, in 1975; the Polovetsian Dances from *Prince Igor*, after Fokine, in 1976; excerpts from *Les Saisons*, after Petipa, in 1977; Danilova's *Les Scènes du Ballet*, in 1978; excerpts from *Le Pavillon d'Armide*, after Fokine, in 1979; Act II of *Swan Lake*, after Lev Ivanov, in 1980; and *Chopiniana*, staged with Frederic Franklin, after Fokine, in 1982.

13. Works from ballets by August Bournonville staged by Stanley Williams for the Workshop Performances include the Pas de Deux from *Flower Festival at Genzano*, in 1968 and 1972; the Pas de Six from Act III of *Napoli*, in 1969; excerpts from Act I of *Konservatoriet*, in 1970 and 1975; excerpts from Acts I and II of *La Sylphide*, in 1971; Pas de Trois from *La Ventana*, in 1976; *La Vestale Pas de Deux*, in 1977; Pas de Trois from *The Life Guards of Amager*, in 1978; Pas de Deux from *William Tell* in 1979; excerpts from Act III of *Napoli* and Jockey Dance from *From Moscow to Siberia*, in 1980; Chinese Dance from *Far from Denmark*, in 1982; Pas de Deux from *Kermesse in Bruges*, in 1983; Pas de Six and Tarantella from Act III of *Napoli*, in 1984.

14. Among the ballets by George Balanchine staged by Suki Schorer for

the Workshop Performances are *Valse Fantaisie,* in 1973 and 1983, and First Campaign from *Stars and Stripes,* in 1973; *Serenade,* in 1974 and 1984; *Concerto Barocco,* in 1975; *Allegro Brillante,* in 1976; *Symphony in C,* in 1977; *Divertimento No. 15,* in 1978; Ricercata from *Episodes* and *Donizetti Variations,* in 1979; *Raymonda Variations,* in 1980; *La Source,* in 1981; Acts III and IV from *Brahms-Schoenberg Quartet,* in 1982; and *Western Symphony,* in 1983.

15. Toni Bentley, *Winter Season* (New York: Random House, 1982), pp. 7–8.

V. THE "BALANCHINE STYLE"

1. Peter Rosenwald, "Lincoln Kirstein's Vision," *Horizon,* May 1980, p. 38.
2. Robert Jacobson, "Full Speed Ahead," *Ballet News,* July 1984, p. 18.
3. Robert Greskovic, "School for Style," *Dance Theater Journal,* May 1983, p. 27.
4. Linda Hirschman, "What Makes a Balanchine Dancer?," *Ballet News,* June 1979, p. 30.
5. Ibid.
6. Ibid.
7. Emily Coleman, "How Balanchine & Co. Changed the Ballet," *New York Times Magazine,* December 1, 1957, p. 101.
8. Michelle Audet and Susan Reiter, "Point of View—Suki Schorer," *School of American Ballet 1983–1984 Calendar of Events,* Fall 1983.
9. Hirschman, "What Makes a Balanchine Dancer?," p. 30.
10. Louis Botto, "Work in Progress," in *Dance as a Theatre Art,* ed. Selma Jeanne Cohen (New York: Dodd, Mead & Company, 1974), p. 192.
11. Jonathan Cott, "Balanchine: Music and Dance," *Ballet Review,* Fall 1983, p. 77.
12. Nancy Goldner, "The School of American Ballet," in *Repertory in Review,* by Nancy Reynolds (New York: The Dial Press, 1977), p. 32.

13. Hirschman, "What Makes a Balanchine Dancer?," p. 32.
14. Virginia Lee Warren, "School of American Ballet," *The New York State Theater Magazine*, June 1970, p. 16.

VI. THE SCHOOL TODAY

1. Alumni and associates of the School of American Ballet who were directing ballet companies in 1984 include: Robert Barnett (Atlanta Ballet), Maria Tallchief and Paul Mejia (Chicago City Ballet), Arthur Mitchell (Dance Theatre of Harlem), Eliot Feld (Feld Ballet), Robert Joffrey (Joffrey Ballet), Todd Bolender, Diana Adams, and Una Kai (Kansas City Ballet), Robert Lindgren (North Carolina Dance Theatre), Francia Russell and Kent Stowell (Pacific Northwest Ballet), Robert Weiss (Pennsylvania Ballet), and Patricia Wilde (Pittsburgh Ballet Theatre).
2. In 1984, the gymnastics class was taught by Lisa Cain.
3. Music theory was taught by Rebecca Schlieben-Scott and Inka Rudnycka, with Mel Brown.
4. Social dancing was taught by Pierre Dulaine and Yvonne Marceau.
5. Teachers for the 1984 summer course were Alexandra Danilova, Andrei Kramarevsky, Richard Rapp, Elise Reiman, Suki Schorer, Antonina Tumkovsky, and Stanley Williams.
6. Martin Mayer, "Are the Trying Times Just Beginning?," *New York Times*, September 28, 1969.
7. The offices were used in 1984 by a staff that included Lincoln Kirstein, president of the School; Natalie Molostwoff, executive director; Nathalie Gleboff, associate director; Mary Porter, director of development; Mari Cornell and Michele DePaolo, secretaries; Sinikka Finn, receptionist; Dinah Lustig, bookkeeper; Anna Petite, Martha Rosenthal, Carol Del Corso, Patricia Romano, and Diane Werner, all members of the development staff; and Phyllis Johnson, finance.
8. The School's accompanists in 1984 were Elfrida Afonina, Gertrude Carroll, Irene Goncharov, Nancy McDill, Tatiana Ouroumoff, Lynn Stanford, Allison Thomas, and Alla Veyrovochkina.
9. John Russell, "Lincoln Kirstein: A Life in Art," *New York Times Magazine*, June 20, 1982, p. 57.

10. The cities in which auditions were held in 1984 were Atlanta, Boston, Chicago, Cincinnati, Dallas, Denver, Detroit, Fort Worth, Honolulu, Houston, Kansas City, Los Angeles, Louisville, Coral Gables, New Orleans, Salt Lake City, San Francisco, San Juan, Seattle, Clearwater, Tucson, Washington, D.C., and Winston-Salem.

11. Natalia Roslavleva, *Era of the Russian Ballet* (New York: E. P. Dutton & Co., 1966), p. 199.

12. Nancy Goldner, "The School of American Ballet," in *Repertory in Review*, by Nancy Reynolds (New York: The Dial Press, 1977), p. 29. I am indebted to Goldner for her clear and cogent descriptions of classes she watched at the School.

13. Jennifer Dunning, "It Could Be Our 'Official' Ballet Academy," *New York Times*, April 27, 1980.

14. In 1984, the Preparatory Division of A1 class was taught by Helene Dudin and Elise Reiman.

15. Elise Reiman taught A1, Children II, III, and V, B1, and Toe classes in 1984.

16. Children I was taught by Dudin and Tumkovsky.

17. Children II was taught by Dudin, Reiman, and Tumkovsky.

18. Children III was taught by Dudin and Reiman.

19. Helene Dudin taught A1, Children I, II, III, IV, and V, B2, C2, and Toe in 1984.

20. Children IV was taught by Dudin, Kay Mazzo, and Tumkovsky.

21. Toe I was taught by Schorer and Reiman; Toe II by Dudin and Reiman; and Toe III by Mazzo and Tumkovsky.

22. Children V was taught by Dudin, Reiman, Muriel Stuart, and Tumkovsky.

23. A-2 girls' classes were taught by Mazzo and Richard Rapp. A-2 boys' classes were taught by Kramarevsky and Rapp.

24. Muriel Stuart taught Children V and C1 in 1984.

25. Alexandra Danilova taught B1, B2, C1, D, and Variations for the C1, C2, and D classes in 1984.

26. Second Intermediate Division girls' B1 classes were taught by Danilova, Rapp, Reiman, and Tumkovsky in 1984. The girls' B2 classes were taught by Danilova, Dudin, Mazzo, Rapp, Tumkovsky, and Williams.

27. Advanced Division girls' C1 classes were taught by Merrill Ashley,